HUNTING & GATHERING SURVIVAL MANUAL

OUTDOOR LIFE

HUNTING & GATHERING SURVIVAL MANUAL

BY TIM MACWELCH
AND THE EDITORS AT *OUTDOOR LIFE*

weldon**owen**

CONTENTS

GATHERING

LIVING WILD

FROM *OUTDOOR LIFE*

LET'S BE HONEST. You probably don't need this book. You can fill your refrigerator and pantry daily from the storehouse of packaged provisions at your local supermarket. You can eat sanitized meat and prewashed vegetables. Everybody does it. I'm sure you'll be fine.

But equally clear is this: If you are reading this, then you know everything is not always fine. You know the supermarket is a flimsy convenience, its freezers and fluorescent lights less reliable than most people think. You know you may not always be able to count on a take-out pizza from the joint on the corner.

If you are reading this, then you are obeying some primitive urge to take care of yourself. I don't mean tuning your head by seeing a counselor or toning your body by visiting a gym. I'm talking about the most basic kind of maintenance: Surviving until at least tomorrow by finding shelter for yourself and your tribe, protecting your possessions, and most fundamentally, gathering and keeping food.

It's easy to ignore these Paleolithic impulses in our digital, ironic age, but if you look deeply, you'll see evidence of our ancient caloric urges: your neighbor's kempt garden, your taste for heirloom vegetables and undercooked meat, the deep satisfaction you feel when you pluck ripe fruit from a wild tree, your tendency to hoard bacon when it goes on sale.

This book is not only a user's guide to accumulating calories in any way possible, it's also a rich celebration of your inner scavenger.

The author of this book, Tim MacWelch, is what I'd call a cheerful skeptic. He's not so sure we'll always have enough rain to grow our gardens or that our neighbors will always be charitable when they run out of food. He's uncertain of our anonymous systems of energy and food distribution. He'd rather rely on his own wits and wisdom to make his living.

Tim is no pointy-headed prepper or deep-woods mystic. He isn't a doomsayer or a conspiracy theorist. Instead, he's pragmatic, practical, and one of the few people I'd like to be stranded with in the wilderness, which can be defined as the remote backcountry or the empty streets of suburban subdivisions. Tim solves problems by calmly, reasonably assessing situations and observing alternatives, and then finding food nearly everywhere he looks. This book is really a series of alternatives to the supermarket.

But it's more than that. It's a manual to living honestly.

Tim teaches you how to catch a fish, but more critically, how to preserve a limit of fish so you can eat them for the next month. Tim teaches you how to recognize edible plants, but also how to save their seeds so you can perpetuate their sustenance. Tim teaches you how to light a fire, cook and cure wild meat, make a food-saving brine, recognize poisonous plants, concoct an herbal remedy, find water, rig a bow, set a snare, and if you get weary of all that solitude, signal for help.

This is a field guide to our collective past as much as it is a user's guide to the future. But ultimately, it's a modern manual for noticing that the world around us is full of food. So buy this book. Take it home and learn how you can gather a wild salad on your way home from work. How you can catch a week's worth of fish by setting out a simple trap in your neighborhood creek. How you can recognize the obscure wildlife in your area by reading their tracks and their scat. How you can make a serviceable bow out of household products.

And, ultimately, how you can recognize calories in all their various and obscure forms in the world around you. Because it's calories—not relationships, or money, or possessions—that will enable you to survive from today 'til tomorrow. And pass this book down to your heirs.

Andrew McKean
Editor-in-Chief, *Outdoor Life*

OUTDOORLIFE

Can you really "live off the land" like our ancestors did?

The truthful answer isn't a simple yes or no—it depends on a dizzying array of factors. The location, the time of year, the weather, and the populations of plants and animals all have a huge impact on the success of a modern-day hunter-gatherer. And how long are you planning to live on wild food? It may be easy to find food for a day, but finding food for a year is a much more daunting task. Cultivating and honing your foraging, fishing, trapping, and hunting skills will play a major role in the amount of food you can bring home—or back to base camp. And in all your pursuits, you'll need to be observant, patient, intuitive, and lucky in order to maintain a full, balanced diet of wild foods.

But it can be done.

You and I are living proof that our forebears collected their meals from the wild. Food harvesting, in fact, is the world's oldest occupation. Once our predecessors secured their shelter, fire, water, and tools, the rest of their daily labor would have been devoted to the gathering of food—as is this book. The *Hunting & Gathering Survival Manual* is designed to be your guide through the world of foraging wild edible foods, harvesting game animals, and providing for your every survival food need.

The art of collecting food from the wild is a synergistic one; all the disciplines are connected. Once you know the basics, your scouting trip for new trapping sites can quickly turn into a wild fruit-foraging mission, just as your quest to harvest cattail plants can easily turn into a profitable fishing trip. These are self-preservation skills that will take you back into the outdoors—your natural habitat. With practice, your eyes will be opened to the amazing variety of foods that fill the parks, countrysides, and wild places all around you. And with luck, you'll never need to go hungry again.

Now, let's eat!

—Tim MacWelch

HUNTING

HOT
OR
COLD
DRINK
Dr
Pepper

In my years of teaching survival classes, I've often been asked about the strangest thing I've ever eaten. The answers always come from the animal kingdom, and the list invariably contains a lot of random animals and animal parts. I've eaten deer hearts, squirrel tongues, opossum lungs, and countless other meats and organs, most of which were surprisingly tasty.

These organs and offal weren't on my plate for some trivial reason; no one dared me to eat anything, nor was I trying to look like some kind of macho survival guy to my friends or students. When I eat most animals, I almost always eat more of them than most folks do, because the organs and other parts are nutritious, and because it's the right thing to do. Taking an animal's life should be a sobering experience—it should mean something. By using the entire animal, I honor the experiences of hunting, trapping, and fishing—and I prepare for a survival scenario in which every calorie counts. This first chapter will teach you the practices of respectful harvesting from nature—not just how to be a predator.

And to that end of conservative collection, I'll show you how to get started in fishing—whether you have tackle or not. You'll build a foundation in animal-trapping skills and learn what to do once you've landed your quarry. From cleaning and preserving to gaining the most nutrition and biggest calorie payouts, you'll get a lot of mileage from this arena of the wild-food realm.

If it's got fur, feathers, scales, or a shell, the following pages will help you turn it into a meal.

001 PICK UP A ROD & REEL

We've all heard the old adage: "Give a man a fish, you'll feed him for a day; teach a man to fish, you'll feed him for a lifetime." There is a lot of truth in those words—often the best way to help someone is by empowering him to be self-sustaining. If you've never fished before, start with the basics, and then share your newfound knowledge with others.

The number of rods and reels on the market can boggle beginners—as can their prices. Sport fishing is a big business, but don't lose hope—you can get by with a lot less tackle than the store would like to sell you.

All you really need to get started is a rod and matching reel, some monofilament line, and some hooks or lures—plus a fishing license. Study up on these different reel styles, find one that works for you, and grab a rod to match.

SPINCAST REEL This is the easiest reel for beginners to use. The top-mounted reel with thumb-button release makes casting easy, and the closed face keeps the line clean and controlled. These reels are also good for night fishing, but they only handle a limited range of lure weights.

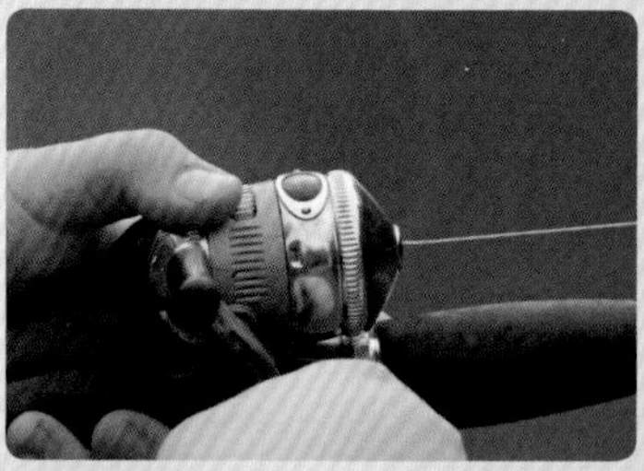

SPINNING REEL Don't let the similar name fool you. Spinning reels come in open- and closed-faced models and are different from spincast reels. This undermounted reel can suit many types of fishing and it can cast far, even with light tackle. The line can have a tendency to unspool in a beginner's hands, however.

BAITCASTING REEL These popular, historic reels, which have a partially exposed spool, are often used for larger fish and can be tricky for new anglers. One bad backlash (in which the spool speed exceeds the speed of the outgoing line), and you'll have a tangled mess of fishing line.

FLY REELS Similar in mechanics to a baitcasting reel, fly reels are a different breed of device used exclusively for fly fishing. Unique rods, fly line, and lures, along with the hypnotic flow of the line, make this a fishing style unlike any other.

TROLLING, CASTING, AND BOAT REELS This group of large, rugged baitcasting reels are almost always used for big-fish sport fishing in saltwater. Marlin, sailfish, tuna, and other big oceanic game fish are often the quarry.

002 GET HOOKED

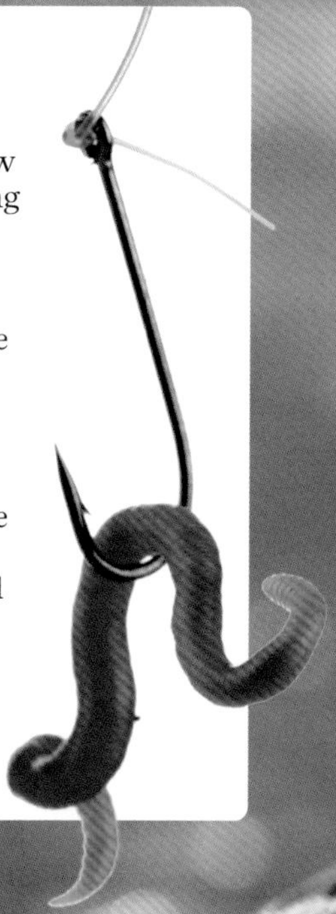

The hook is really humanity's attempt to grow some claws. Eagles have little trouble grabbing slippery trout with their hooked talons, and our ancestors no doubt borrowed the idea.

If you decide to fish with natural bait or something that resembles it, you'll need bare hooks that are appropriate in size and construction for your intended fish.

The variables in hook selection are numerous. The size of wire that made the hook is relevant, along with the length of the hook's shank, the bend of the hook, the eye style and placement, the point and barb, and even the bait-holding slices (barbs) on the shank. The hook packaging may give you some tips about which to choose; when in doubt, select the smaller size, just to make sure it will fit in the fish's mouth.

003 SELECT YOUR FISHING LINE

There are many different brands and styles of fishing line, and most anglers have their favorites for specific fish—though none of these rules are absolute. To start, look for the number that indicates the line's breaking strength (commonly sold in the United States as "pound test"). A light pound-test line will range from 2–6 pounds (1–3 kg) and is good for panfish, small trout, and the like. A 6–12 pound (3–5 kg) test line is good for handling bass, pike, and walleye, while a 10–15 pound (4–7 kg) test line can haul in lake trout, salmon, and striped bass. If you get into saltwater fishing, you may want to try line that is even heavier.

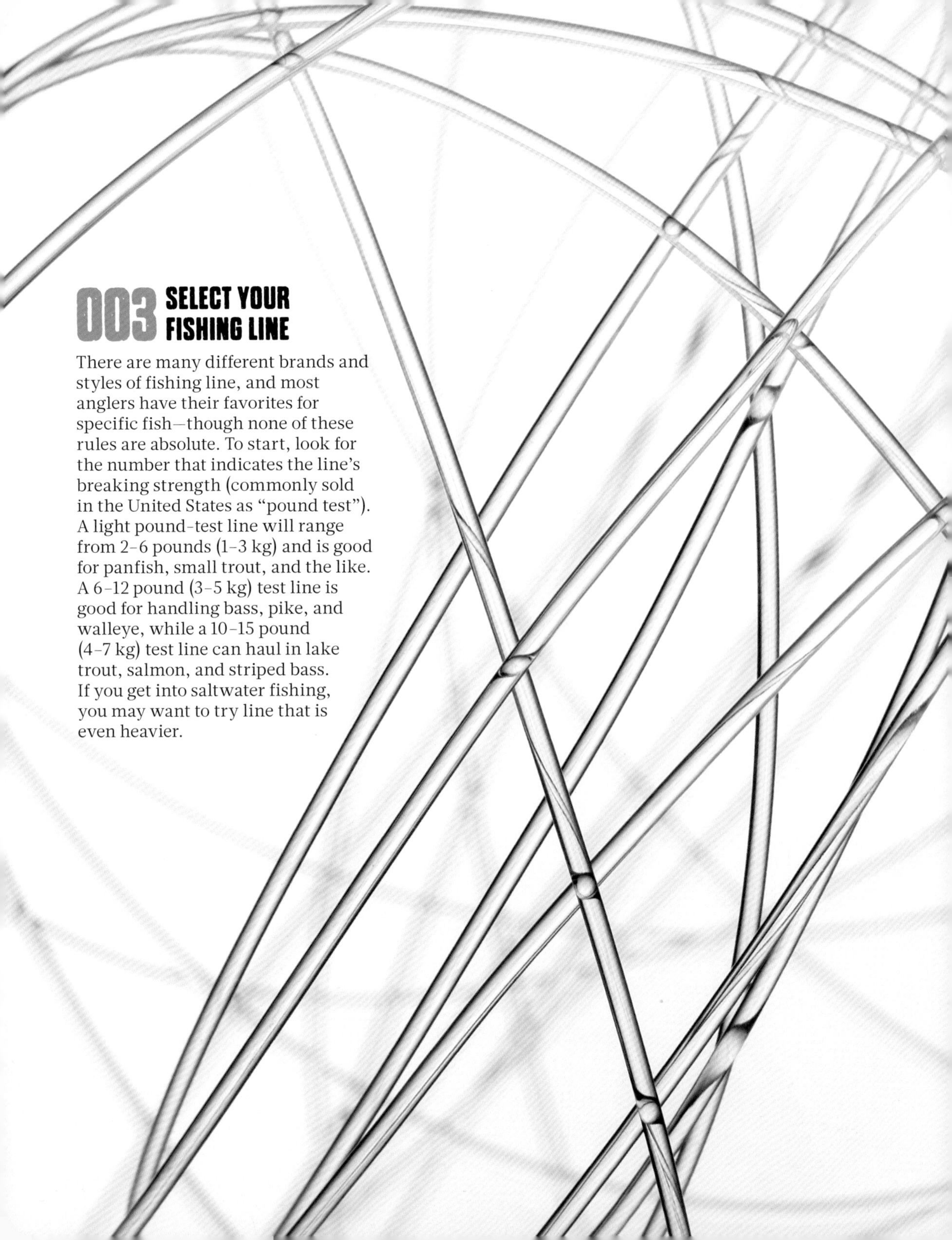

004 LURE THEM IN

Lures are probably as old as the fishhooks themselves. Few self-respecting fish will bite on an empty hook (although it does happen). Lures come in many sizes, shapes, colors, materials, and styles. Don't buy just one—get an assortment of colors and types in order to offer the fish different choices until you find one they want to bite that day.

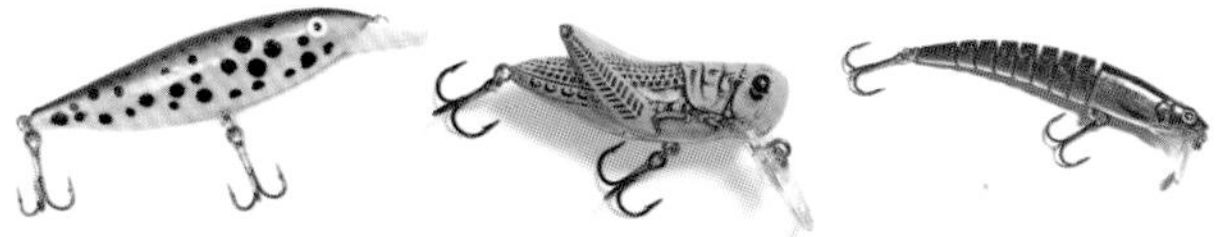

PLUGS These imitate small fish, frogs, and other creatures that fish find tasty. Often clunky, cylindrical, and brightly colored, plain plugs are used as a water-surface lure, and plugs with a lip are able to dive underwater while being reeled in.

SPOONS AND SPINNERS The oldest artificial lures, spoons mimic little fish and are used to catch all kinds of fish. Spinners are a combination of a small spoon-shaped blade and a lure that offers movement to entice the fish. Buzz baits are a large spinner type that makes a buzzing sound and bubbles.

JIGS AND PLASTICS This group is characterized by weighted lure heads attached to rubbery (sometimes plastic) bodies.

FLIES Typically used for fly fishing, hair and fiber combine to make wet flies (which sink) and dry flies (which float). Poppers are a floating fly that with a small, plug-style head.

005 PACK YOUR SURVIVAL FISHING KIT

If you find yourself in a wilderness survival scenario, and you were smart enough to have fishing gear in your survival kit, you can feed yourself and others. Prepackaged survival fishing kits are available, but over the years, I have found that the all-in-one kit is neither packaged correctly nor sized for your success. In fact, all you really need is a small coil of monofilament line and one or two dozen hooks.

Very often, survival kits contain large hooks, presumably to catch large fish during your emergency, in my experience though, smaller hooks are more critical. There may not be big fish in the local waterway, but there are always little ones. For best results, pack some small and medium hooks. And as for your line, bundled monofilament can bend and twist, making it a nightmare to unwind and cast. Store your line in the largest round coils your survival kit will allow, keeping it wound in a similar shape to the spool it came on.

To make your survival fishing most effective, select a long stick or branch to use as your pole and tie your line to it. This will allow you to conserve line and still reach the fish.

006 CARVE A FISH STICK

We're not carving up the kind of fish stick you eat out of the freezer, but the kind you use to catch a fish.

You may already be familiar with the "hobo fishing kit" (if not by that name): a hook and some fishing line wrapped around an aluminum can for a reel. In this still-water fishing technique, you cast the baited hook, weight, and bobber with one hand while unwinding the line from the can with the other. But how can you save line and incorporate a rod?

After a few false starts, I tried using a stick sanded smooth and wound with some fishing line; I cast it out directly off the end of the stick. With the stick held firmly, I pointed it behind me with the hook, weight, and bobber hanging loosely from the end. Then I swung my arm overhead in an arc and pointed my stick out over the water. My hook, line, and sinker sailed out into the water—I had cast the full length of the line I had wound on the stick! It felt like I was standing there holding the original rod and reel.

After working with this technique for some time, I came up with two helpful improvements. Tapering the casting end of the "fish stick" makes the line cast out easier, and winding the line without overlapping helps to prevent tangles.

A word of caution when showing this to first-time fishers: Put a wrist loop on the handle end of the stick so they don't throw your amazing rod into the creek.

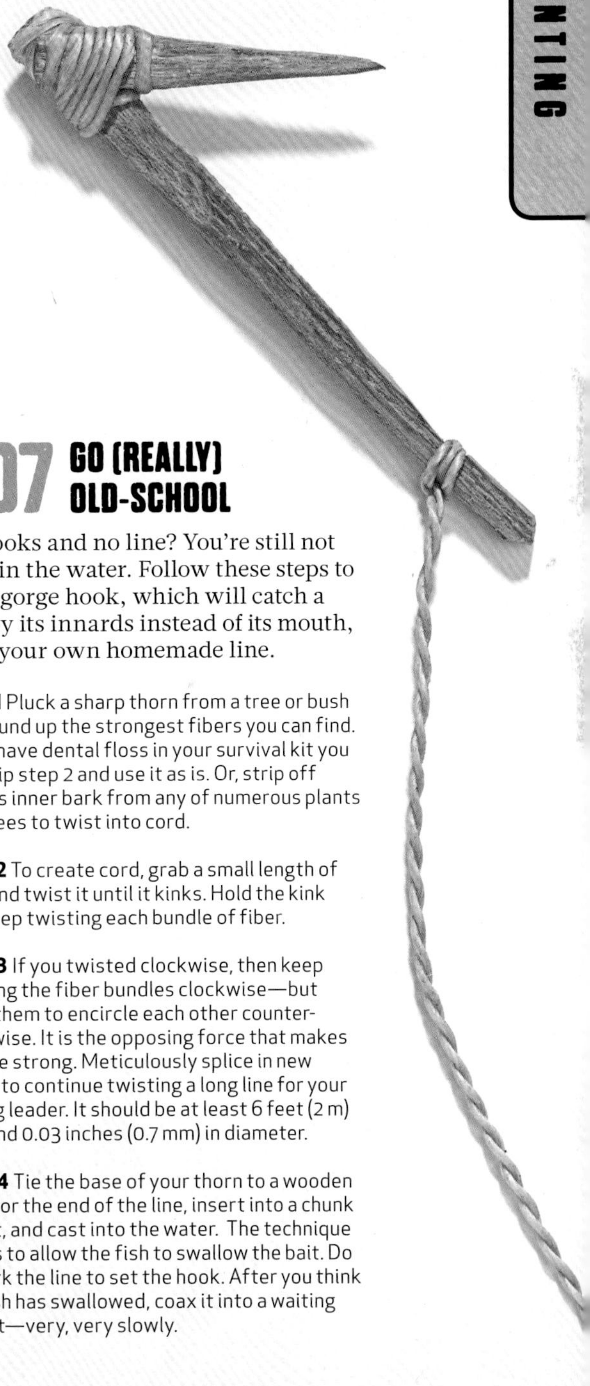

007 GO (REALLY) OLD-SCHOOL

No hooks and no line? You're still not dead in the water. Follow these steps to use a gorge hook, which will catch a fish by its innards instead of its mouth, with your own homemade line.

STEP 1 Pluck a sharp thorn from a tree or bush and round up the strongest fibers you can find. If you have dental floss in your survival kit you can skip step 2 and use it as is. Or, strip off fibrous inner bark from any of numerous plants and trees to twist into cord.

STEP 2 To create cord, grab a small length of bark and twist it until it kinks. Hold the kink and keep twisting each bundle of fiber.

STEP 3 If you twisted clockwise, then keep twisting the fiber bundles clockwise—but allow them to encircle each other counter-clockwise. It is the opposing force that makes the line strong. Meticulously splice in new fibers to continue twisting a long line for your fishing leader. It should be at least 6 feet (2 m) long and 0.03 inches (0.7 mm) in diameter.

STEP 4 Tie the base of your thorn to a wooden shank or the end of the line, insert into a chunk of bait, and cast into the water. The technique here is to allow the fish to swallow the bait. Do not jerk the line to set the hook. After you think the fish has swallowed, coax it into a waiting dip net—very, very slowly.

008 SET TRAPS FOR FISH AND CRUSTACEANS

The beauty of traps is that they work hard to collect your food while you're off doing something else. Fish and crustacean traps can also catch animals that are fast, nocturnal, and resistant to other fishing methods.

The sizes, shapes, and construction materials of traps are as variable as their prey. Wire mesh and wooden slats are common building materials, but netting, plastic mesh, woven vines, plastic containers, and hollow logs can work as well.

Almost all fish traps follow the same principles. Animals are lured into the trap by bait (or because it looks like an inviting shelter). The entrance is a restricted area, typically funnel shaped, leading to the center of the trap's interior. Animals work their way around until they find this entrance, and, once inside, behavior patterns cause them to seek an exit at the corners and perimeter of the trap. Rarely will they go back to the center of the trap to find the only exit; an octopus is usually the only creature smart enough.

You can also add an interior bait cage to keep the bait from being eaten by the trapped animals and enable the trap to keep working. Your aquatic quarry will be trapped—unless it's small enough to fit through the gaps in the trap wall (which is a great way to eliminate undersize animals).

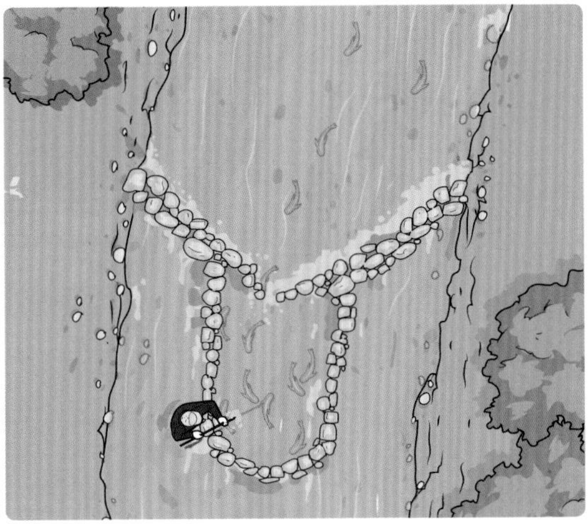

009 MAKE IT WEIR-D

If you're looking to get serious about fish traps, and you're going to be in one spot for a while, add a fish weir to your traps and watch the fish pile up.

A weir can be a wall, circular fence, or larger funnel directing fish into your traps. Some ancient weir construction styles are still used today. Why? Because they work. Weirs can be built of stone for permanent construction or by driving stakes or posts into the mud or sand for semipermanent installations. Weirs also work for spear fishing and net fishing.

010 MAKE A SODA-BOTTLE TRAP

All you really need to make a trap is a container and a funnel entrance. A soda bottle does the trick—with this, you can create a handy trap for catching minnows and other small fish, as well as crayfish. You can then use them as your bait to catch larger animals, or you can eat the little things yourself. All you need is a 2-quart (2-l) soda bottle, a bit of string, a cutting tool, and something meaty for bait.

STEP 1 Tear the label off and cut around the "shoulders" of the bottle. Remove the cap, and insert the funnel-shaped piece inside the bottle.

STEP 2 Poke a few holes near the cut edges of the bottle wall and the funnel piece. Use your string to "stitch" these separate plastic pieces together. Leave one long piece of string attached to one of these ties.

STEP 3 Poke a few small holes around the bottle for water flow. Add some bad meat, fish guts, or crushed insects to the trap, then submerge and tie off with the long string. Then sit back and watch it fill up!

011 CATCH FISH BY HAND

Hand fishing is perhaps our most primitive technique for collecting fish. Depending on your geography, this activity goes by many names, including noodling, catfisting, graveling, hogging, gurgling, grabbling, fish tickling, and stumping.

Check your local fishing regulations before you dive into this activity, as it is illegal in many areas. But if you're lost in the wilderness and in need of food, I say go for it.

Mastering hand fishing requires an understanding of the fish's habitat (for example, flathead catfish, the species of choice in the southern United States, hang out in underwater rock ledges, in holes, and under submerged logs).

These fish can really bite, so wear shoes, long pants, a long-sleeve shirt, and gloves. Feel for structures that could harbor a fish, then reach your hand into the structure. The fish will move forward and bite your hand. Resist the urge to pull away. Wrap your free arm around the fish, being careful to avoid contact with the barbs on its fins. Never try this solo, in case you become injured or entangled.

012 DODGE THE DANGERS

Hand fishing is far from hazard free. Common injuries include cuts, scrapes, scratches, and minor wounds to the bare-handed angler. Most of these small injuries can be avoided by wearing gloves and protective clothing. But the big dangers—well, read on, if you dare.

HAZARDS

DROWNING The most dangerous hazard in hand fishing, drowning is a special concern in rivers full of tree branches and brush that can snag clothing.

INFECTION You can lose fingers and toes from even small wounds when they become infected due to pathogens in the water.

BITES Your intended fish or other aquatic creatures can relieve you of your fingers (or more), particularly if you reach into a hole and discover a snapping turtle instead of a fish.

ANIMAL ATTACKS Waterways with high alligator populations or numerous venomous snakes are extremely high-risk environments, whether or not you're reaching into nooks and crannies.

013 GO NOODLING ABROAD

Hand fishing is not a modern invention, and the southeastern United States is not the only region where it's practiced. If you're feeling adventurous, do some research and wander the world to find this extremely simple extreme sport.

Perhaps the best-known hand-fishing gathering is the Argungu Fishing Festival in northern Nigeria. This annual fish-catching free-for-all began in 1934 as a way to celebrate the peace between the former Sokoto Caliphate and the Kebbi Kingdom. The primary fish caught in this event is the Nile perch, which can reach weights of 165 pounds (75 kg). These fish are caught both bare-handed and with small handheld nets. Whoever catches the biggest fish wins a hefty cash prize.

014 BUILD A BOX

If you live near a waterway with a catfish population, you can create your own underwater structures to entice them to stay for a while. I wouldn't exactly call this cheating, but I wouldn't call it fair play either. It is, however, something to add to your arsenal of fishing strategies, which could be employed if times got tough and your dinner table lay empty.

STEP 1 Gather some lumber, a saw, a tape measure, and galvanized nails or rustproof deck screws. You'll also need a hammer or screwdriver, depending on your choice of fastener.

STEP 2 Build a box roughly 5 feet (1.5 m) long, 2½ feet (75 cm) wide, and 1 foot (30 cm) tall, with solid ends.

STEP 3 Cut out an opening 8 inches (20 cm) tall and 1 foot (30 cm) wide in one end. This is the opening for fish to enter and for you to reach into while fishing.

STEP 4 Submerge the box and weigh it down with stones. In areas prone to flooding, attach a rope to the box and tie it to a nearby tree to keep it from being washed away.

015 CASE STUDY: THE THREE FISHERMEN

Three Mexican fishermen are modern proof that you can survive adrift at sea—for over nine months. Their ordeal began after their fishing boat carried them deep into the Pacific Ocean. Upon their rescue, their hometowns greeted them as folk heroes, and religious leaders hailed their story as proof of the power of faith. However you view this tale, it is a story of amazing seamanship and survival against seemingly impossible odds.

WHO Salvador Ordóñez, Jesús Vidaña, and Lucio Rendón

WHAT Adrift in the ocean

WHERE Pacific Ocean

WHEN Late October 2005 to early August 2006

HOW LONG THEY SURVIVED Nine months and nine days

THEIR STORY Five men left a Mexican fishing village on October 28, 2005, expecting to go on a several-day shark-fishing expedition. Their ill-fated voyage hit its first snag when they lost their heavy tackle. Then the boat ran out of fuel as they tried to find it, shore winds pushed them farther out, and the current caught them—holding them in its grasp for nearly 5,000 miles (8,000 km) across the deep ocean. During this ordeal, the boat's owner and another fisherman died of starvation and were buried at sea.

A Taiwanese fishing trawler spotted the boat and rescued the fishermen on August 9, 2006, near the Marshall Islands. Unimaginably, the three remaining men had survived nine months and nine days lost at sea, making their struggle one of longest episodes on record.

HOW THEY DID IT In the face of a slow death by starvation, the three survivors turned to their trade, fishing (as well as catching and eating raw seabirds). The small group had some knives and other equipment aboard, and they fashioned hooks from engine parts and lines from cables to make up for the tackle they lacked. Salvador Ordóñez was perhaps the most prepared man onboard, as he had taken a course on surviving at sea a year prior to the incident—and he also brought his Bible. Ordóñez was given the nickname "the cat" for his uncanny stealth at stalking the seabirds that landed on the boat at in the evening.

Over the nine-month voyage, Salvador Ordóñez, Jesús Vidaña, and Lucio Rendón spent their time fishing and praying. They learned to live off raw fish and birds, and they drank fish blood when rain was scarce. They weathered fierce fall storms, sang ballads, danced as best they could on the small boat, pretended to play guitar, and read aloud from the Bible. Their most perilous times came in December and January, when several large storms hit; the men were unable to fish and were in legitimate danger of sinking. Their longest stretch without food was thirteen days with only one seabird to share among them.

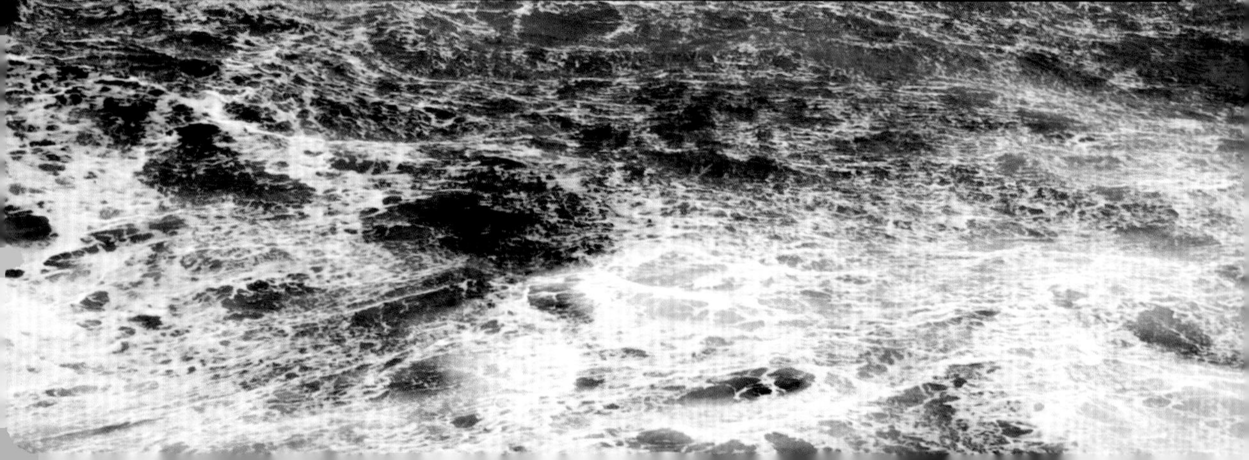

COULD YOU DO IT?

There's a reason this survival story is so epic: The odds are dramatically stacked against anyone lost on open water. Between storms, predators, lack of food and water, and the sun's unrelenting rays, there's a lot that can go wrong.

SHELTER There is no shelter on an open boat. The sun burns mercilessly all day, amplified by the reflection of the water. You're also completely vulnerable to storms. Your only choice is to stay clothed, cover exposed skin as best you can, and huddle for warmth on the cold ocean nights.

WATER Water, water everywhere, right? This must be like looking through a grocery store window, starving and penniless. All you can do is catch the rain, ration it well, and drink the fluids of any creatures you manage to catch.

FOOD Hope you like sashimi. That's all you're going to get if you're stuck in a life raft. Though you may crave many different types of food during your ordeal, you can live off raw fish for quite a long time.

MORALE The fishermen's faith in God kept them motivated and lifted their morale during their epic misadventure. Under similar conditions, concentrate on the things that mean something to you. Morale boosters may come in the form of your desire to see family and friends, your faith in a higher power, or your belief in yourself.

016 DIG UP DINNER

All around the world, tasty treats can be found for the price of a little digging. Clams, mussels, and similarly shelled creatures are often buried in sand or mud, and all you need to harvest them is a pail, a shovel, and a bit of knowledge.

Start by doing your homework on these creatures—find out what's locally abundant, what's in season, and what may be toxic to eat or illegal to collect in your area. Then put on your waders and go digging. The hints that follow are for clams, but many of their relatives can be harvested the same way.

Clams are chewy, rich buried treasures that can be found in tidal saltwater areas across the globe. Other related species make their home in fresh or brackish water. Many are prized for their size and flavor.

For example, the U.S. west coast is home to razor and geoduck clams along with many species of bay clams and other mollusks. Eastern clams include the Atlantic surf and soft-shell, among others. Regardless of the location, most of these creatures can be unearthed from their sandy nests using the same guidelines.

GUIDELINES

FIND THE RIGHT SPOT Learn where your local clam beds are located, and try to discover the "hot spots" in those areas.

GO AT LOW TIDE This means more area to successfully dig. Minus tides are best—get there two hours before peak low tide. During times of less swell, your quarry is likely to be closer to the surface. And closer to the surface means closer to your plate.

LOOK FOR SIGNS A clam's neck near the surface of the sand will produce a distinct "show." Look for small holes, round dimples, or indentations in dry sand, or pound your shovel handle in receding surf. If you're lucky, the pounding will reveal a show—or two.

DIG FAST Some clams are sluggish creatures, but others are lightning fast. The Pacific razor clam is one of the fastest diggers, and it can bury itself faster than some clammers can dig.

018 DIVE FOR LOBSTER

Lobster hunting, or bug diving as it's sometimes called, is about as hardcore a shellfishing technique as you can perform. It puts you in their world, under the water, reaching around in crevices and holes that could contain a lobster—or something much meaner.

Speedy grabs and swatting motions are the most successful method of bagging a lobster. But there's obviously a lot that can go wrong. Since lobsters primarily move around at night, you'll have to find protected spots where they hide during daylight hours. These underwater shelters can also contain sea urchins, moray eels, scorpion fish, and other sea creatures that bite, stab, and sting.

One of the best pieces of gear to make this pursuit safer for lobster hunters is Kevlar gloves. These cut-proof, puncture-proof gauntlets protect against urchin spines and many other dangers of the deep.

017 GET A LINE ON CRABS

The ideal way to catch crabs is with a crab pot (which works on the same principle as a standard fish trap), but making one isn't easy. Luckily, crabs can also be caught with a simple handheld, baited line.

Just tie a piece of bait, such as a chicken leg, to the end of a weighted line. The weight needs to be heavy enough to drag the bait to the bottom, even in a current. Cast the baited line roughly 4–6 feet (1–2 m) out into the water. This short line helps with easy retrieval and avoids wasting time while you battle the currents. Now wait—and remember, patience is a virtue.

When a crab grips the bait, you'll notice the line tightening. Don't yank the line or lift the crab from the water! Haul it in very slowly, until the crab is visible—only a rare one will hang on aggressively enough to make it to dry land, so be sure you have a dip net handy. Try this technique off jetties and piers for the best chances.

019 FOLLOW THE COON'S EXAMPLE

Looking for shellfish away from the sea? Find the nearest rivers with sand bars or mud flats and look for evidence of raccoon mollusk-digging activities. Freshwater mussels and related shellfish are often abundant in these riverine environments.

Look for little holes dug throughout the mud or sand. Also watch for raccoon tracks and empty mussel shells that have been strewn about. These are proof of two things: there are raccoons nearby, and there are shellfish in that mud (that is, if the masked bandit left any for you).

As with clams (see item 016), look for shows, and sift through the sand and mud to collect your prizes.

020 WORK FOR SCALE

Whether by trap, by hook, or by hand, you have caught one or more fish to satisfy your hunger. Now you need to clean the animals and prepare them for cooking. Fish are the easiest animal to skin and gut, but there are a few ways to make things go more smoothly.

Most fish have some sort of scales; they're there to protect the fish against all kinds of injuries. Their toughness also makes them difficult to digest, should you decide to eat the fish as-is. You can always fillet your fish and remove the skin completely, but removing only the scales will preserve the valuable calories stored in the skin. Keeping the skin also helps to preserve the fat contained in the fish, which is important for both flavor and nutrition.

You can purchase simple fish-scaling tools, or you can improvise them on the spot: use a knife, a sharp stone flake, or shells. You can also screw bottle caps to a stick or strip of wood to create a toothed scaler. Whatever you use, just scrape the fish from tail to head to begin removing scales, preferably before gutting. When you don't feel or see any more scales coming off, scrape your fingernails from tail to head to check for stragglers, and scrape again as needed.

021 FINISH THE JOB

Now for the part you've been waiting for: gutting the fish. It's a very easy task, especially with a sharp blade.

You can remove the head by chopping it off, and you're free to snip off the fins, but these steps are certainly not necessary. Don't waste the organs you remove, as they make great fish bait and trap bait. Don't discard the head, either—use it for soup stock to make a broth full of minerals and good fish flavor.

STEP 1 Cut into the fish's underside, starting between the gills and slicing down to the anal vent. It's okay if your knife tip slices through a few organs—fish aren't that germy.

STEP 2 Now use one or two fingers to swipe out the innards, and you're basically done for head-still-on cleaning. You can use your thumbnail to scrape the body cavity of blood and leftover entrails.

STEP 3 It's also a good idea to rinse the fish out. Rinse it quickly in cold water and then keep it out of water for firmer flesh. Store on ice or cook immediately.

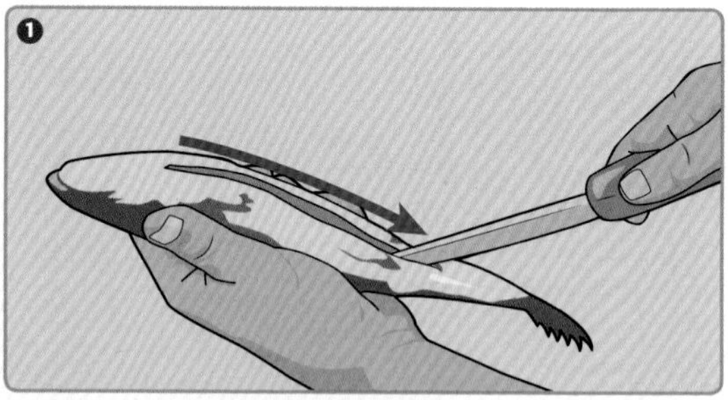

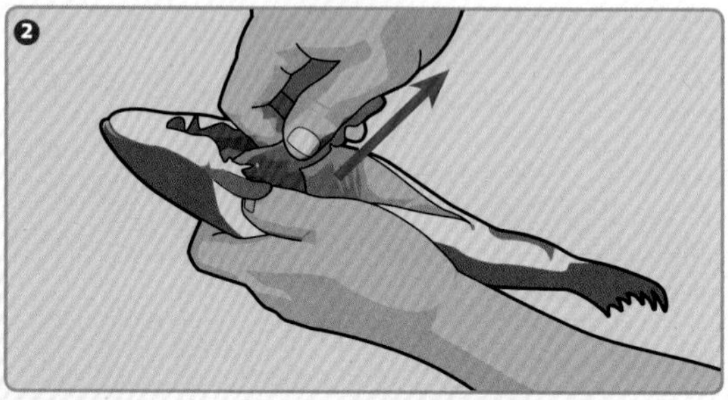

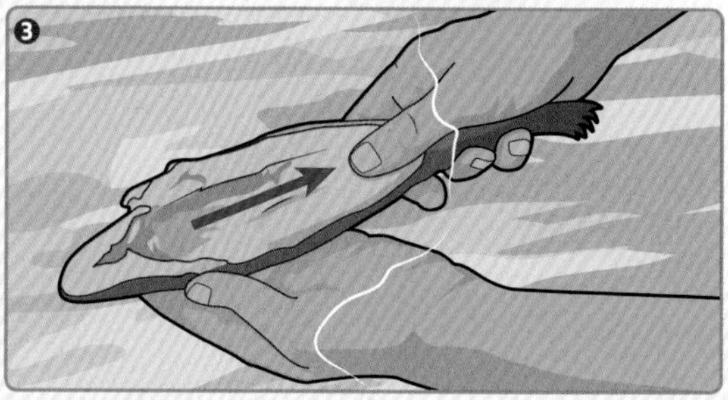

022 ENJOY THE SCALES

Fish with tiny scales and sparsely scaled fish can be gutted and prepared immediately— no scaling necessary. I am a big fan of trout with the scales still on, as well as catfish and smaller fish that I'm lucky enough to catch in small traps. These finger-size fish don't even need to be gutted. Fry them or roast them whole, ideally until they are crispy, and crunch on them (bones and all) like a kind of fishy cracker.

023 LEARN HOW TO FILLET

Bigger fish will yield some big, beautiful fillets, and cutting your own is a great way to portion out a larger catch. This process will differ depending on the fish and its particular bone structure, but here's one way to get started.

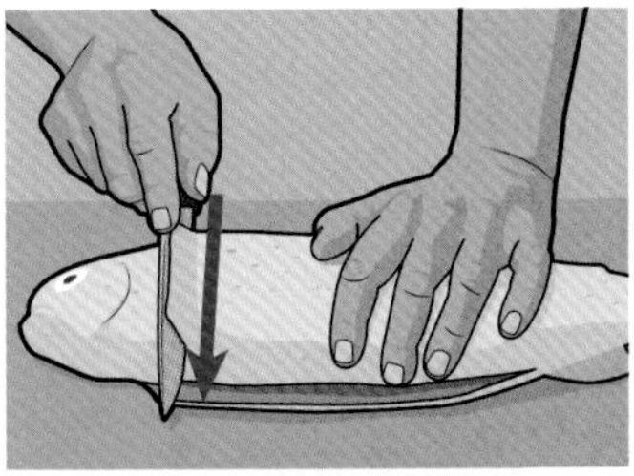

STEP 1 Use a sharp, flexible fillet knife to make a deep cut behind the gill plate and at the tail on one side of your fish.

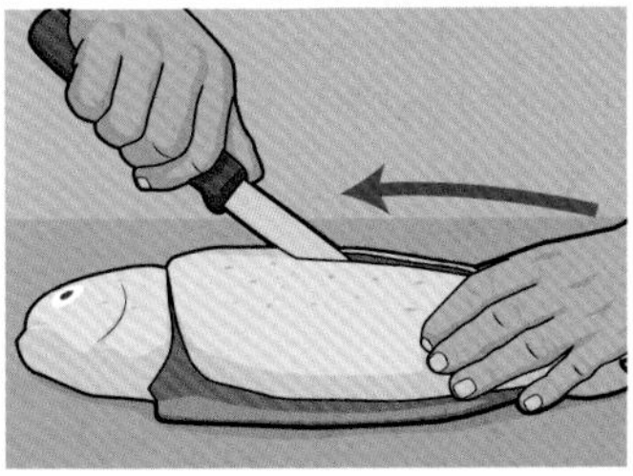

STEP 2 Make a connecting cut down the fish's back to join the gill cut and tail cut.

STEP 3 Begin slicing down the fish, using the backbones as a guide. Make long cuts from head to tail, eventually cutting down to the belly, and peel off the fillet. If you have not gutted the fish, be careful to avoid piercing the body cavity.

STEP 4 Repeat the process on the other side of the fish.

STEP 5 Waste not, want not. Remove the innards, chop up the remaining fish, and simmer in water to create a savory fish stew.

024 PRESERVE FISH WITH SMOKE

Now that you've caught some fish, it's time to figure out what to do with them. Before the days of freezers and canners, smoking, drying, and brining techniques were used to preserve the catch. Today, we can use some of these long-perfected practices to preserve and season the catch of the day.

Smoking fish can produce some remarkably flavorful results, and it can be done without much in the way of modern conveniences. There are two traditional ways (using the same setup) to smoke fish and other foods.

HOT SMOKING This technique uses a closed box to hold in the smoke and the heat. The fish is cooked by this heat and permeated with a smoky flavor. Fish prepared in this manner can last up to a week at room temperature.

COLD SMOKING Cold smoking is done at cooler temperatures for a longer period of time. The goal in this method is long-term fish storage, which requires the fish be dried rather than cooked. It should not get hot enough in the smoker to actually cook the fish: temperatures under 100°F (38°C) are ideal.

025 PUT THE CHIPS DOWN

You won't be smoking anything without a good source of smoke, which means that wood chips are the most vital part of the operation. A modern smoking setup can involve a hot plate (portable electric burner) heating a pan of dampened chips. More traditional methods (sans electricity) involve a pan of hardwood coals from a fire with wet wood chips sprinkled over the top. Determine your method based on your nearby tree species.

Make sure you avoid any local species that are toxic. My local bad guys in the eastern U.S. are black locust, yew, buckeye, horse chestnut, rhododendron, and mountain laurel. You'll also want to skip bitter resinous woods like cedar, cypress, redwood, fir, pine, spruce, and other needle-bearing trees.

TREE	FLAVOR
APPLE	Apple wood, found in orchards, makes a sweet smoke perfect for poultry and pork.
HICKORY	Hickory chips produce a rich, sharp flavor and make hot, long-burning coals.
MAPLE	Chips from maple wood are excellent for smoking tasty cheeses.
MESQUITE	Native to the southern U.S., mesquite wood produces smoke with an earthy flavor.
ASH	Ash wood chips produce a lightly flavored smoke that's great for fish and poultry.
OAK	With a heavy smoke flavor, red oak is good on ribs and pork, and white oak yields lasting coals.

026 SMOKE YOUR CATCH

While it is possible to smoke smaller fish whole, filleting and hanging them properly allows them to smoke more evenly, as the greater exposed surface area lets the smoke penetrate deeper into the flesh. And when you're dealing with larger fish, this step becomes a necessity.

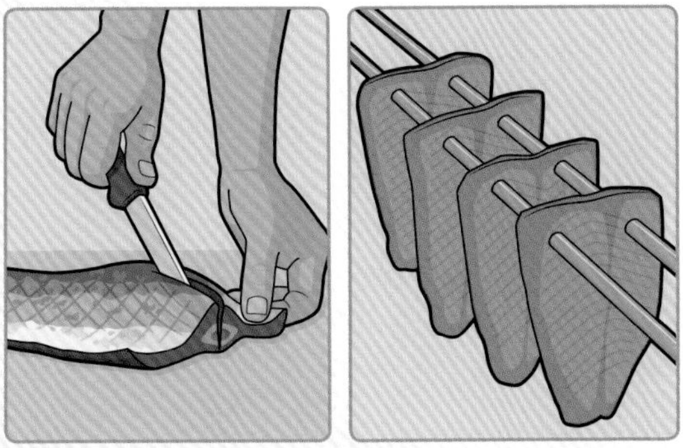

Cut small fish along the backbone and press them flat. These flattened fillets can be hung on rods, laid out flat on a rack, or draped over a pole.

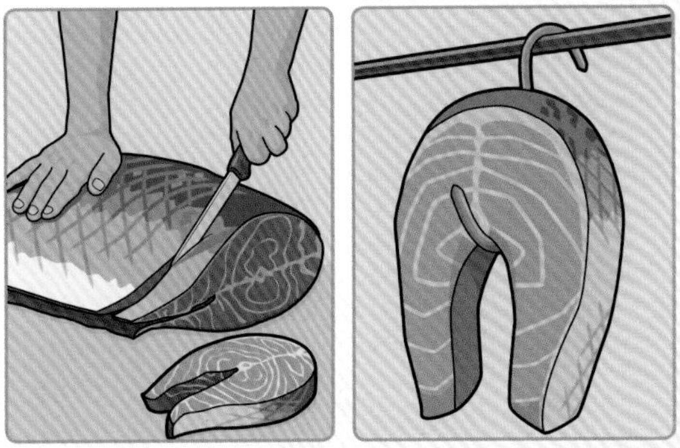

Cut larger fish, like salmon, into U-shaped steaks and hang them on hooks in your smoker.

027 GET SALTY WITH BRINED FISH

Brining can be used as a marinade to infuse the meat with flavor before smoking, or it can be used as a method of preservation in and of itself.

SALT AND SPICE MARINADE Add 1.3 gallons (5 l) water to a stainless or enamel pot and bring to a boil. Pour in 3 pounds (1.5 kg) salt, $\frac{3}{4}$ cup (150 g) white or brown sugar, 2 tablespoons (30 g) whole black peppercorns, and 5 sprigs oregano. Once the salt and sugar are dissolved, cool the brine to room temperature and add several of your fish. Place in a cold spot or in your refrigerator for two to four hours. Remove the fish, allow them to drain, and then smoke as normal.

PRESERVING BRINE Soak the fish for one to two hours in a mild brine made from 1 gallon (4 l) water and 5 tablespoons (75 g) salt. Remove the fish and allow them to drain off all surface moisture, then coat with salt and stack them in a crock or large glass jar. Alternate layers of salt-encrusted fish with layers of salt. Place a weight on top of the fish to press them down. Over the next few days, the salt will pull the fluid from the fish and create a potent brine. Once the salt has drained the fish of their fluid, rinse the fish (and your crock), and refill with a new brine made from 2.5 pounds (1.2 kg) salt and 1 gallon (4 l) water. Store the crock in a cool, dark place, and replace the brine every couple of months.

028 DRY THEM, YOU MIGHT LIKE THEM

One week of low humidity and warm sunshine can turn your fresh, juicy catch into fish jerky, which can be enjoyed as is for up to a year or used to make a tasty broth. Dried fish can be stored at room temperature, provided the flesh stays bone-dry. Avoid fatty fish (like catfish, eel, and salmon), as the fat turns rancid under the skin.

In order to air-dry, you'll need a stretch of dry weather. If your area is damp or you're in the middle of a rainy season, air-drying isn't a safe option. If the weather is right, you're good to go.

First, clean and dress your fish as quickly as possible after catching, then give them a rinse in a salty brine, towel dry, and pack them in salt for 48 hours. Then, rinse them again, and they are ready to dry. Hang them properly (see item 029), then store in a cool, dry place.

To reconstitute, crumble the fish—head, bones, and all—into simmering water as a soup starter.

029 MAKE A FISH SHED

Direct sunlight can melt the fats in fish, thereby destroying all your hard work. Luckily, any kind of simple roof can protect your drying fish from a passing shower and direct sunlight. If you only have a few fish to dry, you can hang them under a porch or the eaves of your house. Those who found more success on their fishing trip will need a fish-drying shed.

Four posts and a flat or peaked roof are all you really need, along with a rack or wire-mesh stand to allow air flow around the fish. During the drying process, you'll need to bring the fish pieces inside at night and on inclement days. You'll also need people nearby to scare off animal marauders. If flies or other insects are a problem in your area, build a small, smoky fire near and upwind of the shed to waft smoke over the drying fish and drive off pests.

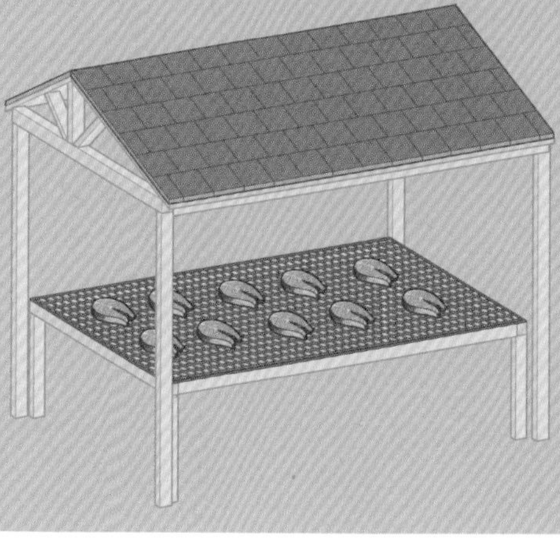

Do not put the fire under the fish, as air-dried fish need to stay raw in order to be preserved safely. Dry them for a week and then test them by pushing your finger into the flesh of the thickest piece: If the dent stays put, you need more drying time; if it doesn't make a dent, or the dent pops back out, you are done.

030 BUILD A SMOKER

Virtually any box, container, or tiny shed can become a smoker for fish, meats, and even animal hides. Take what you have available, and turn it into a serious smoke box.

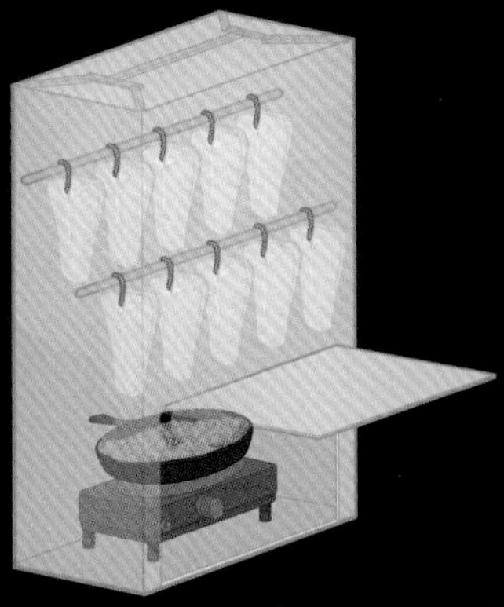

APPLIANCE-BOX SMOKER Use a giant cardboard box or crate from a new appliance to create a cold smoker. Cut out the bottom or leave it open on bare ground. Use sticks or metal rods poked through the box to make a rack for the food. You can even use wire to dangle your catch from the ceiling of the box. Cut a door in the side, and place a pan of coals and wood chips on the ground inside. You can also use a hot plate and a pan of damp wood chips.

ELECTRIC-RANGE SMOKER Repurpose an old electric range into a smoker by cutting a hole in the bottom of the oven compartment and using the metal drawer to hold your pan of coals and wood chips. For an easier approach, just place a pan of coals in the bottom of the oven compartment and use the existing oven racks to hold your fish or food.

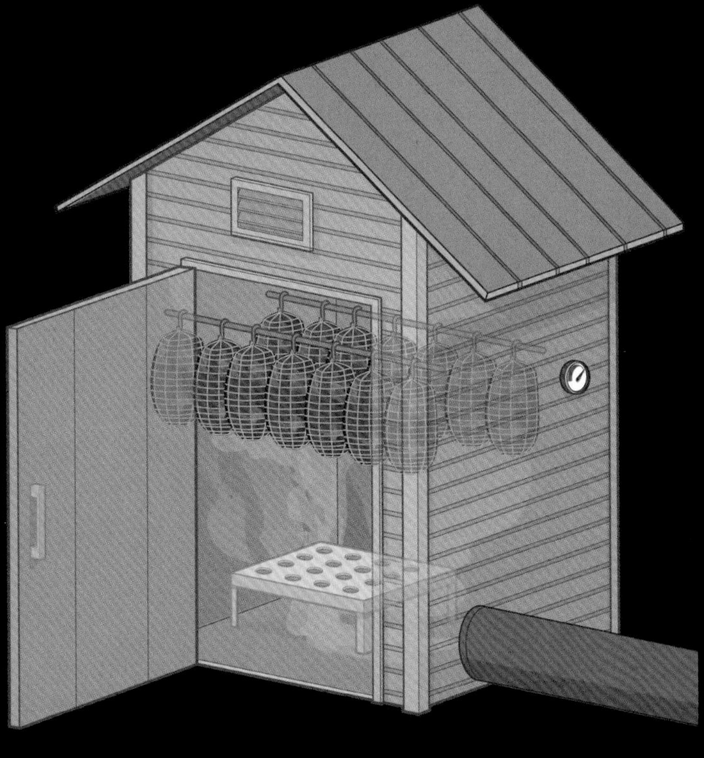

PERMANENT SMOKE HOUSE Build or repurpose a very small shed for hot or cold smoking. Stove piping or a clay drain line can be used to pipe smoke into the structure, and the smoke can be supplied by an old wood stove or a similar fire box.

031 SUPERPLANT: PINE

PINE FOR THIS EVERGREEN

Pine trees can be found throughout the world, and a variety of species are native to the Northern Hemisphere. Pines are easily identified by their needles, which are found in clusters of 2–5 in most of the world, and they also bear telltale pine cones. These versatile trees provide us with food, fuel, glue, and many other useful things. Make sure you have the right evergreen, and go crazy with the plethora of piney products available to you.

KILL YOUR STANK

Few things scream "human in the woods!" like the scent we carry around at all times. Most animals have keen senses, and you'll need to fool their sharp nose to have any success at trapping or hunting. In areas where pine is available, crush the green needles and wipe the slightly sticky material all over your clothing and exposed skin. Your evil human scent will be camouflaged by the biting scent of pine (see item 058 for more).

TRY SOME BARK

Yes, you can eat tree bark. It's a safe and nutritious wild food as long as you use the right part of the bark from the right species of tree. To clarify, I'm not talking about the crusty, corky part of the bark. The bark section of choice is the cambium layer, which lies right next to the wood. It can be obtained in large amounts year-round by "skinning" a single tree or by taking advantage of living limbs that have broken off during storms.

The bark is relatively nutritious, packing about 500–600 calories to the pound (450 g), but it may be bitter depending on the species and the tree's growing conditions. Most inner bark contains digestible starches, some sugar, vitamins, minerals, and tons of fiber—so brace yourself for a good internal scrubbing.

Other trees with edible inner bark include slippery elm, black birch, yellow birch, red spruce, black spruce, balsam fir, and tamarack.

HAVE SOME TEA AND NUTS

In addition to the inner bark, you can also eat pine nuts and needles. The soft, fatty nuts can be picked from large pine cones and eaten raw or cooked. You can get 10% of your daily potassium in 3.5 ounces (100 g) of pine nuts, which have approximately 640 calories. Steep a spoonful of chopped pine needles in a mug of hot water for fifteen minutes to make a tea containing five times your daily requirement of vitamin C. (Note: Pine needles may be harmful to unborn babies. Also, there may be toxins in the needles of the western ponderosa pine and the southeastern loblolly pine, so avoid these species.)

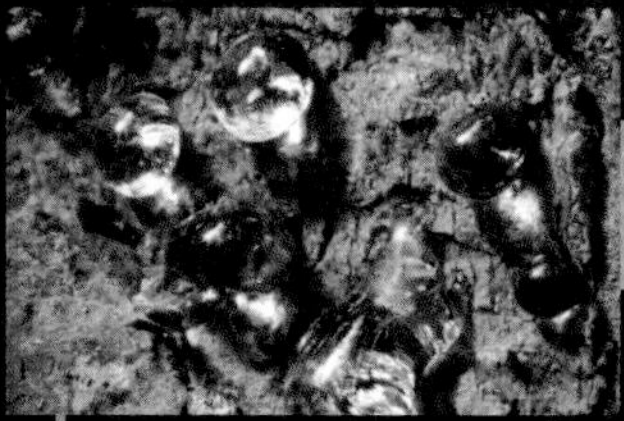

GLUE WITH PINE SAP

Pine-sap glue is a waterproof, resinous glue made from the sap of evergreen trees such as pine, spruce, fir, and cedar. It is ideal for wet conditions because it's impermeable to moisture but will melt easily. To make the glue, gather the sap and pitch from wounds and weeping spots on an evergreen's trunk and branches. The clearer and softer the pitch, the better (although darker pitch is still usable). Heat in a fireproof container for a few minutes, and add ground charcoal as an aggregate. When the pitch cools, it should look like shiny black plastic. Simply heat the glue and the items to be glued, and use while hot (it is okay to heat repeatedly).

BURN IT UP WITH FATWOOD

Fatwood is known by many names, including fat lighter, lighter knot, rich lighter, and heart pine. Whatever you choose to call it, fatwood comes from the same place: the heartwood of pine trees and a few other resinous conifers. As a tree dies, the pine resin can become concentrated in the heartwood, which then becomes hard and very rot-resistant. You may also find fatwood in the joints where pine limbs intersect with the trunk.

Fatwood is prized because it lights readily and burns well even in wet weather. The resin in the wood makes it almost waterproof and very flammable—both great qualities in for starting a fire.

The fatwood can be cut and split into small sticks for kindling or carved into shavings for tinder. To find yourself a ready supply of this fire-starting wonder, look through a pine forest until you come across a stump with only the center remaining. This center should seem solid. Cut off some pieces of this wood, and give them a look and a sniff. If they look like perfectly good wood (not rotten at all), then smell the pieces—if it's fatwood, it will smell strongly of pine (in a chemical way, like scented cleaner) and resin, with the sharp odor of turpentine. Burn it as a final test; good fatwood makes thick, black smoke.

032 KNOW YOUR QUARRY

You've got the tools and the proper permits, but you need a strategy if you're going to bring home the bacon. Or venison. Or squirrel. Study up on these common prey animals, and learn what to expect.

	ANIMAL	STRATEGY	FLAVOR	SEASON
DEER		Place treestands and ground blinds on travel routes and near feeding areas. Take pains to control your scent, and be quiet and still. Various calls, scents, and food supplements (where legal) will help draw them near.	Deer produce rich, red meat that is very nutritious.	Typically fall and early winter depending on region and hunting method.
BEAR		Strategies vary widely by region. Where legal, baiting of bears has been a successful tactic. Other hunters will try to "drive" bears through a stand of timber, sometimes with dogs. Spotting and stalking is popular in the west.	The meat is rich and dark, though a little greasy for some palates.	Depending on the area, bear seasons occur in the spring and/or fall.
ELK		Spot-and-stalk is the most popular tactic with these imposing animals. Glass for elk in likely feeding and bedding areas, and quietly move in for a shot with the wind in your face. Calls are effective during the rut.	Elk meat has a richer, bolder flavor than that of their whitetail cousins.	Throughout the fall, typically broken down by method: bow, rifle, or muzzleloader.
MOOSE		Despite their size, these huge animals can seemingly disappear into their surroundings. During the rut, bulls are very aggressive and will come to calls.	Mild and tender. Many people prefer it to deer or elk meat.	Usually September through November, though tags are hard to come by in the lower 48.
FERAL HOG		Hogs have terrible eyesight, but a great sense of smell. Set up near known feeding or watering areas or stalk them into the wind. In some states (hello, Texas), hogs can be hunted at night.	You already know what these guys taste like—they're made of pork.	Generally open year-round, as wild pigs have become a nuisance species in many areas.
SQUIRREL		Scoped small-caliber rifles (.17s and .22s) are great for picking squirrels out of the treetops. Shotguns loaded with No. 4 or 6 shot are popular, too.	Squirrels have nutty, tender, sweet-tasting meat.	Typically from early fall through winter, although some states have spring seasons.
RABBIT		Rabbits are usually hunted with hounds (usually beagles), but solo hunters can roust them from thickets and brush piles.	These herbivores produce a very lean, healthy, and delicious meat.	Typically hunted from fall through winter.
TURKEY		Turkeys have tremendous eyesight and very good hearing. Camo up and keep your movement to a minimum. In the spring, prey upon their desire to mate and draw toms in with hen calls.	Extremely lean when compared to farmed birds, yet very tasty when prepared right.	Both spring and fall; turkeys are a classic conservation story, prolific in all states but Alaska.

033 PAY ATTENTION TO SEASON

Hunting and trapping seasons exist for many reasons, primarily to preserve the stock. State wildlife agencies take into consideration the animal's mating patterns and rearing of the young. The season also focuses on the animal's preparation for winter as well as other factors. In most areas and for most animals, there are specific seasons when they can be taken, and the rest of the year is left for them to remain undisturbed.

For most wild game, the season runs from fall into midwinter. A few animals have a shorter season, and some (often ones that are considered nuisance animals) have a continuous open season, meaning that you can take them any time hunting is allowed. Any hunting done out of season (or out of place) is considered poaching, and it can carry steep punishments. Pick up a guidebook or research online to clarify your options.

034 SCOUT YOUR HUNTING GROUNDS

If you have the means, scouting your hunting area prior to the season can prove invaluable. You can hang trail cameras on known travel routes to surveil the local animals, or hike into the wild to glass feeding areas from a high vantage.

Alternatively, you might slip through the woods in search of tracks, scat, beds, scrapes, rubs, and wallows. Gather as much reconnaissance as possible ahead of time to get a better idea of your quarry's patterns, habits, and tendencies once the season starts.

035 GET THE RIGHT ACTION

The longer the barrel, the easier it is to aim. This truism works in firearms, blowguns, and tanks, and it's why the rifle (as opposed to, say, a pistol) makes the most sense for hunting. Modern rifles come in a dizzying array of variations; try a few and make an educated purchase.

MUZZLELOADER These single-shot blackpowder rifles are loaded through the muzzle (hence the name), and fired when the hammer hits a cap. Each round is manually pushed down the barrel.

SINGLE SHOT This rifle has a break action, which is often a more familiar action for shotguns than rifles. Single-shot rifles open at the breech, and you manually insert one bullet at a time for each shot. Why is this older style still around? Two reasons: safe operation and strong, durable components.

BOLT-ACTION A classic rifle, the bolt-action rifle requires a little work, but there are fewer pieces that can malfunction than on a more complex rifle action. Each time you close the bolt, you're chambering a new round.

LEVER ACTION A lever-action rifle uses a lever underneath the rifle, near the trigger, to load each fresh round. These were popularized in cowboy shows and movies and have remained high on the list.

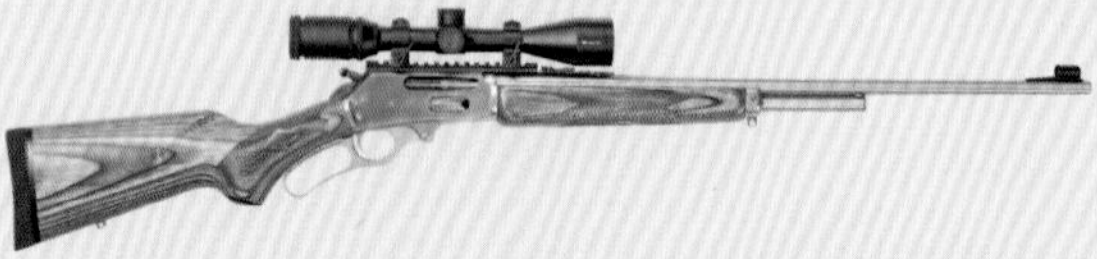

PUMP-ACTION Pump-action rifles chamber a round when you slide the fore-end to the rear—just like a pump-action shotgun.

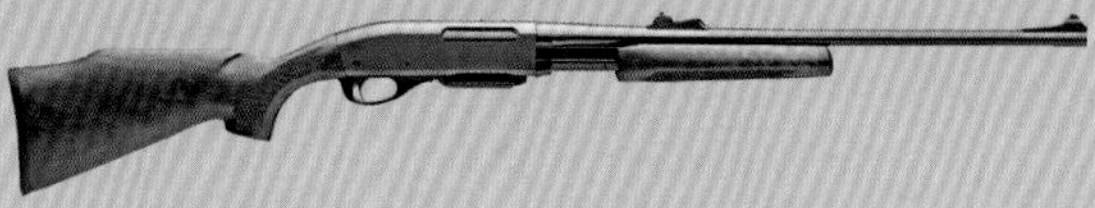

SEMIAUTOMATIC Clever engineering in the semiauto rifle uses part of the energy of each shot to eject the spent cartridge and chamber another round. These rifles offer the fastest follow-up shots.

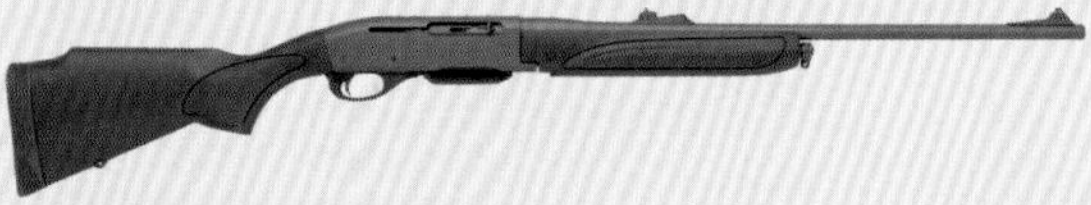

SPORTING RIFLES (AR PLATFORM) With the AR-15's common use in the military and popularity among those who have served, it's only natural that this rifle would have a growing following among hunters and sportsmen. These are versatile, rugged, modular rifles that many people prefer.

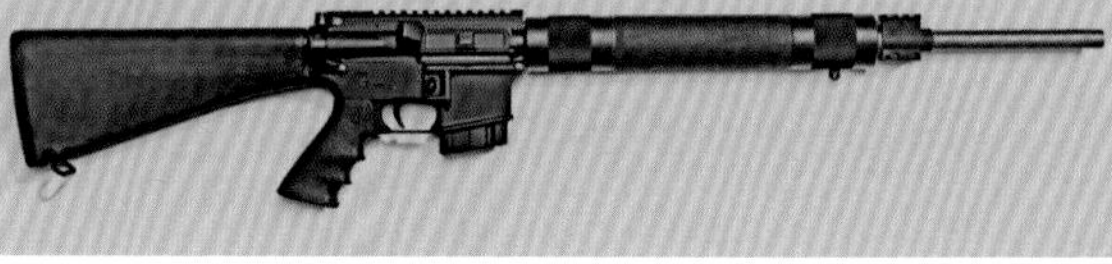

036 SHOOT OLD-SCHOOL

The oldest rifles in the world are simple muzzleloaders. Since the Chinese invented gunpowder in the 10th century, these rifles have been through many iterations, from the matchlock to the wheel-lock to the flintlock—invented especially for King Louis XIII of France.

Muzzleloaders have experienced a resurgence of interest in the past 25 years, and though today's model is still loaded from the business end of the barrel, the rest of the weapon is state of the art.

037 GO THE DISTANCE WITH YOUR RIFLE

Because gravity never stops working, even on a speeding bullet, you'll need to learn to judge distances, adjust your sights or scope accordingly, and shoot accurately at a particular distance. Range finders are tools that help you calculate the distance to the target while you're in the field. You should also spend some time at the range, working on your distances. Practice your shots and sight adjustments at 25, 50, 100, 150 meters, and so on. Remember that the game won't be standing next to a 100-meter sign during your hunt, so you'll need to know what that distance looks like.

038 CLEAN UP THE MESS

Shooting your rifle is all fun and games, but you'll need to do some housekeeping to clean and preserve your investment. Purchase a basic gun-cleaning kit and use it after you're done shooting. Your gun will repay you with years of dependable service.

039 SCOPE IT OUT

If you're going to hunt with a rifle and plan to shoot out more than 50 yards, a scope is a mandatory investment. The right optic will allow for a degree of precision not regularly possible with open sights. Talk to your gun dealer to figure out what kind of scope is right for your rifle and the terrain where you'll be hunting. Rifle scopes are available with either a fixed or variable magnification. That is, it will magnify an image a specific amount (6X, for instance), or across a range (say, 3–9X). Another important thing to consider when buying a scope is the size of the objective lens. In a typical scope configuration, like 3–9x42, "42" represents the diameter of the objective lens in millimeters. The larger the objective lens, the greater the scope's ability to "see" during low-light conditions. The trade-off, however, is added weight.

040 MAKE SOME ADJUSTMENTS

Once you have your scope installed, it's time to learn how to use it. The two adjustments that every scope will have are the windage (side to side adjustment) and the elevation (up and down). These are adjusted by a pair of small dials. The windage adjustment will allow you to correct for the wind's force on the round (which can be surprising). The elevation adjustment can correct for the drop on the bullet over distance. Focus is another common adjustment, and it works just like the focus on a manual camera lens. Just twist the lens bell until your view is sharp.

041 EMBRACE ARCHERY

Want to hunt like your ancestors? Pick up a bow. Native people worldwide developed the bow and arrow to improve upon the hand-thrown spear and spear-thrower (called an atlatl). But when you think about it, the bow is not really a primitive weapon. It is a complicated, intellectual invention created from very random, unrelated items. And, of course, modern compound bows involve all kinds of high-tech innovations.

A flexible stick, strong string, smaller sticks, the feathers from birds, glue from plants, and sharp pieces of stone all converged to become the most lethal long-range weapon until the birth of the firearm. Let's check out the bows that are available for today's archer.

❶ **SELF BOW** A bow made from one solid piece of material, typically wood, is referred to as a self bow. This is the oldest and most traditional bow style.

❷ **RECURVE** The recurve bow, as you might guess, has curved limbs, which store up more energy than a flat bow. These can be self bows with curved limb tips or composite bows glued together from various materials.

❸ **LONGBOW** Popularized in Europe but found everywhere, longbows are self bows around 6 feet (2 m) in length. Their increased power and range changed the nature of medieval warfare.

❹ **COMPOUND** A modern engineering marvel, the compound bow uses fiberglass limbs and a pulley system to store great energy, but is lightweight to hold in a drawn position. The compound bow is the one most commonly used for hunting.

❸

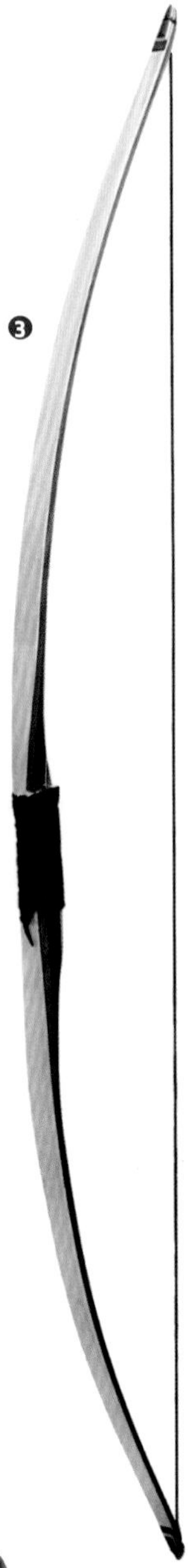

❷

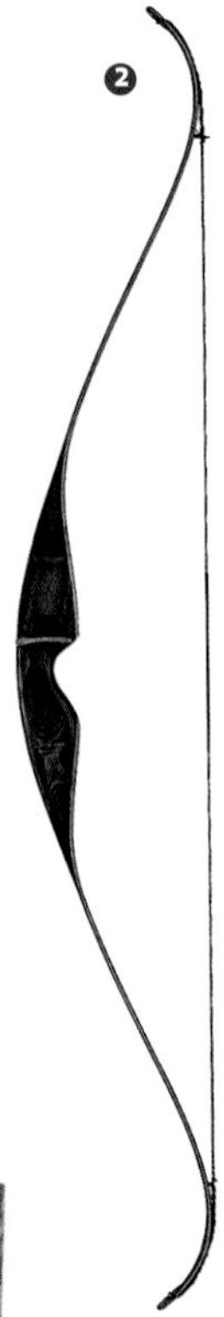

❶

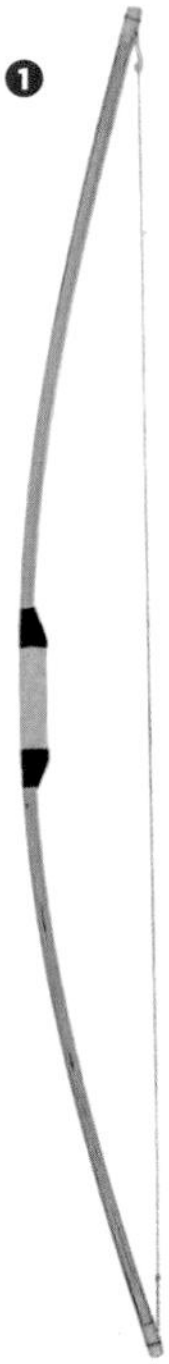

❹

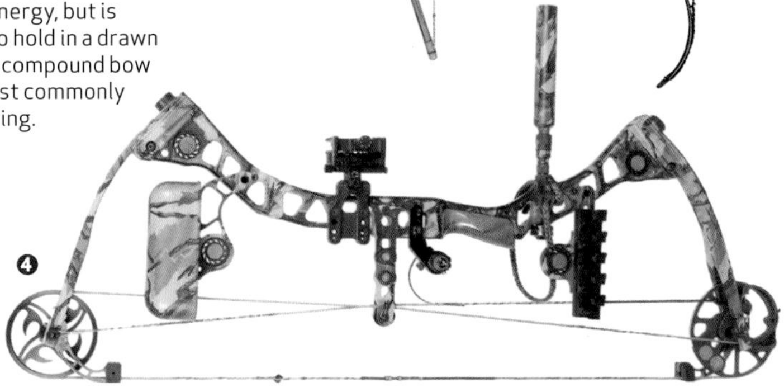

042 ADD SOME SIGHTS

A bow of any kind can have one or more sights attached to it. While some archers may practice instinctive shooting (firing without looking down the arrow) or traditional aiming (looking down the arrow shaft), sights can add accuracy and make your hunt more productive, and they are always present on compound bows. If you haven't been shooting in years and need an edge, the sights will do it.

Compound bows are outfitted with a vertical row of sighting pins. As the target grows more remote, you'll use lower pins, which raises the bow and gives you the arcing trajectory you need to hit the target.

A peep sight (which can accompany the pin sights) is a little donut-shaped disk placed in the bowstring that allows you to look through the center hole at the pin, which should be covering the target. These two visual points give you better accuracy than just the pins—like the front and rear sights on a rifle, they align the entire weapon.

043 GET SOME PROTECTION

A painful discovery that new archers make on their first day of shooting is this: Archery can hurt. Bruised fingertips and scraped inner forearms are the most common complaints, both of which can be remedied with a little protective gear. An archery glove or finger tab will save the wear and tear on your fingertips as you shoot, and an arm guard will save your forearm from worse damage. I once saw a neophyte archer shoot a compound bow with no arm guard and an inward bent elbow. The string slapped his arm with such force that, in mere minutes, he had a fluid-filled blister the size of a hamburger bun. Don't repeat his mistake.

044 AVOID DRY FIRES

If you're just playing around with a bow or have an epic misfire, you might release a fully drawn bow without an arrow on the string. This is called a dry fire, and the only faster way to destroy your bow is with a chain saw. Because the arrow absorbs so much force from the bowstring when shot, normal arrow firing isn't damaging to the bow. A dry fire, however, is a sudden shock and jolt to all of the bow's bent fibers. Whether they're wood, fiberglass, or something else, these fibers are damaged by the dry-fire shock. Will your bow explode if you dry fire? Nope, but it's more likely to break later.

045 CARVE A BOW

Need a bow? Don't have one? No problem—you can make a quickie survival bow and start shooting it immediately. Bow making can be a fun hobby at home and a means for catching some calories in a survival situation. Carve this bow from a sapling or tree branch, then string it with some of the strongest cordage you can get. It is surprisingly quick and easy.

❶ CHOOSE THE RIGHT WOOD Some of the best wood for making bows include Osage orange, yew, ash, black locust, and hickory; most hardwoods (like oak and maple) will work. Start with a relatively straight sapling or branch that is free of knots, side branches, and twists, about 6 feet (2 m) long and 2 inches (5 cm) in diameter. It should be dead and dry but have no sign of rot. Cut it carefully to avoid creating any cracks in the wood. This piece is now your bow stave.

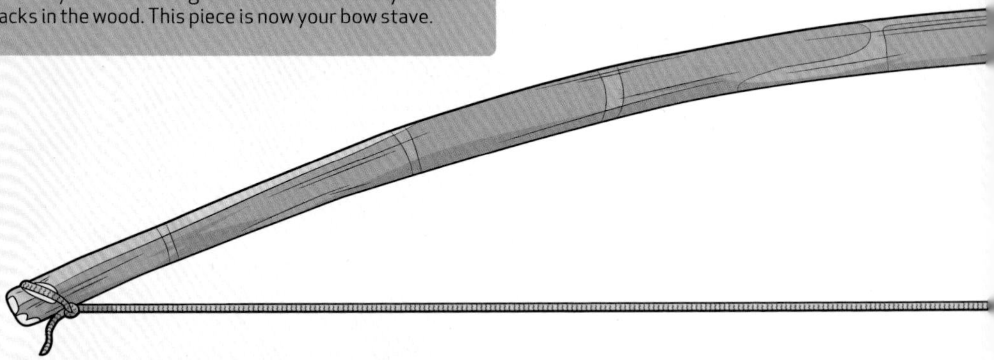

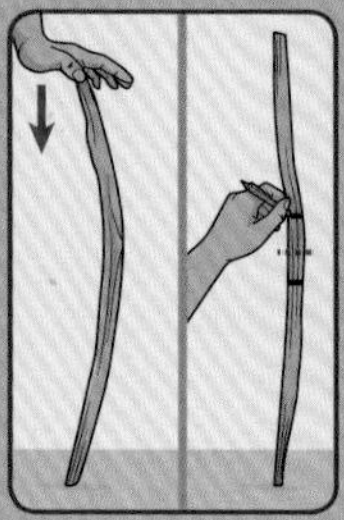

❷ FIND THE BELLY AND BACK Stand the stave upright on the ground, hold the top loosely with one hand, and lightly push down until the middle bows outward. It should swivel to show you which way it is naturally curved or more bendable. The outside bend of this curve is called the "back" and the inside bend is the "belly." Don't touch the back—any damage to it can cause the bow to break. Mark out a handhold area in the middle of the bow by marking 3 inches (7.5 cm) out from the center in both directions. The area above the handhold is the upper limb and the area below is the lower limb.

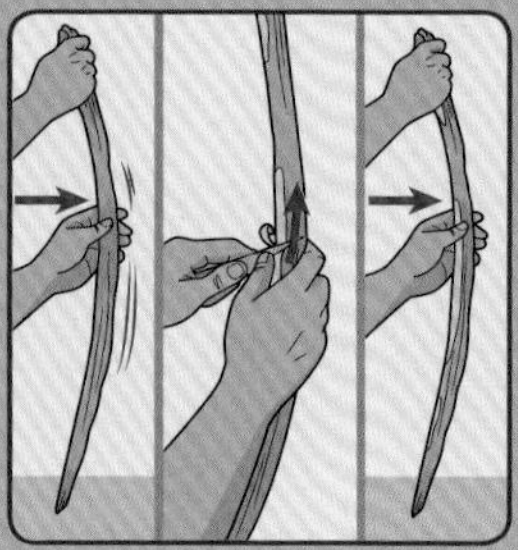

❸ TAKE SHAPE Put the bottom tip of the bow on the ground, hold of the top tip, and push slightly outward from the belly side of the handhold. Observe how the limbs bend and note any areas that do not bend, then use a knife to slowly and carefully remove wood from the stiff parts of the belly. Remember: Only remove wood from the belly side. The goal is to get the limbs to bend in an even curve; double-check the bend frequently until both limbs are flexing evenly throughout their length.

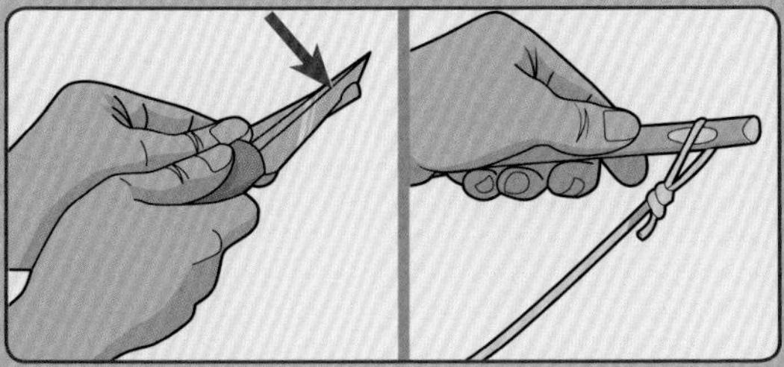

④ NOTCH AND STRING Carve small notches on each tip, being careful not to carve into the back of the bow. They only need to be deep enough to keep a bowstring in place. Tie loops into both ends of a nylon, sinew, paracord, or plant-fiber string. You want about 5–6 inches (13–15 cm) of space between the string and the handhold when the bow is strung. Don't fully draw the bow yet—doing so can break it.

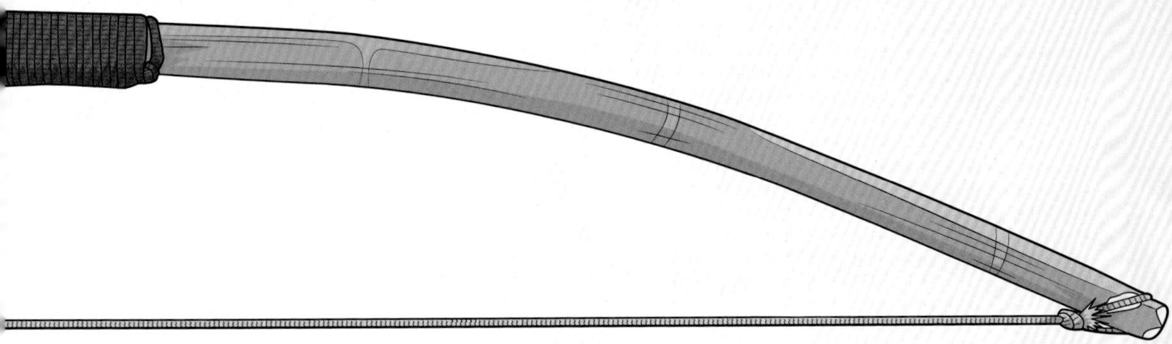

⑤ TILLER Hang the bow horizontally on a branch by the handhold and pull the string a few inches downward. You want each limb to bend evenly and symmetrically. This final shaping is called tillering, and it is one of the most important steps. Shave, scrape, sand, or carve the belly of each limb until both limbs bend equally and evenly. Recheck frequently, pulling down on the string a little bit further each time until you are able to pull it to your draw length (the distance between the handhold and where your fingers hold the bowstring when pulled back to your upper jaw).

The tillering process is complete once both limbs flex equally and evenly and the draw weight (pounds of pressure required to pull the string back to a full draw) is at your desired poundage. You need a 25–35 pound (11–16 kg) draw for hunting small game or 40–60 pounds (18–27 kg) for larger animals.

⑥ FINISH THE JOB For wilderness survival situations, the bow can now be used as is. If you have the luxury of finishing it properly however, you should take the time to sand the belly smooth and oil the entire bow to seal off the wood and prevent over-drying. Many bowyers prefer linseed or tung oil, but animal fat works, too. To care for your bow, shoot and oil it frequently, adjust the tillering as needed, and unstring the bow when not in use. Your quickie bow has the advantages of being quick to build and ready to use right away, but keep in mind that it won't shoot as well as a fine bow and it may break or crack after some use.

046 MAKE YOUR OWN ARROWS

So you've made a bow, but of course it's no good without the arrows. Your arrows need to be lightweight yet strong. They must also be straight, well fletched, have the right rigidity (spine), and be the right length for your bow. The arrow is the part of the operation that has to be flightworthy—the bow is merely the springy stick engine in charge of launching it.

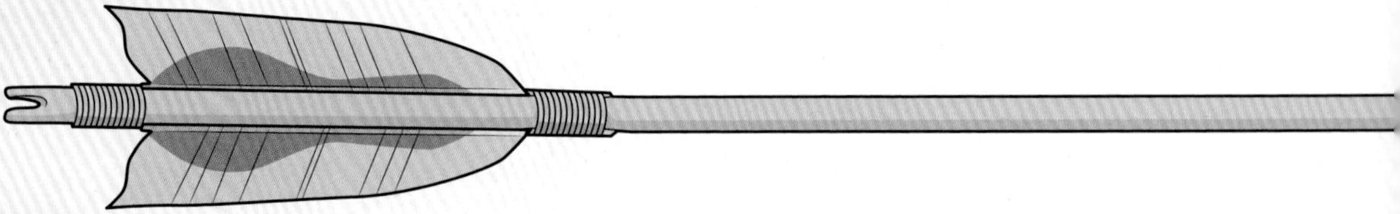

❶ COLLECT SOME SHOOTS Collect branches, shoots, and straight saplings that are at least 30 inches (72 cm) long and 3/8–1/2 inch (around 1 cm) in diameter. Take a ruler to ensure you only gather appropriately sized pieces, and trim off the side branches from the wood as each is collected.

If you are beginning the arrow-making process right away, peel the bark off each prospective arrow shaft, being careful not to cut deeply into the wood. After the shaft is peeled, set the wood aside for a few days, if you have time. Once it's had a chance to dry, sand it to smooth out any knots.

If you are not working on the shafts immediately, bundle them tightly with string and set them in a dry place. Wait one to six months for the wood to dry and harden—this wood will make strong, lightweight arrows. Once it's dry, peel off any remaining bark and smooth out the wood.

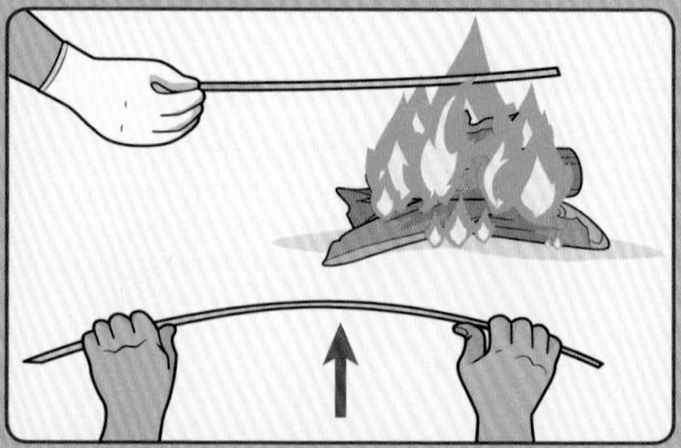

❷ STRAIGHTEN IT OUT Put on protective gloves and straighten the wooden shafts over an open fire by heating the area that needs bending (without allowing it to change color or catch fire). Once heated, the shaft should be slowly straightened and bent a little beyond the point of straight. Hold the wood in the over-straightened position until it cools. It should spring back a little when released, to the desired straightness. It may take several cycles of heating and cooling—it's far from an exact science.

You can determine whether a shaft is straight by tying a string around the length of the shaft, from one end, around the other, and back. Any gaps in the string will highlight where the shaft is bent. You can also look down the shaft with one eye while twirling it to spot these crooked sections.

❸ CUT THE NOCK Cut a notch about $\frac{1}{4}$ inch (6 mm) deep into the end of the shaft to create the nock that holds the bowstring. Cut carefully so as to avoid splitting the arrow. Reinforce the arrow shaft below the cut to keep the powerful bowstring from splitting your arrow upon shooting. String, thread, or sinew can be wound around the shaft and glued in place below the nock to strengthen it. If you're using cut dowels (instead of saplings with concentric growth rings), cut the nock perpendicular to the growth rings.

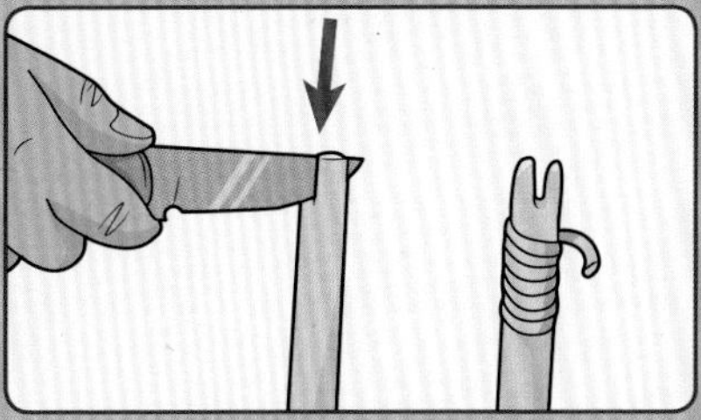

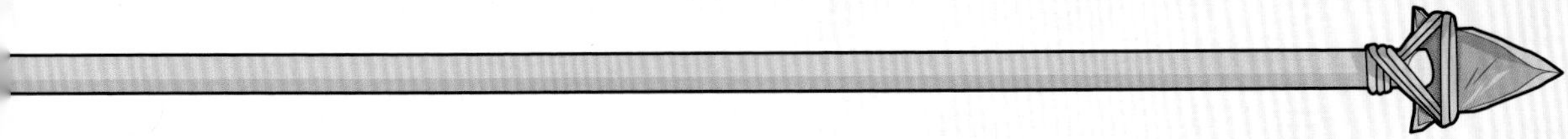

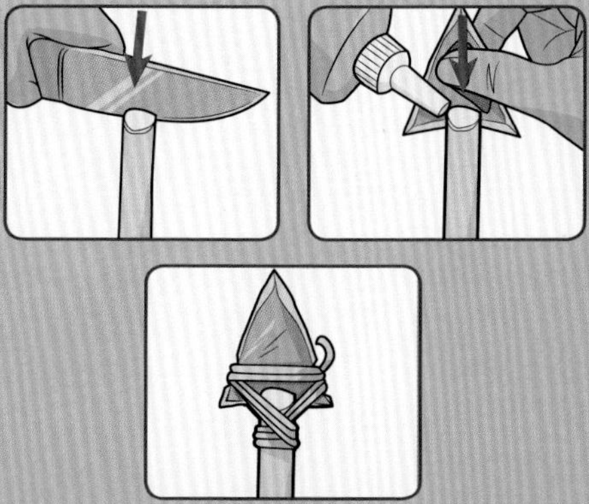

❹ ADD POINTS Make simple arrowheads from thin iron or steel, carved bone shards, or chipped pieces of stone. Use whatever tools you have at your disposal to cut or chip the projectile point into a triangular shape of about $1\frac{1}{2}$–2 inches (4–5 cm) in length and about 1 inch (2.5 cm) wide. Add small notches in each side of the arrowhead for the string binding to sit in, and fit the bottom of the triangle into the arrow shaft by means of a notch similar to a bowstring nock—add glue into the notch to help hold the arrowhead before it's further secured. Wrap twine, floss, dried sinew, or dogbane fiber around the shaft and arrowhead, and seal the wrapping with pine pitch or additional glue to make sure everything stays in place.

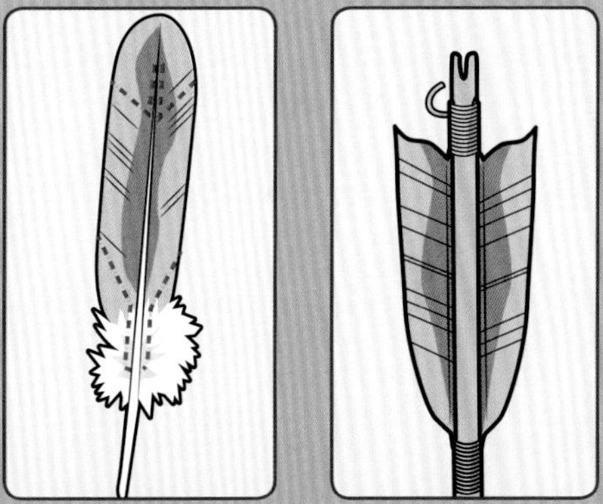

❺ FLETCH YOUR ARROW Collect some bird feathers, but don't mix and match on the same arrow, as different feather types have different shapes. The feathers also need to be from the same side of the bird (right or left), though they don't have to be from a single bird. Split the feathers in half and shorten them to about 4–5 inches (10–13 cm) and $\frac{1}{2}$ inch (12 mm) wide. Space the split seam of the three feathers equally around the arrow and glue them on, securing with the same cord you used for the arrowhead. Make sure the front of the fletching is covered with enough string and glue so that the sharp ends of the feather quills aren't poking out, or they'll deliver a serious scratch. Never use a homemade wooden arrow on a modern compound bow—this can cause wooden arrows to explode.

047 SUCCEED WITH SMALL GAME

You may imagine our predecessors carving huge steaks off big-game animals for their daily meal, but the truth is a little more humble. Most archeologists would agree that small game filled more stew pots than mammoth ever did. Living off small game is really about strength in numbers. You may hunt for days, looking for a large and crafty whitetail buck, and come home empty-handed. Yet in the span of an afternoon, you may come back from a field with several meaty rabbits—each one feeding a person for a day. Don't turn your nose up at the little critters, because there are a lot more of them to go around. Plus, most are delicious.

048 PLACE YOUR SHOT

So you've selected a small-game quarry and a weapon, you've practiced shooting and honed your aim, you've found the animal—now it's time to actually take the animal. Even after all these years as an outdoorsman, I still have a mixed emotional and mental reaction to this event. On the one hand, these animals are beautiful creatures living as nature intended; on the other hand, my ancient hunting instincts boil to the surface.

If you need the meat, and plan to use it thoroughly and respectfully, fire when ready. Aim for the backside of the animal's front shoulder. This area of larger body mass will give you a little room for error if the animal starts moving as you fire or if your aim is off. The lungs, heart, and liver are in this area, and hitting any one of them will take the animal out. After you shoot, give the animal a few minutes to die undisturbed, even if it runs for cover. Chances are it won't go far.

049 SAVOR SMALL-GAME FLAVOR

Rabbits and squirrels are so tasty, I'd rather have them on my plate than any other meat, wild or farmed. A few other small critters, however, can be more of an acquired taste.

CRITTER	FLAVOR
RABBIT	Tender white meat that can easily pass for chicken
SQUIRREL	Delicious white meat, a little tougher than rabbit
OPOSSUM	White meat that will remind you of pork if the animal has a clean diet
RACCOON	Nutritious light meat, but handle carefully in case of rabies
GROUNDHOG	Dark meat, not as tasty as other small game
MUSKRAT	Dark meat that tastes like a musky rat (go figure); good if spiced

050 SHOOT A LEAD HAILSTORM

Much as I love my grandfather's old .22 rifle, I'm a sucker for shotguns. Though it's not a cure-all, the shotgun is a great equalizer for poor marksmanship, fast and unpredictable game, wind, and other factors that contribute to missed shots. If you can't hit something with at least a few pellets, you need to get your glasses checked.

A great all-purpose, versatile shotgun is the 12-gauge pump action. It can shoot powerful game loads for surprising distances. When hunting squirrels and rabbits, #7 1/2 and #6 small-game load shotgun shells are a good choice. Select a load with larger pellets if you decide to try for game larger than a rabbit.

051 START WITH THE BASICS

Animals need the same survival essentials that we do: shelter, food, and water. Small-game animals find shelter in thick vegetative cover, holes in trees, and burrows in the ground, according to the behavior of their species. It's usually pretty predictable—they don't mix it up much, and you'll never see a squirrel coming out of a groundhog hole. Small-game creatures also need water and food, so you'll find them where wild foods are abundant and water is available. Begin with these basics, and move forward when you're ready for more.

SCOUTING TIPS

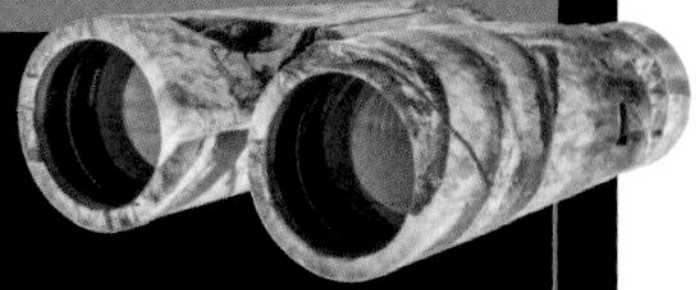

Use a binocular to look for likely cover, food, and watering spots.

Locate tracks and signs to use for positive identification of the local species.

Sit and wait. Watch and listen. Sneak and stalk. See how close you can get to potential game.

052 READ THE SIGNS

Learn how to read tracks, and you'll be learning a new language—one that tells you the hidden stories of the animals. Our ancestors had to be adept at tracking to learn about the unseen game animals and predators in their vicinity. Today, animal tracking provides an invaluable service to the hunter, trapper, nature lover, and photographer. Tracking can also be a lifesaver in a survival situation, warning you about dangerous creatures in the area and helping you to locate wild game. Find some clear prints and you'll be able to read a few pages from the tale of that animal's life. Find a trail, and you might just find the animal itself.

BEAVER
Castor canadensis

It's easy to spot a beaver's tree-felling work at a distance, but it's harder to find its prints. Inspect areas with gnawed trees and check waterway banks for a beaver slide (a well-worn, muddy run leading to water). The rear beaver foot is unique, with five long toes and signs of webbing. Front prints are about 3 inches (7.5 cm) long, while rear can be more than 6 inches (15 cm). Beaver can be found in the continental U.S. and Canada.

EASTERN COTTONTAIL RABBIT
Sylvilagus floridanus

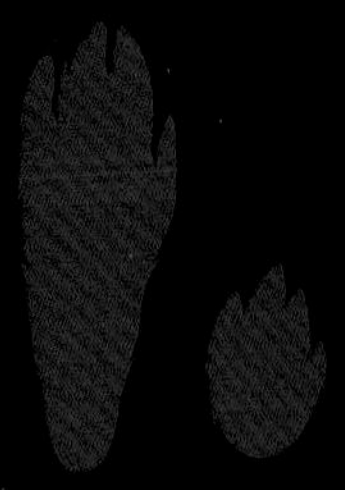

The eastern cottontail rabbit lives in the open, seeking shelter in the brush rather than a den. Because rabbits primarily gallop, the prints you'll see are due to two large rear feet hitting the ground in front of the tiny front feet, the trail resembling a series of Cs or Vs. Snowshoe hares and jackrabbits have similar trails. A cottontail's front feet are about 1 inch (2.5 cm) long and their rear feet are about 3 inches (7.5 cm) long.

RACCOON
Procyon lotor

A raccoon's front and rear prints both resemble a human hand—look for five toes that point forward on each foot, nearly parallel. This helps differentiate from the wide-splayed toes of the opossum and the rarely imprinted fifth toe of a muskrat. Raccoons move in a diagonal track pattern, like deer. The front feet measure 2–3 inches (5–7.5 cm), the rear 3–4 inches (8–10 cm), with a longer heel on the rear feet.

GRAY SQUIRREL
Sciurus carolinensis

Squirrel sign (chewed nut shells or holes) is often abundant, but clear tracks are rare. When you do spot them, you'll see that squirrels gallop, like rabbits. Their patterns show the rear feet preceding the front, with more symmetrical track patterns than rabbits. Like other rodents, they have four toes on their front feet and five on the rear. Gray squirrel prints are about 1 inch (2.5 cm) long, with a sometimes longer hind heel pad.

COYOTE

Canis latrans

Coyotes, found throughout North America, favor open plains, brushy areas, and woodlands, but can live anywhere. Their four-toed tracks look a lot like a dog's footprints, but upon closer inspection, you'll notice the coyote's tracks are farther apart, and where dog trails wander and are whimsical, coyote trails are straight and purposeful. The front feet are larger than the rear feet, and roughly 2½–3 inches (6–7.5 cm) long.

RED FOX

Vulpes vulpes

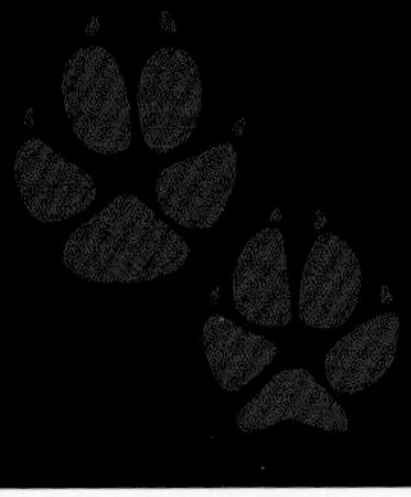

The red fox is one of the most elusive canines in North America, so use your ears—if you hear a yelp in the woods on a spring evening that sounds like a woman yelling "help," it's probably a red fox. Their front prints usually measure 2½ inches (6 cm) and rear prints around 2 inches (5 cm). Foxes are diagonal walkers, and they place their rear feet into the front prints. Their trails often reflect their punchy little steps and quick feet.

BLACK BEAR

Ursus americanus

Identifying a black bear's tracks is important for your safety, as bears can be very dangerous. Though generally shy, a 200–400 pound (90–180 kg) bear will defend itself—with speed and strength—if threatened. Black bears leave large tracks; their front footprints average 4 by 4 inches (10 by 10 cm), and the rear feet average 3–4 inches (7.5–10 cm) wide and 6–7 inches (15–18 cm) long when the heel pad is imprinted.

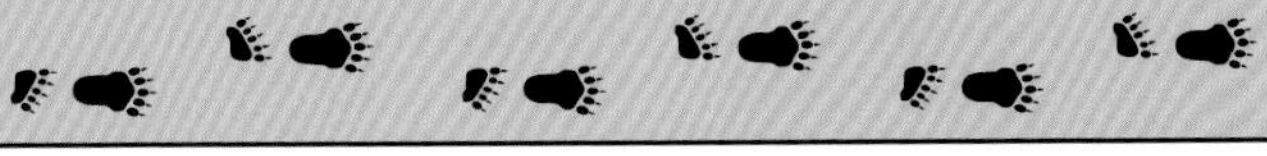

BOBCAT

Felis rufus

Bobcats, found in most of the lower 48 states, spend most of their time alone, except during the midwinter mating season. Bobcats are diagonal walkers, with a pattern so precise that the rear feet land in the front footprints (like foxes). Bobcat tracks are about 2 inches (5 cm) in diameter, with front feet slightly larger than the rear, and resemble those of a small dog, but with a small notch in front of the heel pad.

WHITE-TAILED DEER

Odocoileus virginianus

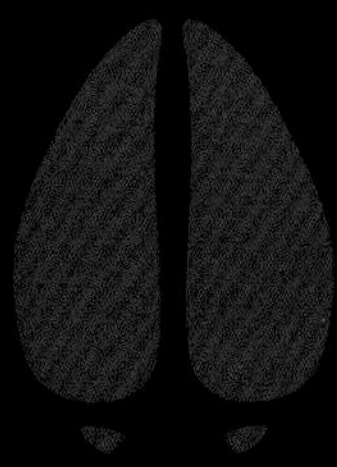

White-tailed deer, found throughout central North America, are easier to track than most animals. Their small, sharp-edged hooves leave distinct impressions, and they leave plenty of sign, from bedding-area ovals to scrapes and rubs. Find a single, heart-shaped track, and you'll likely find many more. Whitetail tracks average 2–3 inches (5–7.5 cm) in length, and though the deer are diagonal walkers, they're not as careful, so look for smaller rear feet hitting near or on top of the larger front foot prints.

053 STUDY THAT SCAT

Scat is a commonly used technical term for droppings, leavings, and, well, poop. This animal evidence is often more obvious than tracks, and it gives us great clues as to the identity of local animals (as well as proof positive of their diet). Don't get too involved with it, as you are at risk of contracting some pathogens. If you accidentally get scat on your hands and then eat something later, you could potentially catch a disease. Some pathogens are also able to go airborne. With safety in mind, just look at scat—don't interact with it.

FOX

Tapered ends and full of hair. Fox scat may also have seeds, feathers, and small bones. Often deposited on prominent spots as territory markers.

COYOTE

Looks similar to fox droppings, but twice the size. Large foxes and small coyotes have very similar scats.

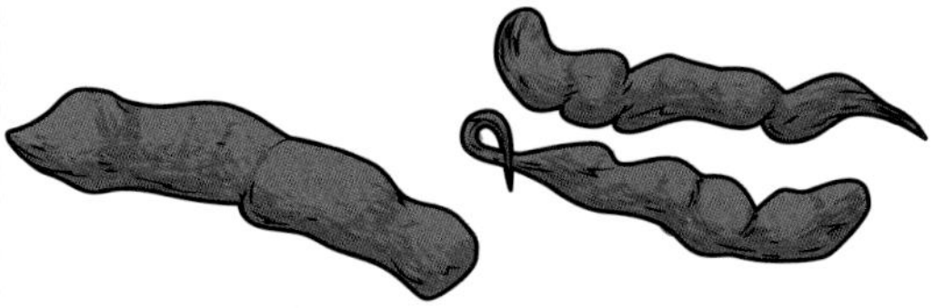

RACCOON

Blunt-ended and uniform scats, often reminding trackers of a Tootsie Roll (that's where the comparison ends). These scats can have anything in them, but crayfish parts are an especially good indicator of raccoon.

OPOSSUM

Variable and sometimes runny. These scats may contain hair, feathers, seeds, insects, or berries. Typically smaller than fox scat and differently shaped from raccoon.

SKUNK

Uneven, and highly variable.

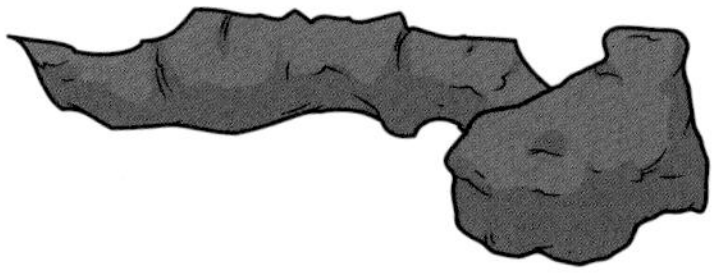

PORCUPINE

Various shapes and full of plant material and bark pulp.

GOOSE

Tubular, like raccoon scat, but more slender. These scats are entirely plant material, often with some whitish coloring like bird and reptile droppings.

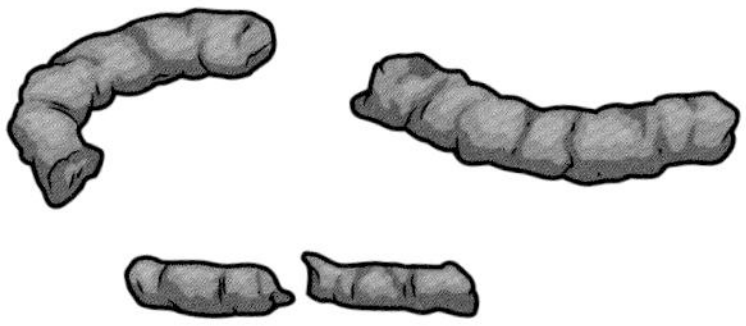

RABBIT

Small, round pellets of finely chewed plant material. This scat can be flattened and several colors, from greenish to tan or brown.

RAT

Dark brown or black, like large grains of rice.

CHIPMUNK

Similar to rat scat, but more uneven.

GROUNDHOG

These round or oval pellets, composed of plant material, can be found on the dirt mound outside their den or inside the den.

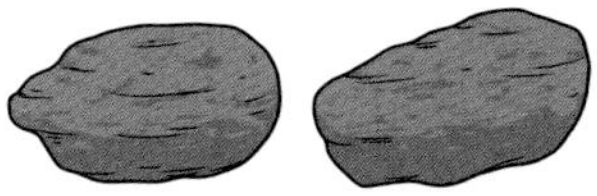

DEER

These pellets are highly variable. Some are round and others are tapered. They're generally found in a small pile and are full of vegetative materials.

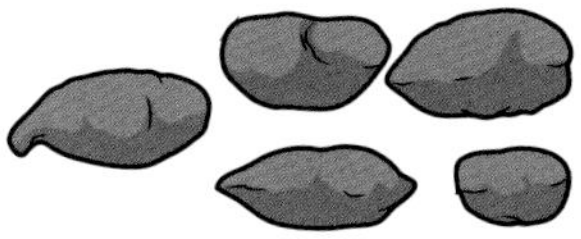

054 LEARN TO TRAP

Hunting and trapping have a lot in common. They each consist of broad skill sets that allow you to collect animals for food (or other uses, like fur). Traps are the satellite hunters that you can place across the landscape to catch your food for you while you hunt or do other tasks elsewhere.

Some animals are legal to trap in any fashion, while others may have a limited range of harvesting methods in certain areas. But sometimes the rules go out the window; when you or your family start going hungry, you'll be very glad to have trapping skills to add to your food-gathering strategies.

Most traps are activated in one of these two ways—learn how they work, and you'll be able to pick the right one for your situation.

TRAPS	EXAMPLES
BAIT DRIVEN	These traps use bait to entice an animal into activating a trigger. The animal may have to pull or push the bait to set off the trap; other traps fire when the animal steps near the bait. These are often successful traps, as the scent of the bait lures in animals that might otherwise pass by.
TRAVEL DRIVEN	Set to engage when an animal travels through a specific area, this type of trap relies on you knowing the animal's typical habits (snares placed on animal runs are a common example).

055 SELECT YOUR TRAP

While you can build effective low-tech traps with materials you'd find in the wilderness, in some situations it just makes sense to use more modern options, such as cable snares, leghold traps, and body-grip traps to improve your odds of success. Choose from the following trap types, based on your needs and the animals in your area.

SNARES You can build primitive snares with materials gathered on-site, even weaving your own string out of bark fibers—but many animals will be able to chew through string. Cable snares made from braided steel cable are more secure.

FOOTHOLD TRAPS Common foothold traps are clamping jaws that grab an animal when it steps on the trigger. They do not kill the prey outright; the trapped animal is usually shot by the trapper.

BODY-GRIP TRAPS Two heavy springs move the trap bars together, snapping the animal's neck, breaking its back, or strangling it. They can be treacherous to set.

LIVE-CATCH TRAPS The typical cage trap is a live-catch trap. This forgiving trap allows you to release animals that you didn't intend to catch and is ideal for urban, suburban, or farm settings.

056 OBEY THE LAWS

The art of trapping is a legal method of taking wild game in many areas, but it doesn't mean that you can do whatever you like. Local areas have their own regulations about the practices of trapping, and they may be very different from another region. Rather than worrying about the history and politics behind those regulations, it's better to simply obey them. Those laws are generally in place for a good reason, and unless it's an emergency situation, they apply to you. Learn what you are required to do when trapping, so you don't run afoul of the game wardens.

GET A LICENSE Many areas require them, and they're generally inexpensive and good for a year.

GET PERMISSION If you are trapping on private land that you do not own, get a signed letter that grants you permission to trap. Be specific in the letter to avoid misunderstandings.

OBEY THE SEASON Certain animals are only legal to trap at certain times. If you start trapping too early in the season, or your traps are still set after the season is over, then you are in violation.

CHECK YOUR GAME Most areas require that you "check" your trapped game, both to observe your personal limits on taking the animals and to keep count of the trapping in the region. Take the animal to an authorized game-checking station so they can verify the species and other information. In most areas, catching animals without verification by the game authorities is considered poaching.

VISIT YOUR TRAPS DAILY Some areas require this daily walk of your trap line; regardless of the rules, it's a good trapping practice.

057 HIDE YOUR SCENT WITH NATURE

It's hard to trick an animal's nose. Although trappers may use many different types of traps to catch a meal, they all have the same problem: They've got human scent smeared all over them. Trapping is never as much about fooling an animal's eyes or ears as it is about fooling the nose. To have any luck when dealing with wild animals, you'll need to remove as much human scent from your traps and your skin as possible. De-scent everything—and often—until you set the trap on your trap line. Try these steps to de-scent your traps with elements from nature itself.

STEP 1 To de-scent your hands before handling or making trap parts, start by washing them in the local waterway. Use sand, clay, mud, or silt as an abrasive and oil absorber.

STEP 2 As your hands and any trap parts dry, wipe on powdered black charcoal from the campfire. Don't use the white or gray ashes, just grind black charcoal chunks into a powder and apply.

STEP 3 Now layer on a strong-smelling local plant as another cover scent (see item 058). Just make sure you stay out of the poison ivy, poison oak, and sumac!

STEP 4 The final touch on this layering system is fresh, damp local dirt. Rub it generously on your hands and the trap parts as a final cover scent and odor absorber.

058 GET CREATIVE WITH COVER SCENTS

The rich smells of plants are a normal part of a terrestrial animal's daily life. They smell crushed pine needles when they step on them in the forest. They smell the wild onions when they brush against them in the field. If these smell strong to us, imagine how intense these odors are to the animals. Use these strong-smelling, local, nontoxic plants on your skin and your traps—it'll just smell like everyday life for the animals.

PLANT	HOW TO USE
PINE NEEDLES	Evergreen needles can be chopped or crushed to release the strong pine resins and oils.
MINT LEAVES AND STEMS	The entire plant can be rubbed to spread their mentholated oils.
ONIONS AND GARLICS	While not generally food for animals, their sulfurous stink can help to turn the animals into food for us.
YARROW LEAVES	These feathery leaves can be bruised to release their piney oils and resins.
WINTERCRESS AND WILD MUSTARDS	Crush the leaves for a strong scent that is short-lived but pungent.

059 TRAP LIKE A PRO

The complex art form of trapping has been practiced for millennia, and experience has taught us plenty. The next time you're out trapping, review and remember the following tips. Put them into action, and greatly improve your results.

TOP TRAPPING TIPS

ROTATE YOUR BAIT Meat and other perishable baits may need to be replaced daily. And don't bait with something that is already available (like corn in the cornfield or acorns near oaks).

PROTECT YOUR TRAP Ants, mice, little birds, and other bait stealers can pick the bait clean in a jiffy; try to set the trap out of their reach.

LOSE THE STINK De-scent in order to get the animals to approach your trap (see item 57).

BE PREPARED Any given bait may catch a variety of animals. Make sure that the trap is strong enough for the biggest animal you might catch.

JOIN THE RESISTANCE When setting a fixed snare, make sure the animal can't tear it loose from its point of attachment, and put a swivel in the line so the rolling and flipping animal can't kink and break it.

AIM HIGH With snares involving spring poles or other methods of lifting an animal in the air, make sure there's enough lifting power to get the heaviest member of that species off the ground—and high enough to be out of the reach of scavengers like coyotes, at least 5 feet (1.5 m) up.

060 FIND THE RIGHT BAIT

Trapping requires focused preparation. When you begin a new trap line, you should choose the right bait for each trap. Sure, cheese or peanut butter will work on a mousetrap, but what if you're not after mice? You often need very specific baits depending on your goals (meat, fur, predator reduction)—which is why the knowledge of trap baiting is such an important part of the overall art of trapping.

HERBIVORES

There are plenty of vegetarian baits to choose from. Groundhogs go for sweet apples cut into pieces so their fragrance is released. Squirrels are very fond of whole peanuts, and they have a hard time resisting crushed sweet pecans and hickories. Just don't try using them under a tree full of those nuts. The animals won't go for the human-tainted bait when there is plenty of the same food lying nearby.

CARNIVORES

Meat eaters tend to have specific tastes. Coyotes love beaver meat. Foxes love rotten, hard-boiled eggs. Mink, ermine, and fisher cats love fish. Bobcats love fresh organ meat like liver and lung. You can also use various scent baits—it doesn't have to be food. Coyote and beaver scent can be used for coyotes. And coon urine can be a useful cover scent against other animals, as well as for attracting raccoons.

OMNIVORES

Omnivores, by definition, will eat anything. This can make them either easier or harder to bait. For raccoons, you can use canned tuna or sardines. The fouler and cheaper the fish are, the better. You can often trap for raccoons alongside creeks and streams, pouring the tuna juice into the creek so they'll follow the smell to get their treat. Possums love lunch meat, hot dogs, and other processed meats.

061 LEARN YOUR FOOTHOLDS

Foothold traps date back as far as the 16th century, and are the only sensible method for trapping larger animals. Historically, even bears were trapped with super-sized (and toothed) clamping jaws. While the toothed versions of these traps are rarely legal, smaller smooth-jawed traps can allow you to trap furbearers, game-meat animals, and dangerous predators successfully. Check out this array of footholds and track down the one that's right for your needs.

TRAP	QUARRY	NOTES
DOG-PROOF TRAP	Raccoons and opossums; excludes all canines and most other animals.	Protects pets; larger versions can be used to catch small primates who will reach in for the bait.
COIL-SPRING TRAP	Vast number of options, from small mink to large coyotes.	The modern style uses small—but powerful—coiled springs to close its jaws.
LONG-SPRING TRAP	Also good for everything from small mink all the way up to large coyotes.	Powered by one or two flat springs; stronger than a coil spring, but requires a wider hole.

062 KNOW THE WHOLE TRUTH

More than any other trapping method, foothold trapping has been responsible for negative stereotypes and unfavorable reactions from nontrappers throughout the last hundred years. Here are some of the common misconceptions about this method and the mechanisms that make it happen.

MYTH	TRUTH
FOOTHOLD TRAPS ARE DANGEROUS TO HUMANS AND KILL PETS.	Smaller traps could break someone's toes if they hit it in bare feet, but only the largest footholds could injure a person in boots. If your pet steps in the trap, the jaws can be pried open by hand.
FOOTHOLDS CATCH MORE "INNOCENT" NONTARGET ANIMALS THAN THEIR INTENDED QUARRY.	This is simply not the case. These traps are set in specific ways, with species-targeting baits and setups, which minimizes the chances of catching the "wrong" animal.
FOOTHOLDS ARE CRUEL AND TORTURE THE ANIMAL.	When a foothold trap catches an animal's leg, the pressure from both sides of the trap will cause the foot to go numb, much like your leg falling asleep when you've sat on it too long.
FOOTHOLD TRAPS ARE OUTDATED AND ANTIQUATED.	These traps are constantly being redesigned for effectiveness. Yes, antique traps may be substandard, but purchasing new traps will get you the best there've ever been.

063 SET AN EFFECTIVE FOOTHOLD

For the best chance of success, place your foothold traps logically and carefully, considering your target animal's haunts, habits, and favorite foods. Here are three classic sets that you can use to catch a wide range of game animals.

FLAT SET The flat set is a lightly buried foothold with a nearby scent stake. Lay down a small tarp to work on and to collect excess dirt. Dig a small, shallow depression, about 1 inch (2.5 cm) deeper than the trap is tall, and stake the trap to the ground with a chain and swivel inside the hole. Place a sheet of wax paper over the set trap to keep dirt from filling the space under the pan trigger. Lightly bury the trap and drive in the scent stake nearby. Use logs, rocks, clumps of vegetation, or anything else to create a fence or funnel to direct the animal to step on your trap. You could also dangle a bird wing or feathers near the trap to attract bobcats (where legal).

DIRT-HOLE BANK SET Find a dirt bank, stream bank, logging road cut, or a similar location. Drive a stake into the bank to create a hole that resembles a small rodent hole. Poke some bait deep into the hole with a twig, and place some freshly dug dirt below the hole to mimic a recent animal excavation. Set your foothold as you would with a flat set. For best results, know the distance from the target animal's nose to its front feet, and place the trap that far from the fake rodent hole. Then figure out half of the width between its feet, and go to the right or left by that much. These measurements tell you how far out and how far to the side to place the trap so that the animal steps right into it.

WATERLINE POCKET SET Excavate a bigger fake animal burrow right at the waterline (or use an existing one), and you can let a very small amount of water (instead of dirt) camouflage the foothold.

064 TAKE CARE WITH BODY GRIPS

Body-gripping traps (also known as conibear traps) are some of the most devastating traps you'll ever set. Think of them as giant rat traps without the attached board. They can be set in a remarkable variety of ways, horizontally and vertically, on land and underwater. Many sizes are available, from small single-spring traps to huge double-spring traps that are downright frightening to set. Here's what to use for your desired prey.

TRAP	QUARRY	NOTES
SMALL-BODY GRIPS	Weasels, muskrats, minks, martins, fishers, and rats	These start small, at 4-inch (10-cm) jaw spreads.
MEDIUM AND LARGE BODY GRIPS	Opossum, raccoons, skunks, bobcats, foxes, groundhogs, otter, and smaller coyotes	These pose a greater risk to trappers, as the larger springs store up more energy when set; these are the most likely to catch pets.

065 SAFELY SET A BODY GRIP

The most important part of the trap is the safety clip on each spring, because your safety is always paramount. Get to know this strong little metal hook; it's meant to hold the springs of the trap in a closed position while you set the "dog" (the trigger). When the safety clips are properly engaged, the trap cannot close on your hand or body. Carefully follow these steps to get it right.

STEP 1 Once you're at the trapping site, lay your trap out so that the safety clips will be on top of the spring when clipped in place. Use your setting tongs to grab both rings on the trap spring and squeeze them together.

STEP 2 When the rings are squeezed together, hold the tongs with one hand and clip the safety onto that spring. Repeat on the other side for double-spring traps.

STEP 3 Using your hands or your setting tongs, squeeze the trap together even more. This will compress the springs further and loosen your safety clips. The trap must be in position so that the clips stay on top of the springs, as the trap clamping will cause the clips to fall free if you're setting the trap "upside down."

STEP 4 Clip the "dog" onto the trap so that it is in the proper position in the center of the trigger. The dog should release if the trigger is pushed in either direction. With safety clips still in place (but loose), set the trap in your desired spot and flip open the safety clips.

Note: If you're setting this trap in flowing water, make sure the clips are loose on the downstream side of the trap. There have been cases where the flowing water actually pushed the clips into place (locking the trap open) when they were on the upriver side.

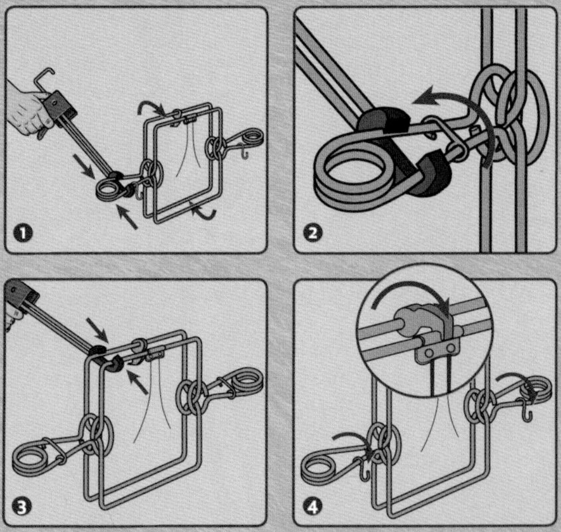

066 USE ROPE FOR SAFETY

This rope trick can replace the need for setting tongs or allow you to make quick resets in the field. Start off with a length of strong, slender rope, and tie a large loop tied at one end. Place this loop over your foot (with boots on, please). Thread the free end of the rope through the rings on the spring, and loop around and through a second time so that you have wrapped a loop of rope around the rings. Pull up hard on the free end of the rope (while keeping tension with the foot loop) and the spring will close. Securely place the safety clip to hold the spring closed and remove the rope.

If you keep this handy, you can release yourself with one hand if you ever get an arm or hand stuck. And on the subject of safety, never walk around with set traps on your person; you should always wait to set them until you're placing them.

067 GET READY TO GET SET

Here are a couple of interesting set to use in common locations:

THE BURROW SET Use this easy set for groundhogs and other hole-dwelling creatures. Prop up the body grip vertically in front of a burrow mouth, or lay it horizontally over a burrow mouth that goes straight down. The horizontal set is less effective, as it tends to jump up in the air when tripped.

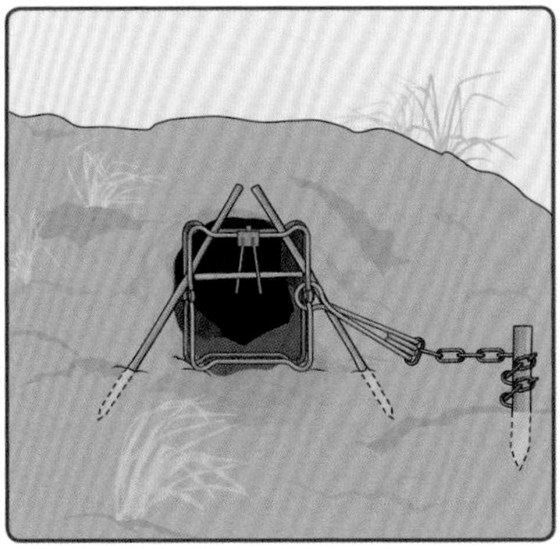

THE BOTTOM EDGE SET Find a steep stream bank in a sluggish waterway with abundant animal sign. This body-grip set is particularly effective on muskrats. Anchor the trap vertically at the bottom edge of the waterway, and connect a snare wire or similar trap keeper, in case you catch a tail or foot, or the water becomes faster.

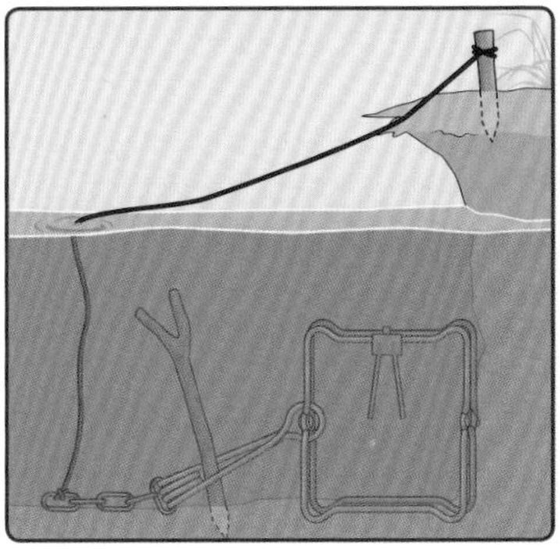

068 CATCH 'EM ALIVE

If you're a student of pop culture (aka Saturday morning cartoons), you may think of a live-catch box trap as little more than a crude box propped up with a stick, and a hungry person lying in wait to pull the stick away. This setup can actually work, but there are far better methods available to the modern trapper. After all, the whole point of using a trap is that you don't need to be present to pull the trigger. To get started in box trapping, you just need to decide between store-bought and do-it-yourself options.

PURCHASED BOX TRAPS

Box traps are available from different manufacturers that offer a few different sizes and features to choose from. They're typically made from galvanized wire (for years of dependable service) and can open either at both ends or just one. There are fewer moving parts with a trap that only opens on one end, but easily frightened animals (like rabbits) will be more likely to go into a trap with both ends open.

HOMEMADE BOX TRAPS

The best of the homemade bunch are made from durable wooden or metal boxes with a sliding door that closes behind the animal. They can be made with a number of different trigger mechanisms (in contrast to the commercially available box traps that only use a pan trigger—a flat metal strip that the animal steps on to activate the trap). The downside of these traps is that they take some time to build, and gnawing animals can damage or chew their way out of wooden box traps.

069 BUILD A BETTER BOX TRAP

A few tools, a little scrap lumber, and a few odd bits of stick and string can provide you with the material to build a trap that can catch a variety of animals and last years.

STEP 1 You'll need 4 wide boards about 1$^1/_2$ feet (46 cm) long, 2 small strips of wood about 8 inches (20 cm) long, a handful of small nails, 20 inches (50 cm) of string, a piece of wire mesh, 2 pencil-diameter sticks, a hammer, a drill, and a saw.

STEP 2 Cut a piece from your longest board to act as the door for the trap. Nail the four boards together to create a wooden tunnel. Make sure you do it so that your door will slide up and down freely. Nail the mesh at one end of the tunnel and nail the two small wood strips at the other end as guides so the door can slide down securely.

STEP 3 Drill a hole about 8 inches (20 cm) from the mesh end of the box. This should be slightly larger in diameter than the stick you will place into it as a trigger. Whittle a notch on the shorter stick, and tie the string to the other end of it. Tie the string to the top of the longer stick, near the shorter stick, and tie the free end of the string to a bent nail in the wooden trapdoor.

STEP 4 Now comes the tricky part: adjusting everything. You'll probably have to untie and retie the string to get it right. The trigger stick may need to be recarved to make it more or less sensitive. You can also carve a point and/or barbs on the tip of the trigger stick to skewer bait on it.

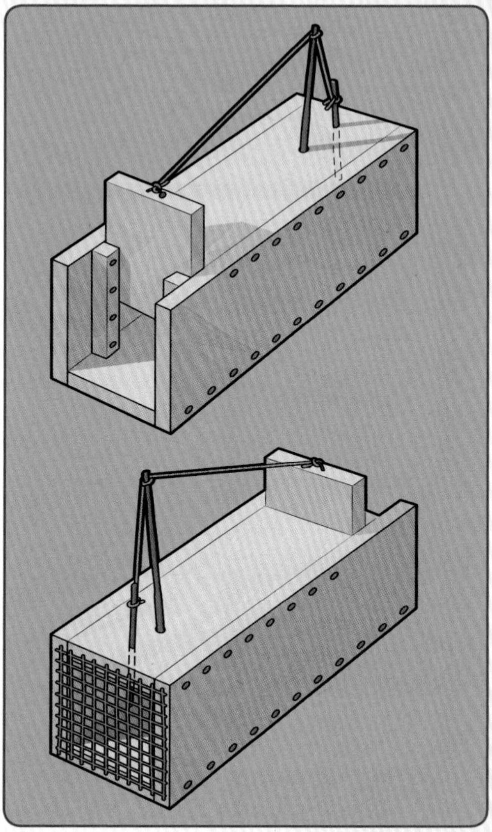

070 BENEFIT FROM BOX TRAPS

No, you can't fit a bunch of box traps in your pocket like you can with snares. But box traps can offer a few benefits that other traps cannot.

BOX BENEFITS

You can safely release pets and other unintended catches. The critter may have a scuffed-up nose from trying to get out, but overall, they'll be no worse off from the experience.

Live catch allows you to examine the animal before making the decision to dispatch it. It's easier to identify illness in a live, whole animal (if it is foaming at the mouth, for example, or exhibiting other diseased symptoms).

The traps are easy and fast to set. No more smashed fingers!

071 PUT YOUR TRAP TO WORK

You could have a perfectly functional box trap and still not catch a thing—especially if you're in the wrong spot, frightening the animals, or failing to lure them in.

DO	DON'T
Place the trap in a field, forest, swamp, or glen with lots of animal sign such as (scat, tracks, beds, and trails).	Place your trap in a heavily used trail. The large, unexpected blockage will scare the animals and cause them to detour around your trap.
Set the trap near the animal's water source, as this will be a popular place for them to visit.	Set a trap where it will wash away. Wooden box traps are particularly vulnerable to floating away in rising water.
Bait the trap for local animals. Follow the tracks, look at the dropping, and use these signs to identify the local species.	Forget about de-scenting. Human scent soaks into wooden traps particularly well.

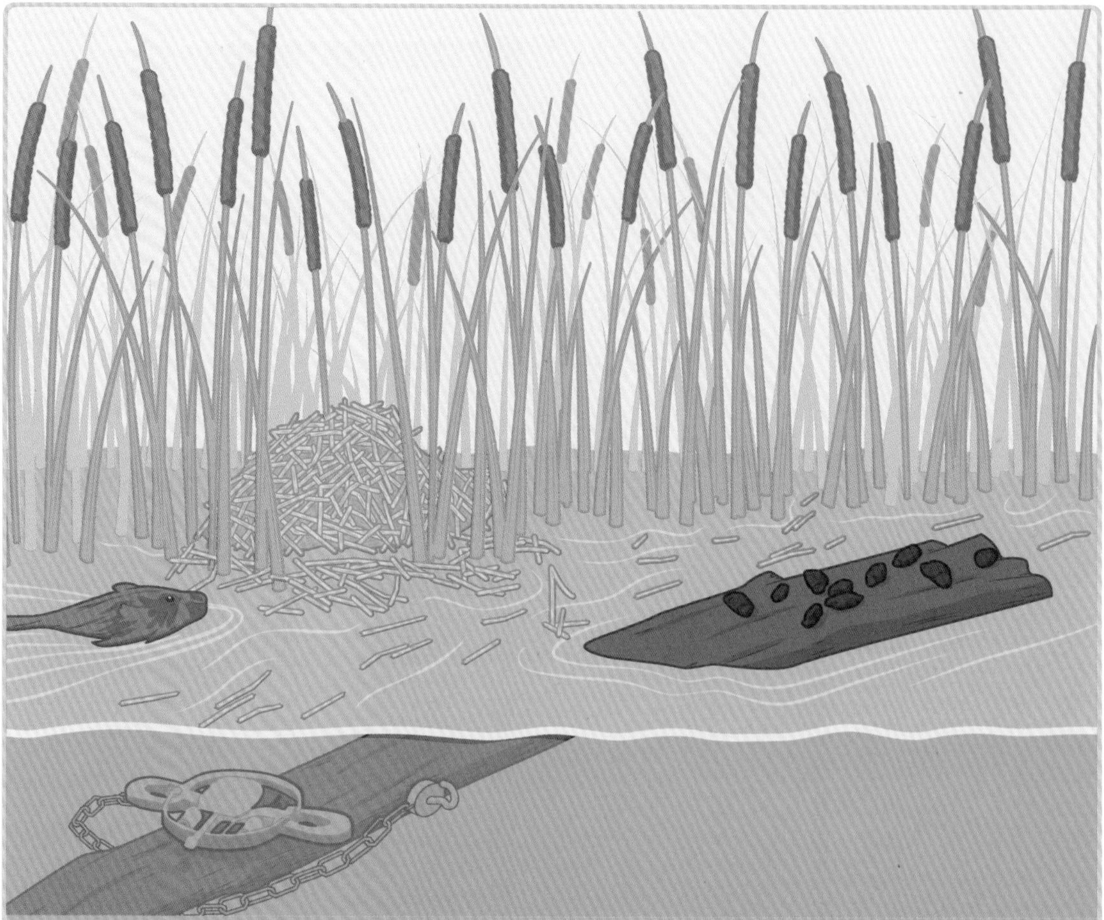

072 MASH A MUSKRAT

Resembling something between a beaver and a rat, the muskrat is an aquatic furbearer that can be a tasty dark-meat meal. The warm, thick fur can also serve many purposes.

Body-grip sets similar to the underwater beaver trap can work well, as well as foothold traps, when properly placed in muskrat-laden wetlands. Look for muskrat feed beds (piles, mounds, or even floating mats of cut vegetation—spots where the muskrat sits to eat), and logs or rocks that they use for toilets (you'll see plenty of scat). Feed-bed foothold traps need to be anchored to a pole driven into the mud, if no shrubs or trees are present for attachment. Drive the pole in deeply, not only to hold the muskrat, but in case a stronger animal like a raccoon steps into the trap.

You can also place footholds underwater, on the submerged portion of logs that muskrats climb up onto for a toilet, or attach them to floating logs, secured underwater by protruding rocks.

Use poles with flags to mark each of your underwater traps, and any other hidden traps on wetland trap lines, as they are easy to lose in swampy conditions.

073 HARVEST A HARE

Fast and wary, hares and rabbits are often tricky to catch. In my home state, rabbits can only be legally caught in live-catch box traps. These can work, but the trap needs to open on both ends to reassure the animal that it can escape. Try baiting the box with apple slices or fresh vegetables like sweet peas and lettuce. Snares can be effective, too, when placed in the critter's run. Make the noose large enough for those big ears, but small enough so your potential dinner doesn't jump straight through.

074 PICK UP A 'POSSUM

Opossums are strange and tasty beasts, and they'll be plentiful in areas abundant with wild foods. These omnivores eat fruits, berries, seeds, and anything else that happens to be available. Processed meats are good, but almost anything has potential. I once caught an opossum in a box trap with the tail of another opossum as the bait. I'd like to believe that he smelled his absent friend and was coming to check on him, but with this species, you can't rule out cannibalism.

Since they are not averse to confined spaces, a medium or large box trap is a good choice when targeting these critters. Snares can work, but the setup has to be flawless, because opossums are excellent climbers. They also have 50 teeth and can chew through softer snare wires and cables (among other things—don't get on the wrong side of an angry one). If you don't catch an opossum by the neck with a strong snare noose, it has a good chance of getting away.

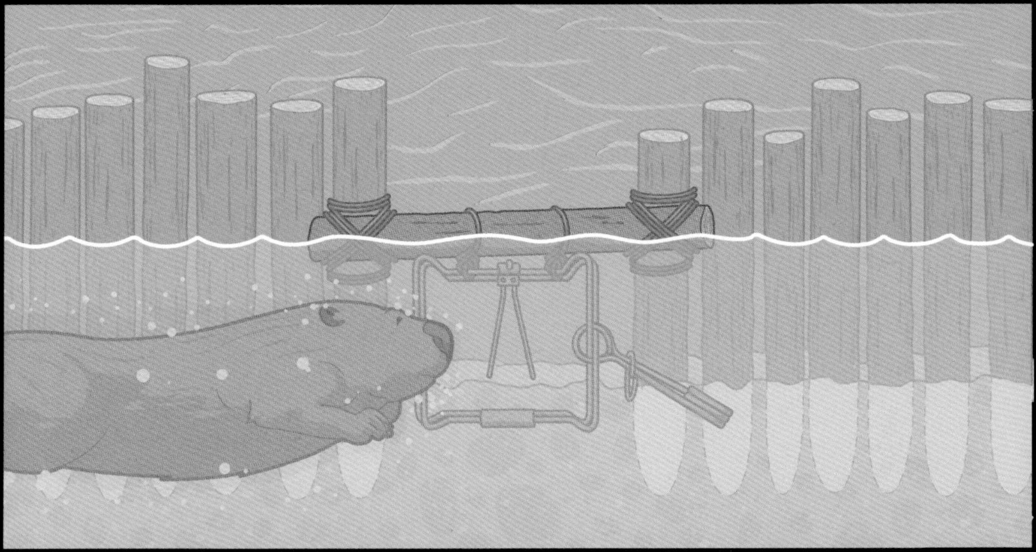

075 BAG A BEAVER

In cold northern climates, beaver can reach massive proportions—100 pounds (45 kg) is not unheard of. Beaver castor (an oily secretion) can be used as bait for foothold traps on land, but the best trap for beaver is a large body-grip trap. These can be set on a beaver's "slide," a place where they routinely slide down a bank into the water, but an even better location is underwater.

An underwater set will take some work to build, but it can last for a long time and be very effective. To construct one, drive poles into the muddy bottom of a heavily traveled beaver waterway. Create a fence with a gap in the center, and tie a log at the water level over this gap, which will encourage a swimming beaver to dive under the log for passage.

Attach the body-grip trap underwater, at this fence opening. This is best done in sluggish waterways, as fast water will eventually destroy your work. And make sure the trap is on the upriver side of the fence, otherwise the current—even a slow one—can lift the trap out of position.

076 REAP A RACCOON

Raccoons are exceedingly smart and nimble, and can grow much larger than opossums. You can use many different kinds of bait for raccoons—they tend to have a sweet tooth, so confections and pastries can be a big success, but they also like fishy flavors.

Snares are more successful with raccoons than opossums, due to their greater body weight. They will usually fall for a box trap as well, smaller raccoons are candidates for body-grip traps, and any raccoon could be caught with a foothold trap. Be aware that they have a greater risk of carrying rabies than other animals, so use disposable gloves when dressing, use antimicrobial soap when you're finished, and cook the meat well done.

077 SUPERPLANT: WILD ONION

SPICE THINGS UP WITH WILD ONION

Winter can be a cold time of year to run around outside, but if you brave the weather you can still forage for something spicy. Some tougher wild onion species (the pungent wild relatives to cultivated onions and garlic) are out from January through spring and are well worth the trouble. Not a fan of the cold? Then wait for the larger, more solitary onions and garlics of summer. Grab a small shovel and a bag to hold your greens—it's time to hunt down one of nature's superfoods.

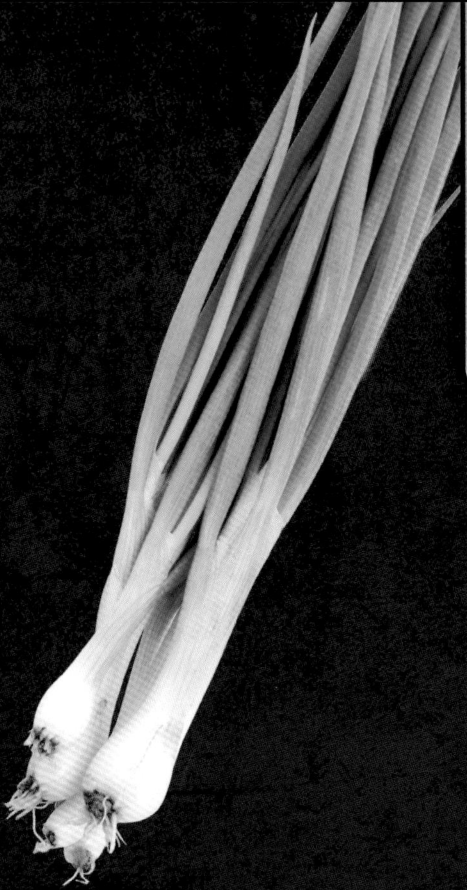

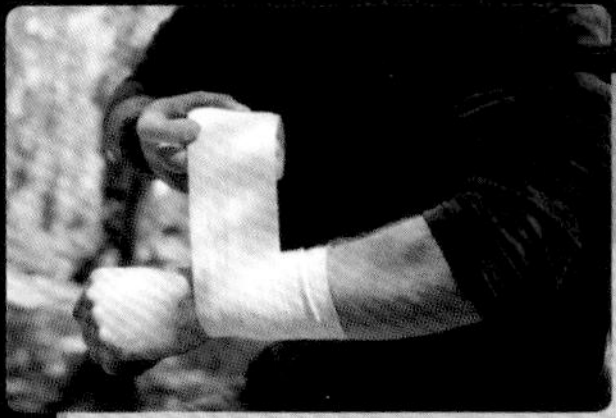

POUND A PUNGENT POULTICE

The tear-inducing, sulfurous compounds contained in wild onion and garlic—along with another compound called allicin—possess some antibacterial properties. Since wild onions are both healing and tasty, this is a combination that's hard to beat. Eat more onions, and you may find your immune system boosted. But for an on-the-spot treatment, pound onions into a poultice, which you can use as a topical field dressing for wounds.

SPOT THE RIGHT PLANT

There are roughly a dozen different species growing in North America that could fall under the name *onion*. Some species grow even in the dead of winter, favoring open ground and sunny conditions.

Look in fields and meadows for some species, and look no further than your yard for others. Some are closer to garlic in appearance and flavor, others closer to chives or leeks. The critical factor for all is their membership in the *allium* genus.

Allium plants are edible and generally very tasty. But don't just wolf down everything shaped like an onion. The broader family they belong to is the lily family, which can be problematic for foragers, because some are toxic.

Your first step in making sure a plant really is an onion or garlic is looking for the classic shape: a bulbous root and a rounded stem. Once you've established a passing grade here, move along to the scratch-and-sniff testing phase. Scratch the bulb or bruise the green tops, and you should immediately smell the familiar oniony odor. If a few tears well up in your eyes, all the better—then you know you have an onion or garlic for sure.

DE-SCENT WITH ALLIUM

The powerful stink of onions and garlic can be a valuable de-scenting tool for traps and hunting clothes. Crush some up and wipe them on your skin before building or setting traps. Rub some on your clothing before the hunt. You can even chew the leaves or bulbs to hide your breath. If there are onions around, they are your top pick for hiding human scent.

078 MAKE DEADFALLS FROM SCRATCH

Deadfalls are a set of traps that use a weight to crush your prey. They can rely on bait or simply be placed in the animal's path. Their triggers can be a little tricky, but they are very versatile—most can be used with a crate or box (instead of a rock or log) to switch a lethal trap into a live-catch box trap.

Deadfalls are often persnickety to set up. Everything has to be balanced and stable for the trap to stay standing. And everything has to work just right in order for the trap to fall correctly, so pay attention to these basic tenets.

WEIGHT ANGLE The deadfall weight is always propped up by the trigger mechanism. Don't worry so much about the height of the weight—instead, look at the angle. The weight should be propped up between 30 and 40 degrees off the ground. If higher, it takes too long to hit the prey. If lower, the weight doesn't build up as much velocity.

SOLID SURFACE The deadfall weight should impact a solid surface. Rather than setting up your weight over sand or mud, set up your trap where the weight will hit a flat stone or other solid surface.

RIGHT ANGLES Many trigger parts work best when they are at right angles to each other, or carved with notches that are exactly 90 degrees. The figure-4 trap (see item 079) is the least forgiving if you don't carve perfect notches and square edges.

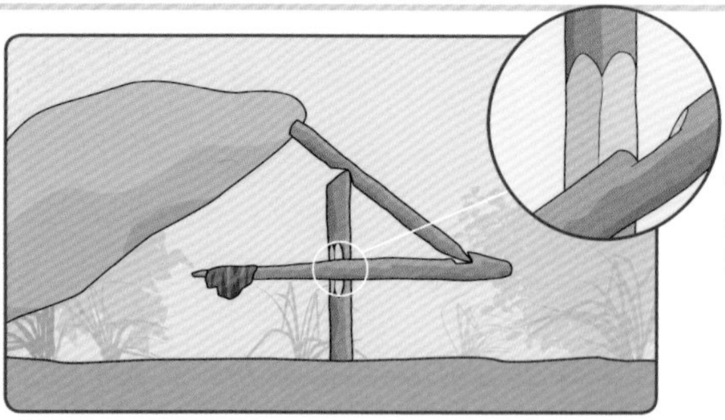

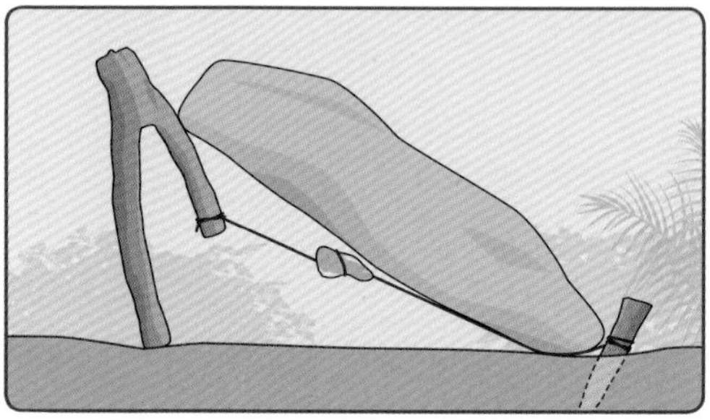

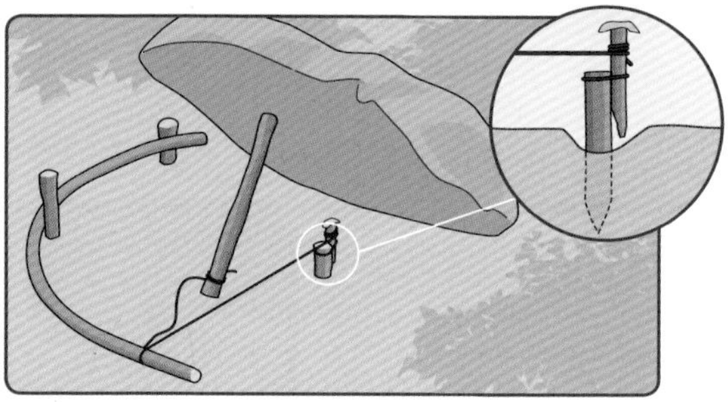

079 CREATE SOME OPTIONS

You can use rocks, logs, or stacks of lumber as the weight for a deadfall, and the variety of triggers available is even more numerous.

FIGURE-4 This trigger is just three straight sticks. The vertical post needs a chisel-shaped top and a 90-degree facet carved on the side. The diagonal lever has a chisel on one end and a side notch on the other, while the horizontal piece has a notch at the end, a notch on the side near the middle, and a point on the end for bait. Put some bait on the horizontal stick, lock these three pieces together, and lower the weight.

GREASY-STRING TRAP You'll need a forked stick, some string, some bait, and a small stake. Tie the string to one leg of the fork and the other end to the stake. Drive the stake into the ground and apply some bait to the string. Set the weight in place so it's propped on the fork and the string is tight. Once the animal gnaws the string in two, the weight will fall.

SPRING-POLE DEADFALL You'll need three stakes, a springy pole, three strings, a small toggle, a prop stick, and some bait. Make a little hole, and drive one stake near level with the ground. Tie a loose ring of string around the stake. Connect the end of the spring pole to the toggle with string, place bait on toggle, and tie the prop stick to the spring pole with another string. Prop your weight with the prop stick, put the toggle into the string ring on the stake, and use the remaining stakes to create tension on the spring pole. When the baited toggle is jostled, it slips free, pulling the prop stick out from the weight.

080 BUILD A PAIUTE TRAP

One of the best "tool-free" traps is known as the Paiute deadfall. This very clever trap dates back hundreds (if not thousands) of years to the early Paiute Indian nations. Like all other deadfalls, it uses some type of weight (often a rock) and a trigger system to hold part of the rock up in the air until your future meal gets under there. But the difference between this deadfall and the rest of them is its stronger and more sensitive trigger, which you can create even if you don't have a knife. To make this trap, just break a few sticks into the right size and shape, scrounge up a bit of string, and locate a flat rock.

STEP 1 Gather the sticks and other supplies. To catch an average-size rodent, you'll need the following: a Y-shaped stick thicker than a pencil and about 8 inches (20 cm) long; a straight stick thicker than a pencil, about 9 inches (23 cm) long; a 2-inch (5-cm) stick that is a little skinnier than a pencil; a slender bait stick half the diameter of a pencil and about 12 inches (30 cm) long; about 8 inches (20 cm) of string; appropriate bait for your critter of choice; and a flat rock that weighs 5–10 pounds (2–5 kg).

STEP 2 Take your 9-inch (23-cm) straight stick (this is called the lever) and tie one end of the string to it. Tie the other end to the 2-inch (5-cm) stick (the toggle). Square knots are fine. Wipe or skewer the bait on the 12-inch (30-cm) bait stick.

STEP 3 Set the trap by laying the rock down on a hard patch of ground. Stand the Y-shaped stick (the post) up by the edge of the rock. Put the stringless end of the lever in the fork of the post, with a small portion of it sticking out toward the rock. Place the rock on the tip of the lever. You should be able to support the weight of the rock by only holding down the string end of the lever. Now wrap the toggle halfway around the post. Place the baited end of the bait stick between a rough spot under the stone and the tip of the toggle. When you can let go of the lever and the rock stays up, you know you did it right.

081 STUDY SURVIVAL SNARES

Snares are a group of traps that restrain or strangle game animals. They can be stationary fixed snares or dynamic traps with complex triggers and engines to lift animals off the ground. Understanding the different parts and purposes of these traps will help you choose one—thousands are available, but the following are trusted performers in the realm of survival. Find out about local trapping regulations, and test the traps that are legal in your area. Here are the two types to know.

FIXED SNARES With rope, cord, or wire that is connected to an immobile object, like a tree or a stake, fixed snares are typically unbaited and restrain an animal until you dispatch it.

ACTIVE SNARES With moving parts in addition to a constricting snare noose, active snares either use bait or rely on habitual animal movement to set off the trap. The classic example is a spring-pole snare that lifts small game by a flexible tree branch or sapling tree.

082 GET YOUR FIX

Fixed snares are simple to make and generally easy to set. They rely on the animal's passage through the noose to tighten the trap around the animal's body, preferably its neck.

FIXED-LOOP SNARE The fixed-loop is easy to make and uses wire (solid wire or, better yet, braided steel cable that is designed for trapping) for its odd combination of strength, rigidity, and flexibility. These are usually single-use traps, as the animals often bend and kink the wire, making it vulnerable to future breakage. Sometimes animals can even break or chew through the wire. Balancing out these flaws is the fact that the fixed snare can be the fastest to create and set.

Here's a quick way to make a fixed snare from solid wire. Find a (breakable) twig that is about $^{1}/_{10}$ inch (2.5 mm) in diameter. Wind one end of your wire around the twig two or three times, then twist the twig like a little propeller, which will twist the end of the wire closed. Break the twig and remove it to reveal an eye, which you can use to make your noose. Place these snares over burrows, in small-game trails, or attach them to spring-pole snares for a more secure snare line.

DROWNING SNARE This simple trap can acquire food for you while putting the critter out of its misery faster than many other traps. The drowning snare is easiest to set when you have a steep-banked waterway frequented by creatures of habit. It requires a snare line with a noose, a heavy rock, a float stick, and a stick to prop up the rock in a precarious position.

To make this trap, simply tie the snare line to the rock, leaving a length of line free to tie the float. Set the noose in a run or slide that is heading straight down into the water. Prop up the rock so that it will fall if the noose is tugged, or tie the prop stick to the snare line. Once snared, the animal pulls the rock in after them, which holds your prey underwater. The wooden float lets you see where the rock and animal are located. This trap makes the most sense in cold conditions, as the cold water will keep the animal intact and away from most scavengers.

SQUIRREL POLE SNARE This trap caters to the squirrel's love of shortcuts. Select a 5- to 6-foot (1.5- to 2-m) pole that is about the diameter of your arm, and cover it with small wire snare loops. It's best if the pole has a rough, natural look to it, so don't carve off all the bark. It's also helpful if the pole has a fork at one end, which you can stick into the ground or pin against the tree to keep the pole from twisting out of place.

Begin making wire snare loops from 1½-foot (45-cm) lengths of wire (22-gauge or 24-gauge wire is a good squirrel-size line). Make the nooses just under 3 inches (7.5 cm) in diameter, and zigzag the wire between the pole and the noose to give it some slack. Twist these snares around the pole, and place them all over it. Don't put all your eggs in one basket by just using two or three snare loops: Do a dozen or more on the pole, with some on the top and some on the sides. Now, pin the squirrel pole against a tree that has a squirrel sign nearby—or a squirrel nest in it.

083 SET A BAITED SNARE

There are many effective baited snares to choose from. Since the scent is doing the work of drawing the animal to the trap, you won't have to be as precise in your trap placement, but note that many of them will require a tree or other elevated source to anchor to.

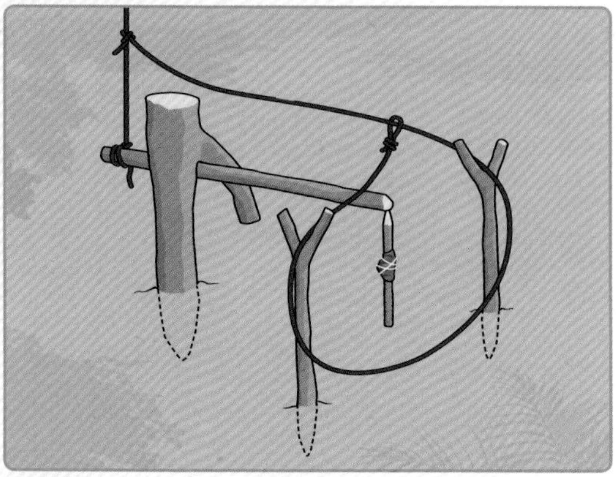

GRAVES' BAIT STICK SNARE This bait-activated spring pole snare, from the long-out-of-print book *Bushcraft*, by Richard Graves, is my go-to. You'll need a spring pole, a forked stake, a pencil-diameter toggle, a snare line with an attached trigger line, a bait stick, and bait. Tie the snare line to the end of the spring pole, bend until the snare touches the ground, and drive the stake in—keeping the line plumb is vital. Tie the toggle to the end of the trigger line (attached to the snare), and run it under the fork, keeping it parallel to the ground and at a right angle to the stake. Set your baited trigger at the end of the toggle to set the trap, and test it. If it springs quickly, you're ready to set up some twigs to support the noose. Then reset. (Note: Never handle the noose with your bare hands after the trigger is set. A misfire can rip skin—or digits.)

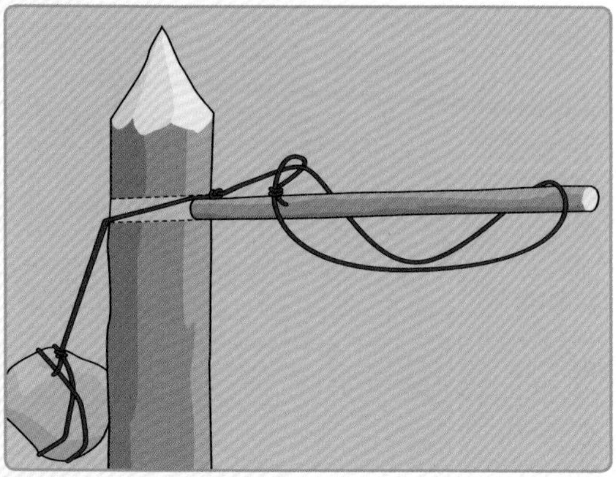

OJIBWA BIRD SNARE You can use this versatile trap year-round and in all conditions. You'll need a pole, a drill to make a 0.4-inch (1-cm) hole, a pencil-size stick for the perch, 3 feet (1 m) slender cord or thick string, and a 3.5-ounce (100-g) rock.

Carve a point on both ends of the pole. Drill a hole through the pole as cleanly as you can. Tie a small bowline knot in the end of your snare line, and pass the line through the loop, creating the snare. Tie the other end of the line to the rock. After you've picked a trapping site and driven the pole in the ground, use a twig to thread the snare line through the hole in the pole. Tie a knot cluster in the line close to the snare noose (this stopper knot coupled with the twig forms the trigger system). Lay your noose over the perch once the stopper knot has engaged the twig, and the trap is set. If your noose keeps blowing off the perch, wipe a little sticky pine pitch on the contact points.

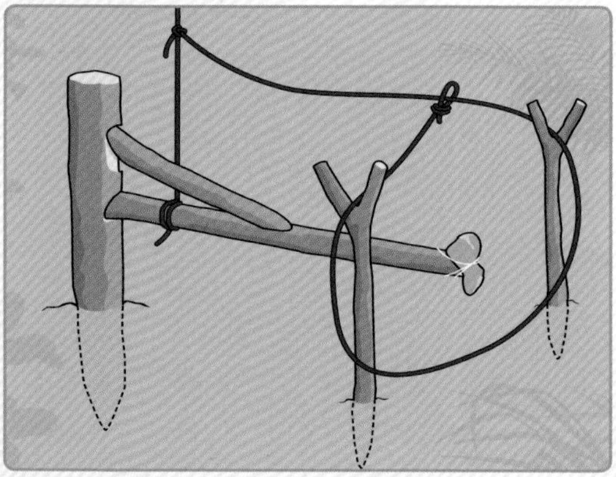

FIGURE-4 SNARE The figure-4 snare combines the sensitive leverage trigger of the figure-4 deadfall with the lunch-launching capability of a spring-pole snare. For this trap, you'll require a good, snappy spring pole, snare line with noose and a side line to the trigger, bait, and the three sticks to make up the "4" shape.

Tie the snare line to the end of your spring pole. Make sure the pole has enough lifting power. Then drive the vertical piece of the figure 4 deep into the ground. This will hold the energy of the spring pole, so drive it 1 foot (30 cm) deep to keep it from being sucked up out of the ground. Assemble the figure 4 by notching the vertical and horizontal pieces to receive the diagonal. Bait the trap, tie on the trigger line, and suspend the noose with a pair of twigs.

084 MAKE A BAIT-FREE SNARE

These snares eliminate the need for bait, though you'll have to take pains to make sure the animal still has a reason to go through the noose and activate the trigger. These traps are usually set on an animal's trails or outside their burrows.

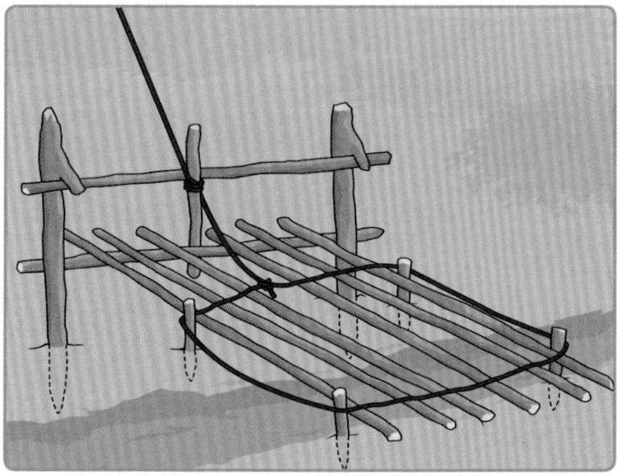

TREADLE SNARE This "spring pole and noose" trap is set off by an animal bumping the treadle stick, stepping on it, knocking it down, or knocking it out of its way while running down its trail. The treadle snare requires a spring pole, a snare line with noose and trigger line, a pencil-size toggle stick, the treadle trigger stick, and a support to hold the trigger stick.

Tie your snare line to the end of the spring pole and tie the toggle stick to the end of the trigger line. Pull the spring pole down, then lap the toggle over the support, using the treadle trigger stick to hold the toggle in place. Set the noose of the snare line so it hangs beside the treadle, and wait for your dinner. A snare hung on each side of the treadle is even better, as it will catch an animal coming or going.

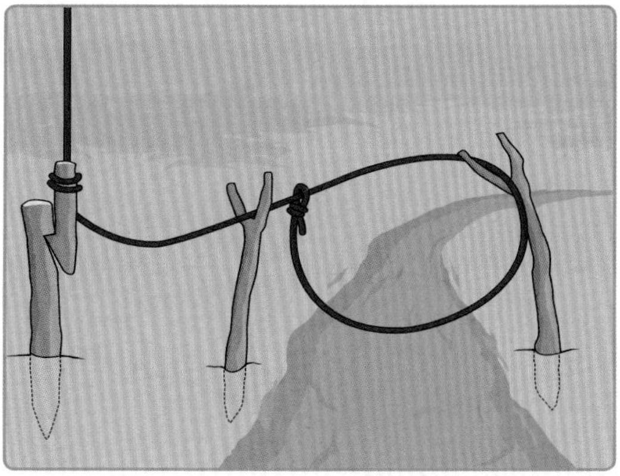

PEG SNARE This trap is easy to set up and to carve. You'll need a spring pole, a peg driven into the ground, a snare line with noose, a peg to act as a trigger, and maybe some bait. That last part will depend on whether you want the trap to be bait-activated or to wait for the animal to pass through.

Drive your peg into the soil, and carve a hook near the top. You could also saw off the top of an existing bush or sapling, which could provide an anchor for your trap. After you make your peg in the ground, carve your trigger peg with a matching hook, which will grab onto your peg in the ground. Tie your snare line to the spring pole and tie the trigger peg onto the line, tying the knot on the side of the peg you have cut the hook into. Attach bait to the trigger peg with the noose hanging around the baited part, or set the noose in a trail near the peg trigger.

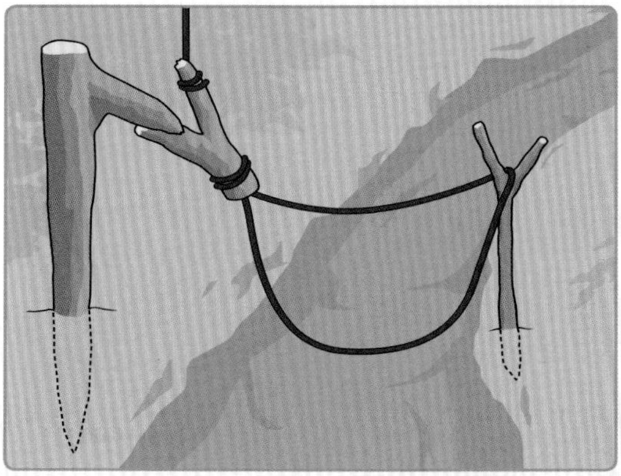

ROLLING SNARE The rolling snare uses a pair of wooden hooks to trigger a motion-activated spring-pole snare trap, and is ideal for trails and runs. You'll need a couple of forked sticks and a snare line with a noose.

Find a slender forked branch and cut a point on the nonforked end to drive it into the ground near the edge of a small-game trail. Find a similar, smaller fork to tie to the snare line. Engage the two hooks so that the free one will roll off the hook that is staked to the ground (not so they will hook together, which would prevent the trap from going off). Set your noose in the trail, propped up with twigs or tied in place with thread. No baiting is required.

IT COULD HAPPEN
085 BADGER ATTACK
I WAS HIKING DEEP INTO THE WOODS TO CHECK MY TRAP LINES.
I SHOULD HAVE KNOWN TO DISPATCH IT PROPERLY--
--IT WAS TOO LATE NOW!
I WOKE UP HOURS LATER, MY HEAD KILLING ME AND VERY DISORIENTED.
I FELT TOO WEAK TO HEAD BACK TO THE TRUCK; LUCKILY ANOTHER TRAP HAD CAUGHT ME SOME DINNER--AND, MUCH TO MY SURPRISE, A FAMILIAR FOE.

I CAME ACROSS A BIG BADGER IN THE FIRST TRAP AND PREPARED FOR A FEAST!
I THOUGHT THE ANIMAL WAS OUT COLD, BUT WHEN I LOOSED THE TRAP, IT SPRUNG UP! VERY MUCH AWAKE . . .
. . . AND MAD!
A FEW SCRATCHES LATER, HE RAN OFF, AND I WENT TO RESET THE TRAP, A LITTLE SHAKEN UP.
SUDDENLY . . .
?
DINK
WWWAP
AND, BOY, WAS HE DELICIOUS!

086 POACH SOME WILD EGGS

Stealing songbird and game-bird eggs is illegal in most areas, but if you're in desperate straits and you happen upon a nest of fresh eggs, you can fry, hard boil, or poach your way to a delicious, protein-packed meal. And the good news is that there are no poisonous eggs. Just be aware that bird eggs develop at different rates, so you may end up with a yellow chick inside that shell instead of the yellow yolk you were expecting.

Collecting eggs for food has been around as long as we have been around—and in a dire situation, it shouldn't be ruled out. Sure, ostrich eggs are the biggest wild-bird eggs, but goose eggs are pretty big, too, and more likely to show up in your hunt. They're the largest wild bird eggs you'll find in North America, and a female goose can lay half a dozen at a time, each twice the size of a chicken egg. Due to the size, their standout white color, and the protective presence of both parents, goose nests are often easy to spot—but that's where the easy part ends.

Fiercely protective, the geese will not give up their eggs without a fight. Running at the nest and grabbing one or two eggs is your best approach. This keeps you from impacting the bird's population too much—or from getting bitten. Goose eggs are typically found in late March or early April, depending on the latitude and temperatures. They also take about a month to hatch, giving you about a week before the eggs start to look like embryos.

087 BECOME A SHORT-ORDER SURVIVAL COOK

They say hunger is the best spice, and if you sprinkle that atop a meal that already tastes good, you may have the makings of a five-star feast. Here are some of my favorite wild-egg meals.

WILD CHEF SALAD Collect tender spring greens and flowers like chickweed, violets, dandelion, sorrel, and whatever else is locally abundant and tasty. Wash the greens in safe water and plate them like a salad. Hard boil your wild eggs for fifteen minutes and allow them to cool. Remove the shells and crumble the eggs over the green salad.

SPICY GOOSE EGG OMELET Pour scrambled goose eggs in a nonstick camping fry pan, and add some minced wild onion. When the omelet is ready to fold, add chopped watercress and any other spicy greens you can find, such as wintercress, bittercress, and any of the peppergrasses.

EGGS IN GAME BIRD This dish is not quite as over-the-top crazy as a turducken (in which a chicken is stuffed inside a duck that's stuffed inside a turkey), but it's not exactly conventional, either. To make this dish, dispatch a game bird, pluck and clean it, and then fill it with whole raw eggs. Bake it slowly at a low temperature in a Dutch oven (or similar) until the meat is falling off the bone. Enjoy your finished roasted bird with cooked eggs.

088 MAKE A LOW-TECH X-RAY

Most people have a natural aversion to cracking an egg over a hot frying pan and having a partially formed chick fall out. A simple trick can help you to discern the egg's level of development.

"Candling" refers to the old practice of placing a candle or light source behind an egg and observing the condition of the air cell, yolk, and white.

Many species of birds (but not all) have translucent eggs, and the light passing through can help you detect bloody whites, blood spots, or meat spots, enabling you to see how far along the chick inside is.

You should candle your eggs in a darkened room or outside at night by holding the egg before the light at an angle. White-shelled eggs that are only a few days old will still clearly show the yolk and white. Older eggs will have a reddish area with blood vessels extending away from it like a huge red spider—this is the embryo inside the egg. If the whole egg is dark, you have a chick inside. The egg is in fact edible throughout all of these stages, even if you'd rather not take advantage of that fact.

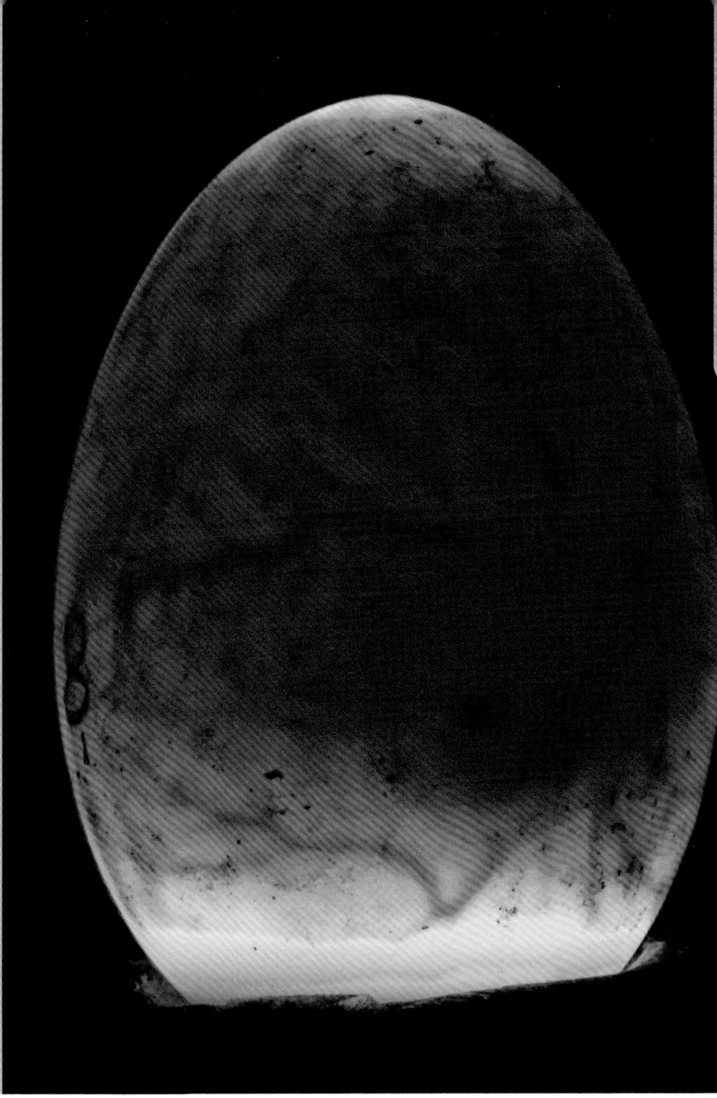

089 COOK IN THE SHELL

For maximum calorie conservation, hard-boil your eggs. This process is just the same in camp as it is at home—but if you have no pot or water is scarce, then it's time to try cooking your wild eggs in the shell.

STEP 1 Use a knife or sharp stone to chip the pointy end off the egg. Remove less than 1 inch (2.5 cm) of shell for best results.

STEP 2 Use a twig to poke the yolk and stir up the egg contents. Think of this as making a scrambled egg inside the shell.

STEP 3 Place the egg in the ashes near your fire, turning periodically. Keep it close enough to cook, but not so close it boils over. Never put a whole egg close to the fire: It will explode, wasting your food source and leaving you with egg on your face—for real.

090 EAT THE BUGS

Maybe your fishing trip isn't going so well. Perhaps the only "catch of the day" is the bait you've wrangled up by flipping over rocks, ripping open logs, and scouring the bushes. Well, as long as they're not poisonous, you can eat your bait bugs. Here are a couple of creatures that you can munch on when the fish aren't biting.

TERMITES Ripping open a rotten log may seem like a lot of work, but the payoff might be worth the trouble. Termites have the highest calorie count of any bug you'll find. You'll have to work to get it, though, as these little guys will go scurrying for cover anytime you damage the wood they reside in. Once you've got them, roast them in a dry pan—some species even take on a shrimplike flavor.

SLUGS Let me say from the beginning that the choice between eating slugs or starving is not one I would relish. I've eaten slugs before, and I hope I never have to repeat the experience. But they will pass for food in a pinch. Terrestrial slugs and snails (those found on land, not in the sea) are generally safe for human consumption—always after a thorough cooking. And their nutritional value certainly justifies the effort. These critters have about 90 calories per 3 1/2 ounces (100 g) of meat, and they're high in protein (12–16 percent) and rich in minerals.

091 ORDER THE ESCARGOT

If you did have to (or wanted to) eat slugs and snails, the safest choice is the snail. Slugs are more likely to eat toxic mushrooms, while snails tend to eat plant material—when they're not eating dung, of course. If you want to try slugs and there are toxic mushrooms in season nearby, put the slugs in a container for a week with some damp cornmeal or moist lettuce to allow them to purge. Psych yourself up for a challenge, and try cooking these mollusk meals.

FRIED SLUGS Scald the slugs in boiling water for two minutes. Dredge them in egg and then in bread crumbs. Deep fry in oil until golden brown and serve hot.

CLASSIC ESCARGOT Let your snails purge themselves in a container of damp lettuce for 24 hours. Bring 1 cup (250 ml) water or white wine to a boil in a large sauté pan, and pour in 2 cups (17 oz) snails. As the liquid boils off and the snails begin to cook, add one stick of butter to the pan and several cloves of minced garlic. Sauté for three to four minutes and serve.

SLUG STIR-FRY In a wok or skillet, fry some of your favorite veggies with oil, add a couple handfuls of blanched slugs, and season with soy sauce to taste.

BACKWOODS BOIL Put the slugs or snails in water with whatever seasonings you can find and boil for ten minutes. Wild onion and other strong flavors are a solid choice. Eat as a soup, or simply pick out the mollusks and eat them on their own.

092 CRUNCH SOME CRICKETS

Crickets, katydids, and grasshoppers are a very diverse group of bugs that are generally safe to eat if you avoid the colorful members of these families. Red, orange, yellow, and blue are usually colors you should stay far away from. Make sure to remove the heads and small legs, and cook thoroughly. Bugs with crunchy shells (exoskeletons) are often the most laden with parasites. Hunt for them in the early morning, when they are less active due to the colder temperatures. This group of bugs yields approximately 4–5 calories per gram. Their flavor ranges from flavorless to fatty tasting.

093 COOK A CICADA FEAST

Each summer, the roar of the cicadas signals a feast in the animal kingdom. Why not join the other animals that are gobbling up this winged windfall of calories? The newly hatched cicadas (called tenerals) are considered the best for eating because their shells are not too hard.

Your prep work for cicadas is easy: Harvest the slow-witted and slow-moving things in the early hours of the morning. They should be blanched (boiled for four to five minutes) soon after collection and before you eat them. Not only will this solidify their insides a bit, but it will kill any bacteria and parasites. Remove the wings and legs, and at this point you can either freeze them for later use or cook immediately. When you're ready to take the plunge with a cicada meal, here are three options to try.

THE OLD-FASHIONED This simple snack involves skewering and roasting cicadas on a slender green wood stick for five minutes over a fire. You can also make these in your kitchen—use a metal skewer and roast in the oven for seven minutes at 400°F (204°C). Brush on a little oil or butter toward the end so that any salt or spices you add will stick.

EL CHIRPO TACO Fry the blanched cicadas in a bit of oil and mix in your favorite taco seasonings. If your guests are squeamish, use crunchy corn shells to camouflage the crunch of the bugs.

CHOCOLATE CHIRP COOKIES Mix up a batch of cookies, and press one blanched cicada into the top of each raw cookie on the sheet. Then bake them according to your cookie-mix directions.

094 DRESS SMALL GAME

Even if you take your deer to the game processor for professional cutting and packaging, there's no reason you can't do the work yourself on rabbits, squirrels, and other small animals. Once you get the hang of it, you should be able to dress out a small animal in less than ten minutes.

STEP 1 Take your legally hunted, trapped, or road-killed animal and your sharp knife to a clean wooden surface, like a board or a weathered, barkless log. Cut off the head and all four feet. The easiest way to do this is to use a small club of wood as a baton to strike the back of the knife blade and drive it through skin, muscle, tendon, and bone.

STEP 2 Lay the game on its back and set the knife-edge above the anus. Tap the knife with the club to cut off the anus and tail. You could also cut a circle around the anus to isolate it, but this can be time-consuming and tricky on small game.

STEP 3 Make an incision in the belly skin and muscle starting at the sternum (breastbone) and cutting down to the anal cut. Slice shallowly, being careful to keep stomach and intestines whole. Scoop out the guts from liver to colon.

STEP 4 Now that the abdominal guts are gone, you can insert the knife into the chest cavity, blade edge up, and slice through the center of the rib cage all the way to the throat cut. Remove the heart and lungs (the only contents of the chest cavity). Save the "good" guts for sausage or soup. The lungs, heart, liver, and kidneys are definite keepers. If you're starving, flush out the stomach and intestines and cook those, too.

STEP 5 Peel off the hide. Start at the hind section, which is thinner and easier to remove. Work your thumb under the skin and cut it loose a little with the knife if needed. Once you get a handful of hide, you can peel it off from tail to head (or where the head was formerly located). Save the skin for tanning, or scald the fur off with hot water and some scraping and use the skin for food.

STEP 6 Pick off any remaining hairs and give the carcass a rinse with clean water to remove blood and any dirt. Cook right away as a whole animal, or cut it into quarters with a little more baton work, then bread the quarters and fry them. You can also freeze the carcass in a vacuum-sealed plastic bag for later.

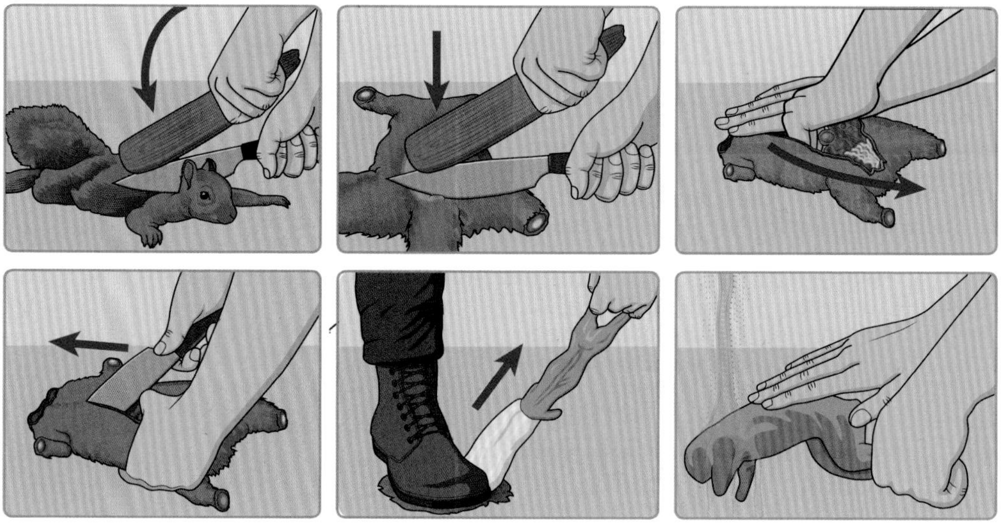

095 WASTE NOTHING

For a macabre treat, place the whole animal head in a small bed of coals from a hardwood fire. Allow it to roast, turning it often by rolling it around with a stick. When the ears have burned off, take the head out and see if it's done. The tongue and the brain are the edible bits (you'll see these on creative—and fancy—restaurant menus); they can be removed by cracking the skull with a stone. If anything seems too mushy, throw the head back in the fire for a few more minutes of cooking.

096 PROCESS YOUR OWN GAME

Don't be intimidated by big-game processing. These animals generally have the same parts and pieces as small game, and they come apart in the same way.

The first job that must be done with big game is the field dressing—the removal of the animal's internal organs so the body can cool more quickly and the abdominal contents don't taint the meat. This can be done while laying the animal on the ground, but many people get some help from gravity by hoisting the animal by the neck into a tree.

Let's start with the hard part: Cut a circle around the anus, pull the rectum outward, and tie it off with a piece of string. This keeps any feces contained and contributes to cleaner field dressing. Once that's done, create an incision from the ribs to the anus through the skin and muscle of the belly. You'll know when you first pierce the abdominal cavity, as a whiff of foul gas will hit you right in the face—and it will be worse if the animal has an abdominal injury or if you accidentally cut into the stomach or intestines.

Cut to the side of male organs, as these will be removed later, and when the cut is complete, reach in and pull out the stomach, liver, intestines, and any other innards. You may have to do a little cutting to get the stomach loose on really large animals, but smaller creatures have thin enough tissues that the digestive organs will all tear free.

You may also have to cut the connective tissue around the rectum, a bit like coring an apple, to get the large intestine free. Finish the field dressing by cutting the diaphragm muscle where it attaches around the rib cage and pulling the heart and lungs from the chest cavity. You may also sever the esophagus to aid in removing the cardio-pulmonary system.

097 HANG IT UP

Hanging the animal lets the animal cool, keeps insects off, and makes your job easier. Using a gambrel hook (which looks like a clothes hanger), you can hang your big- game animal with its tail upward. Make a slit in the skin of each rear leg, between the tendon and the bone. This hook can be replaced by tying a rope to each Achilles tendon, or threading a stout pole through these leg cuts. You can leave the animal hung like this for a short while in warm weather, or several days in cold weather. It can keep for weeks in subfreezing weather.

098 SKIN YOUR CARCASS

Carefully cut around each rear leg to cut the skin but not the meat or load-bearing tendons. Make cuts down each inner thigh, a circle around the neck, and a cut down the chest so they all meet up with the initial field-dressing cut. Then cut circles around the front leg joints and connect to the chest cut. Peel the hide forcefully from the animal's rump to its neck. The head can be cut off at any time, but don't skin until you're ready to cut up the meat, as the hide acts as a natural barrier to insects, scavengers, and bacteria.

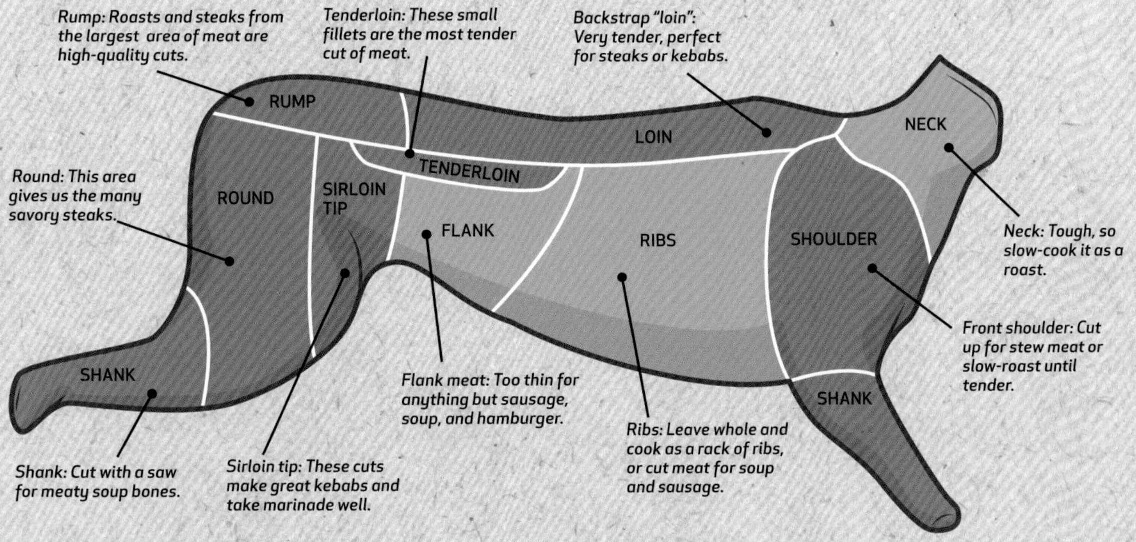

099 PULL THE CHOICE CUTS

Here's the part where things can get either really complicated or really easy. You can study a book on fine cuts of meat and learn where each type of steak comes from, or you can cut off a hunk of meat, impale it on a pointy stick, and roast it over the open fire. Remember to use every little scrap. It can be soup stock, hamburger, sausage, or something else to make thrifty use of your resources. And all the bones can be used to make broth, which provides vital minerals.

100 DISCOVER WILD-GAME NUTRITION

Ever wonder how many calories are in a squirrel? I have. It's 900, and it's not necessarily something you need to memorize. But failing to understand the nutritional value of your wild game meats can lead to malnutrition and even death in extreme cases of living off the land. There was a malady among fur trade–era trappers that came to be known as "rabbit starvation"—today we might call it protein toxicity, and it's still fatal. Eating only lean muscle meats, as the trappers sometimes did (without eating the animal fat and organs or any carbohydrates), puts the body deep into ketosis and leads to rapid weight loss, diarrhea, and ravenous feelings. If the weight loss and accompanying hunger led to more lean meat consumption, a person could be dead from "starvation" in just a few weeks—with a full belly of meat! And that's why you need to know about nutrition—so dig in.

DEER

Nutrition Facts
Serving Size: 100g

Amount Per Serving	
Calories: 158	
	% Daily Value
Total Fat 3.5g	**5%**
Cholesterol 112mg	**37%**
Protein 31g	**62%**
Iron	**25%**

ELK

Nutrition Facts
Serving Size: 100g

Amount Per Serving	
Calories: 137	
	% Daily Value
Total Fat Less than 1g	**1%**
Cholesterol 67mg	**22%**
Protein 22.8g	**46%**
Iron	**17%**

DUCK

Nutrition Facts
Serving Size: 100g

Amount Per Serving	
Calories: 120	
	% Daily Value
Total Fat 5g	**8%**
Cholesterol 75mg	**25%**
Protein 19g	**38%**
Iron	**25%**

CANADA GOOSE

Nutrition Facts
Serving Size: 100g

Amount Per Serving	
Calories: 236	
	% Daily Value
Total Fat 14g	**22%**
Cholesterol 95mg	**32%**
Protein 28g	**56%**
Iron	**14%**

WILD TURKEY

Nutrition Facts
Serving Size: 100g

Amount Per Serving	
Calories: 163	
	% Daily Value
Total Fat Less than 1g	**1%**
Cholesterol 55mg	**18%**
Protein 26g	**52%**
Iron	**25%**

GROUSE

Nutrition Facts
Serving Size: 100g

Amount Per Serving	
Calories: 165	
	% Daily Value
Total Fat 1g	**2%**
Cholesterol 119mg	**40%**
Protein 28g	**56%**
Iron	**22%**

COTTONTAIL RABBIT

Nutrition Facts
Serving Size: 100g

Amount Per Serving	
Calories: 173	
	% Daily Value
Total Fat 3.5g	**5%**
Cholesterol 123mg	**41%**
Protein 33g	**66%**
Iron	**27%**

GRAY SQUIRREL

Nutrition Facts
Serving Size: 100g

Amount Per Serving	
Calories: 173	
	% Daily Value
Total Fat 5g	**8%**
Cholesterol 121mg	**40%**
Protein 31g	**62%**
Iron	**38%**

ALLIGATOR

Nutrition Facts
Serving Size: 100g

Amount Per Serving	
Calories: 211	
	% Daily Value
Total Fat 4g	**6%**
Cholesterol 83mg	**28%**
Protein 31g	**62%**
Iron	**22%**

OPOSSUM

Nutrition Facts
Serving Size: 100g

Amount Per Serving	
Calories: 221	
	% Daily Value
Total Fat 11g	**17%**
Cholesterol 129mg	**43%**
Protein 31g	**62%**
Iron	**25%**

RACCOON

Nutrition Facts
Serving Size: 100g

Amount Per Serving	
Calories: 255	
	% Daily Value
Total Fat 14g	**22%**
Cholesterol 96mg	**32%**
Protein 29g	**58%**
Iron	**40%**

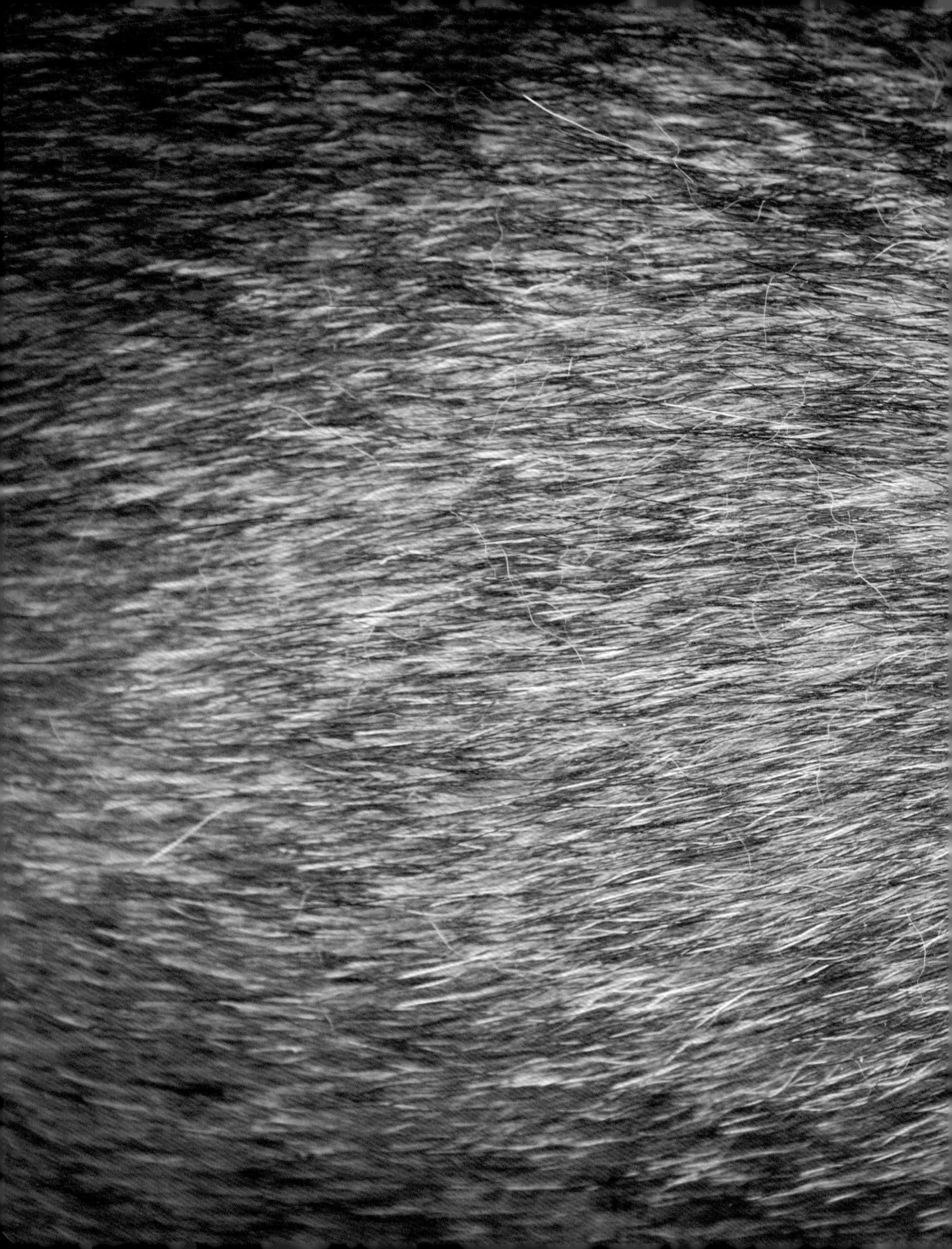

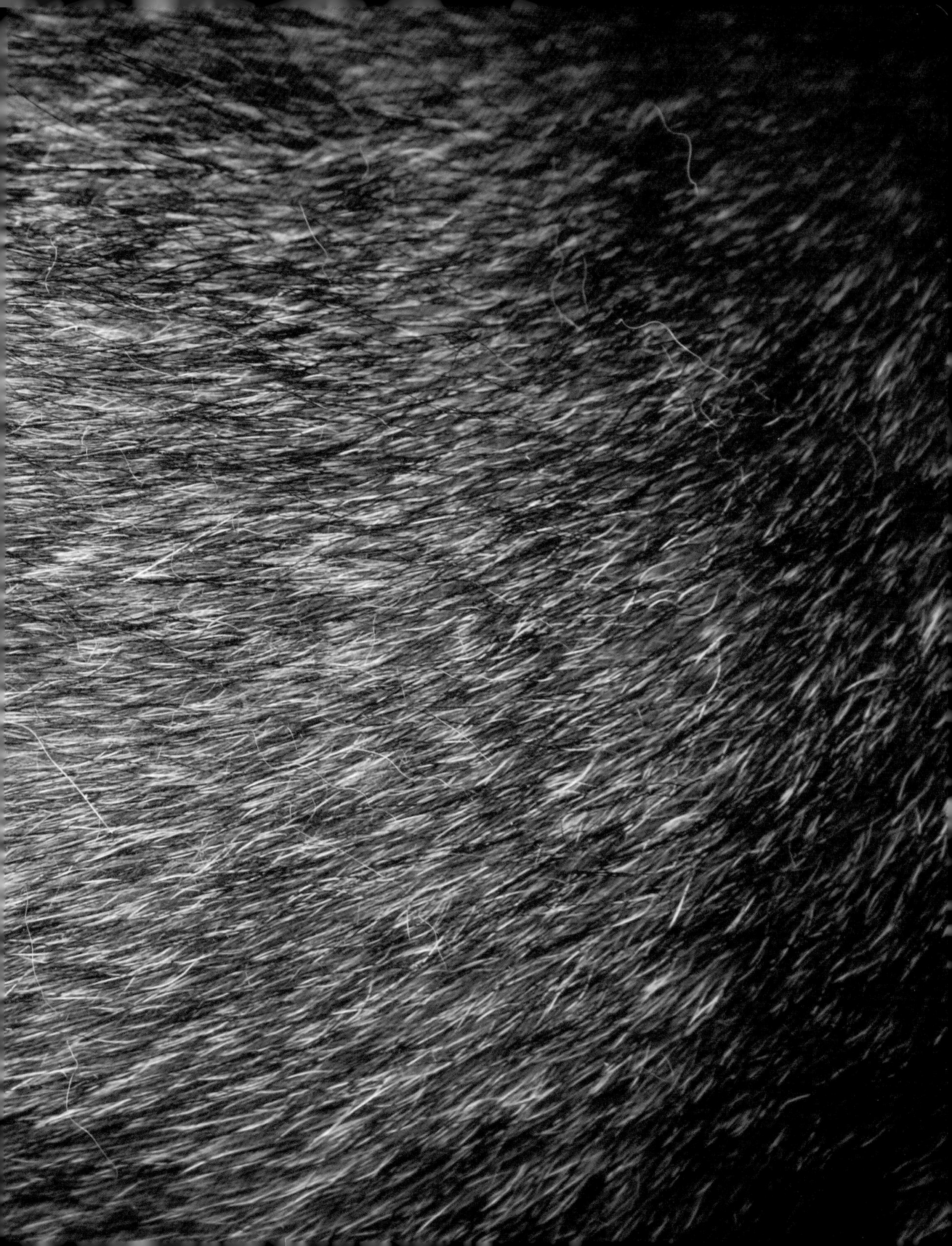

GATHERING

Let's continue our wild-food finding with the plant kingdom—or, as I like to think of it, the food that can't run, fly, or swim away. Safe, nutritious, wild edible plants are abundant across much of the world during warmer seasons, and often these tough plants survive into the colder seasons, too. Even if you don't succeed at fishing, trapping, and hunting, there are almost always plant foods available.

It's not just the stuff of legends and survival shows—out there in the wild, there really are nuts, berries, twigs, and roots that will make you a feast. Whether your goal is to survive an emergency in a remote area, or simply find something unique to put on the family dinner table, the following pages will guide you through the complex world of botanical terms and plant structures, inform you with food-gathering knowledge for survival, and provide intriguing ideas for preparing these wild foods.

When it comes to learning about how to identify good food plants and avoid the dangerous ones, the devil's in the details. Small structural differences between plants can make a big difference as to their identity, which in turn affects their safety as a consumable good. You'll need to train your eye to look for the little things, and exercise caution if you're not certain of the plant's identity. Don't be afraid to use your sense of smell to assist with plant identification, too. Some plants have very characteristic odors.

Study the details of these plants, and soon you'll be seeing familiar wild-plant foods everywhere you go.

101 FOLLOW THE BOY SCOUT MOTTO

Before you run out to go berry picking, fishing, or 'shroom hunting, you should always take a moment to consider what would happen if you were injured, lost your way, or otherwise ran into trouble. In other words, be prepared!

COME PREPARED If you're going outside your normal stomping grounds, be sure to bring a map and compass. Even if you're on familiar ground, carry a survival kit and first aid kit in case of the unexpected. Traveling with a friend is also good for safety—and fun.

LEAVE A TRAIL Tell someone the details of your trip so there will be someone who knows where you went and when you should return, and who can contact the authorities if you don't show up on time.

DON'T DISCONNECT Carry a fully charged cell phone so that you can call or text for help if you get into trouble (but don't assume you'll always have a signal).

102 PACK A KIT

A well-stocked survival kit can be a literal lifesaver in an emergency situation. Although many of these items are inexpensive, their value in the field is immeasurable. It's far better to have the gear and not need it than to need the gear and not have it. Build your own survival kit and first aid kit with these components.

SURVIVAL KIT

- ▢ Space blanket
- ▢ Butane lighter
- ▢ Waterproof matches
- ▢ Ferrocerium spark rod
- ▢ Collapsible water bottle
- ▢ Water disinfection tablets
- ▢ Whistle for signaling
- ▢ Mirror for signaling
- ▢ Metal cup to boil water
- ▢ Cordage material
- ▢ Snacks or emergency food rations
- ▢ Large trash bag
- ▢ Roll of dental floss
- ▢ Monofilament fishing line
- ▢ Small and medium fish hooks
- ▢ Compass

FIRST AID KIT

- ▢ Alcohol swabs
- ▢ Antibiotic cream packets
- ▢ Burn gel packet
- ▢ 10 adhesive bandages
- ▢ 1 blister patch
- ▢ Small roll of waterproof tape
- ▢ 4 nonstick gauze pads
- ▢ 4 butterfly strips
- ▢ 8 acetaminophen tablets
- ▢ 8 ibuprofen tablets
- ▢ 8 aspirin tablets
- ▢ 8 antidiarrheal tablets
- ▢ 8 antihistamine tablets
- ▢ 1 pair of nonlatex exam gloves
- ▢ Thermometer
- ▢ 1 large needle

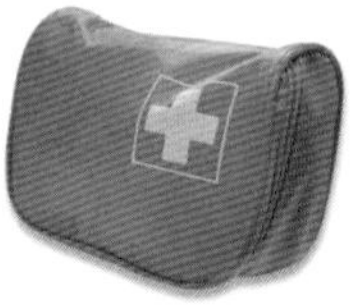

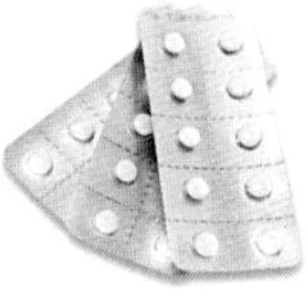

103 BECOME LOST-PROOF

Getting lost is one of the main reasons that people find themselves in survival situations, and it's one of the easiest problems to prevent. Avoid losing your way by using these navigation tricks.

PRE-GAME

Get a map of the area that you are traveling to and study it before going.

Use the map and a compass while you're there.

Imagine looking down on the terrain from a "bird's-eye view" and find where you are on the map.

Look behind you frequently to familiarize yourself with the views and terrain, especially if you will be returning in that direction.

Look for landmarks, memorize them, and use them to travel in straight lines.

IF YOU DO GET LOST, DO THE FOLLOWING IN ORDER:

1. STAY PUT.
2. MAKE CAMP, FOLLOWING THE PRIORITIES OF SURVIVAL (SEE ITEM 104).
3. SIGNAL FOR HELP OFTEN, USING DIFFERENT METHODS.
4. TAKE TEST TRIPS OUT AND BACK FROM CAMP TO SEE IF YOU CAN DETERMINE WHERE YOU ARE AND WHICH WAY TO GO.

104 PRIORITIZE YOUR SURVIVAL TO-DO LIST

If the worst happens and you need to survive until you're found or can find your way out, you need to prioritize—and fast. Here's what you should concentrate on, in order, starting with your most immediate need and moving toward less-pressing issues.

SHELTER This is always your top survival priority (unless there is a dire medical issue). Your shelter will need to protect you from the cold or the heat, depending on the scenario. Build a thick, insulated shelter for cold conditions. Construct a shady, open one in hot, sunny climates. Remember that your clothes are a form of shelter, too. Stuff them with insulation if you're getting too cold.

WATER You can only make it a few days without water. Boil or treat your water for safety if you can. When faced with the choice between drinking questionable water or dying due to dehydration, drink the water. It's better to be sick and alive than pathogen-free and dead.

FIRE AND SIGNALING Fire is an outstanding distress signal. It also boils your water, cooks your food, and gives you light and heat. Carry multiple fire-starting methods to ensure your success, no matter the weather conditions.

FOOD While the average person could survive a month without eating, there's usually no need for that kind of suffering. Follow the tips, tricks, and information in this book, and you'll have the food priority covered.

105 ENJOY YOUR WEEDS

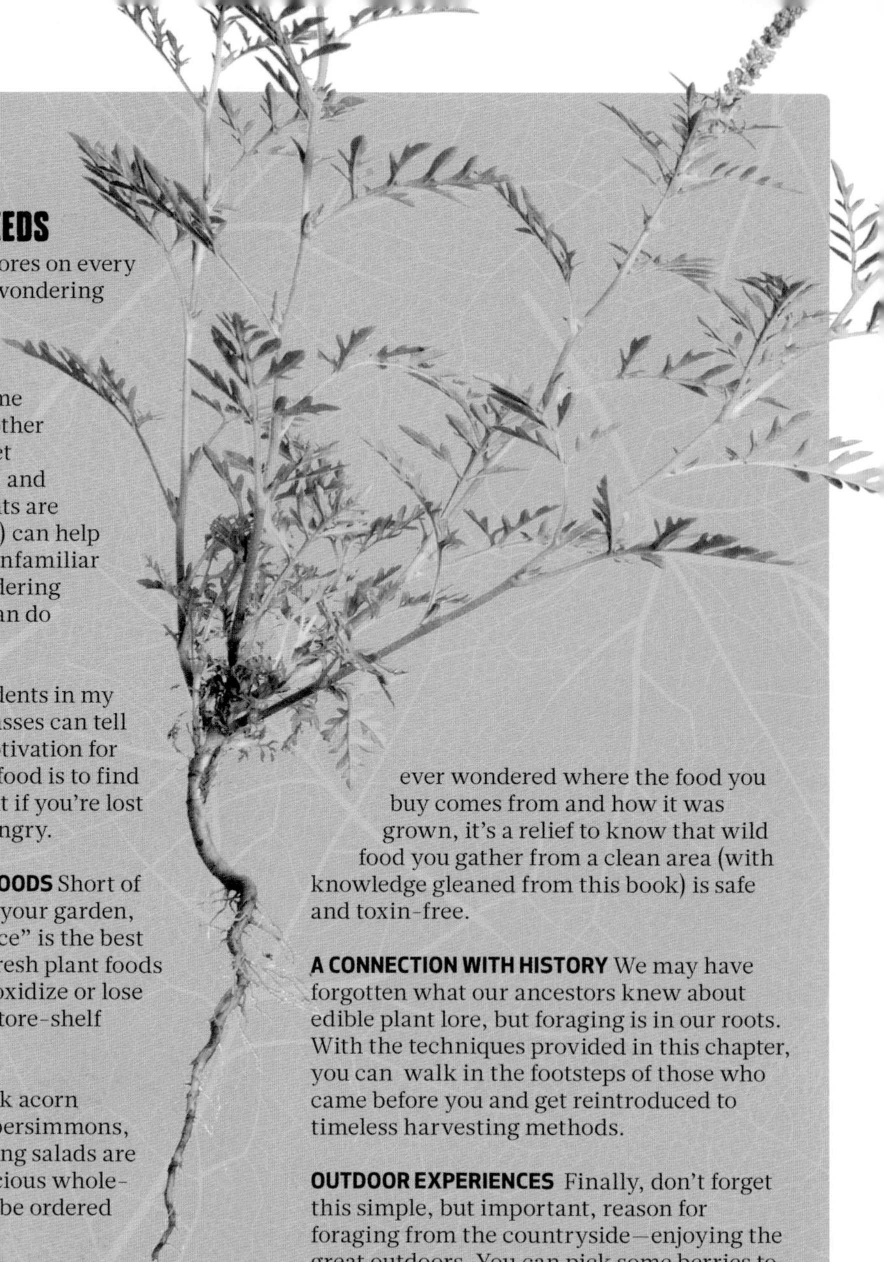

With convenience stores on every corner, you may be wondering why people would need to scavenge for wild plants. But there may come a time when foraging in Mother Nature's supermarket becomes a necessity, and knowing which plants are edible (and delicious) can help you navigate those unfamiliar aisles. If you're wondering what weed-eating can do for you, read on.

SURVIVAL As the students in my seasonal foraging classes can tell you, the primary motivation for learning about wild food is to find out what plants to eat if you're lost in the woods and hungry.

FRESH, NUTRITIOUS FOODS Short of eating directly from your garden, picking wild "produce" is the best way to "eat local." Fresh plant foods haven't had time to oxidize or lose nutrients like their store-shelf counterparts.

GOURMET TREATS Dark acorn bread, gooey sweet persimmons, and spicy, crisp, spring salads are just a few of the delicious whole-food dishes that can be ordered in the wild.

ORGANIC PRODUCE If you care about the techniques used in growing the food you eat, munch a bunch of weeds. Naturally self-sustaining, non-GMO, and poison-free, wild edible plants are completely organic. If you've ever wondered where the food you buy comes from and how it was grown, it's a relief to know that wild food you gather from a clean area (with knowledge gleaned from this book) is safe and toxin-free.

A CONNECTION WITH HISTORY We may have forgotten what our ancestors knew about edible plant lore, but foraging is in our roots. With the techniques provided in this chapter, you can walk in the footsteps of those who came before you and get reintroduced to timeless harvesting methods.

OUTDOOR EXPERIENCES Finally, don't forget this simple, but important, reason for foraging from the countryside—enjoying the great outdoors. You can pick some berries to snack on while out for a quick walk with the kids or supplement the food you packed for a rock-climbing, kayaking, or backpacking trip with plants you find. It's a great way to connect with nature.

106 STAY SAFE OUT THERE

Never for a moment think that foraging for wild edible plants is a risk-free endeavor—there's plenty that can go wrong. You may misidentify a plant, have an allergic reaction, or even get sick from what should be a totally safe plant (specimens can be contaminated). Follow this tried-and-true list of wild-plant harvesting guidelines for best results.

HARVESTING TIPS

Be 100 percent positive about your identification of all plants and plant parts.

Research poisonous plants, and heed warnings about dangerous plants in your area and abroad.

Know how to use the plants, which parts to use, and when to use them.

Learn to recognize plants through different growth stages and seasons.

Wash greens, vegetables, and fruit to avoid pathogens from the droppings of birds, insects, and other animals.

Don't collect plants near roads, dumps, trains, industrial areas, or other contaminated sites.

Eat only small amounts of plants that are new to you, try just one new plant at a time, and know which plants should be eaten in moderation.

Cook all aquatic plants and their parts in order to destroy waterborne pathogens.

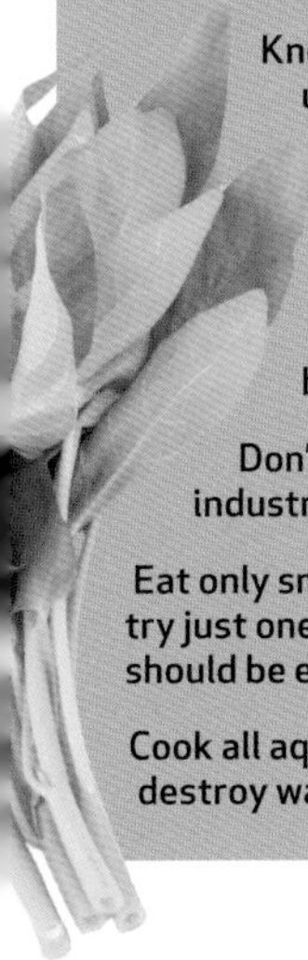

107 GIVE SOMETHING BACK

In the beginning, it's easy to think of the great outdoors as your own personal grocery store. When you're just starting out, you may tend to over-harvest, especially since everything is *free*. But you don't want to leave devastation in your wake—or leave your fellow foragers empty-handed.

It's okay to take some plants, and in some cases, you may actually be providing a service. By cutting back plants where they are thick, you are making room for healthier growth. By harvesting invasive species, you are expanding the habitat for native ones. By spreading the seeds as you go, you are planning ahead for your future crop of edibles. In short, don't use this book to descend on the landscape like a hoard of locusts—give something back.

108 LEARN BOTANY BASICS

Understanding the different parts of plants and the way they grow will pay off quickly as you begin foraging. Plants can be divided into many categories, but these two are a great place to start.

HERBACEOUS PLANTS The herbaceous group of plants consists of annuals (plants that live only one year), biennials (plants that live only two years), and other fleshy plants that are not usually long-lived. These plants have soft and green (not woody) leaves that die at the end of the growing season, leaving only the roots (the entire plant will die in the case of annuals). While most are small, some herbaceous plants can grow to the size of trees, such as the *Musa* genus, which contains the treelike banana plant (left).

WOODY PLANTS The woody group includes shrubs, trees, and many vines. These plants produce wood as one of their structural tissues and are typically perennials, living more than a few years. The stems, branches, and larger roots are reinforced with wood produced from plant tissue called secondary xylem. Those structures usually have a bark covering, which is built up from a corky material. Woody growth allows these plants to keep growing year after year, making them the largest and tallest terrestrial plants.

109 GET DOWN TO THE ROOTS

Learning the scientific names of plants (and all other life-forms) may seem boring and kind of nerdy—but there is no better way to cross-reference different species of plants. Using a categorical system called "binomial nomenclature," every recognized species has been given a two-part scientific name. With only a few exceptions, these scientific names are the same around the world. The names are often Latin, with some Greek and other languages thrown in for good measure. Botanists' names are sometimes honored in plant names, as well as the location where the species was discovered. Below are just a few of the merits of understanding how to interpret scientific names.

RED OAK (*Quercus rubra*)

1 = RED OAK; 2 = *Quercus*; 3 = *rubra*

1. **COMMON NAME** Most plants have several common names, which are the ones people use every day. These can be confusing or refer to more than one, which is why the scientific name is the only way to be sure everyone's talking about the same plant.

2. **GENERIC NAME** Also known as the *genus*, this part of the name tells you which plants a given specimen is related to. For example, everything in the genus *Allium* is some kind of onion or garlic and is edible for humans.

3. **SPECIFIC NAME** This term tells you the species and is an easy way to tell the difference between closely related things. One species may be edible, while another species is not, even though they are in the same genus.

Descriptive elements are often hidden in the scientific names. *Rubra*, for example, means "red" (as in ruby).

110 DIVIDE AND CONQUER

This may seem really fussy, but trust me, knowing about leaves can mean the difference between life and death—or the difference between foraging a dinner and living on pocket lint. To quickly identify plants, start by looking at their branch patterns and leaf structures. They'll fit into one of six categories: simple leaves, compound leaves, alternate branching leaves, opposite branching leaves, whorled leaves, and basal leaves.

SIMPLE LEAVES
These leaves grow as a single main body, though it may have multiple lobes or points.

COMPOUND LEAVES
Multiple leaflets that count as just one leaf grow from different locations on the main stem.

ALTERNATE BRANCHING
In the most common branch pattern, alternate branching, leaves grow in a zigzag pattern.

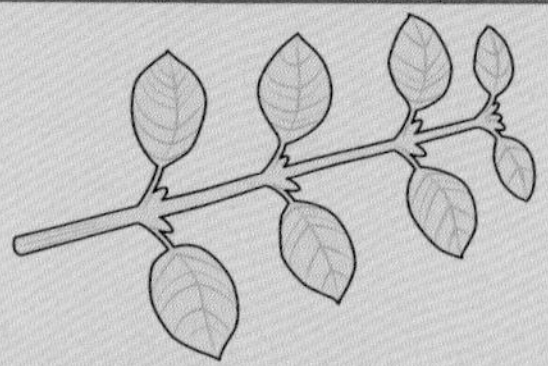

OPPOSITE BRANCHING
In this symmetrical pattern, leaves grow directly opposite each other on a branch.

WHORLED LEAVES
This uncommon pattern of leaves grows in rings at intervals along the stem.

BASAL LEAVES
These leaves grow in a circular ring at the base of a plant.

111 NOTE THE MARGINS

Next identify the names and shapes of leaf margins (the edges of the leaf).

1. Entire
2. Sinuate
3. Crenate
4. Serrate
5. Dentate
6. Lobed
7. Double serrate

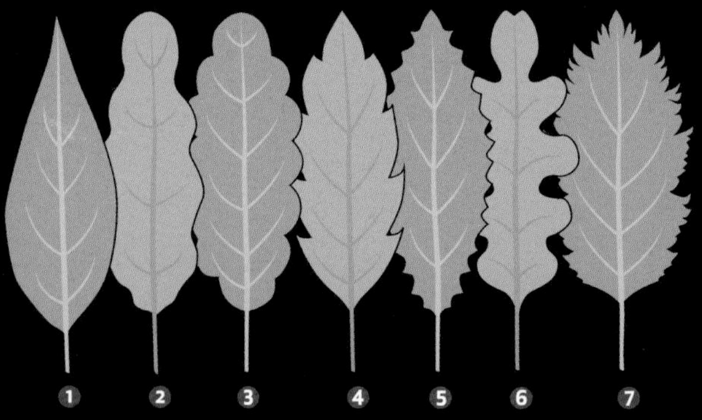

112 FOLLOW A PATTERN

Once you've figured out branch and leaf patterns, your next step in identification is to determine what *kind* of leaves the plant has. Most plants follow a few common patterns, and though they may look similar at first, you'll soon learn to spot these key characteristics and be well on your way to knowing what the heck you just picked.

❶ Pinnate veins
❷ Palmate veins
❸ Parallel veins
❹ Pinnately compound
❺ Bipinnately compound
❻ Palmately compound

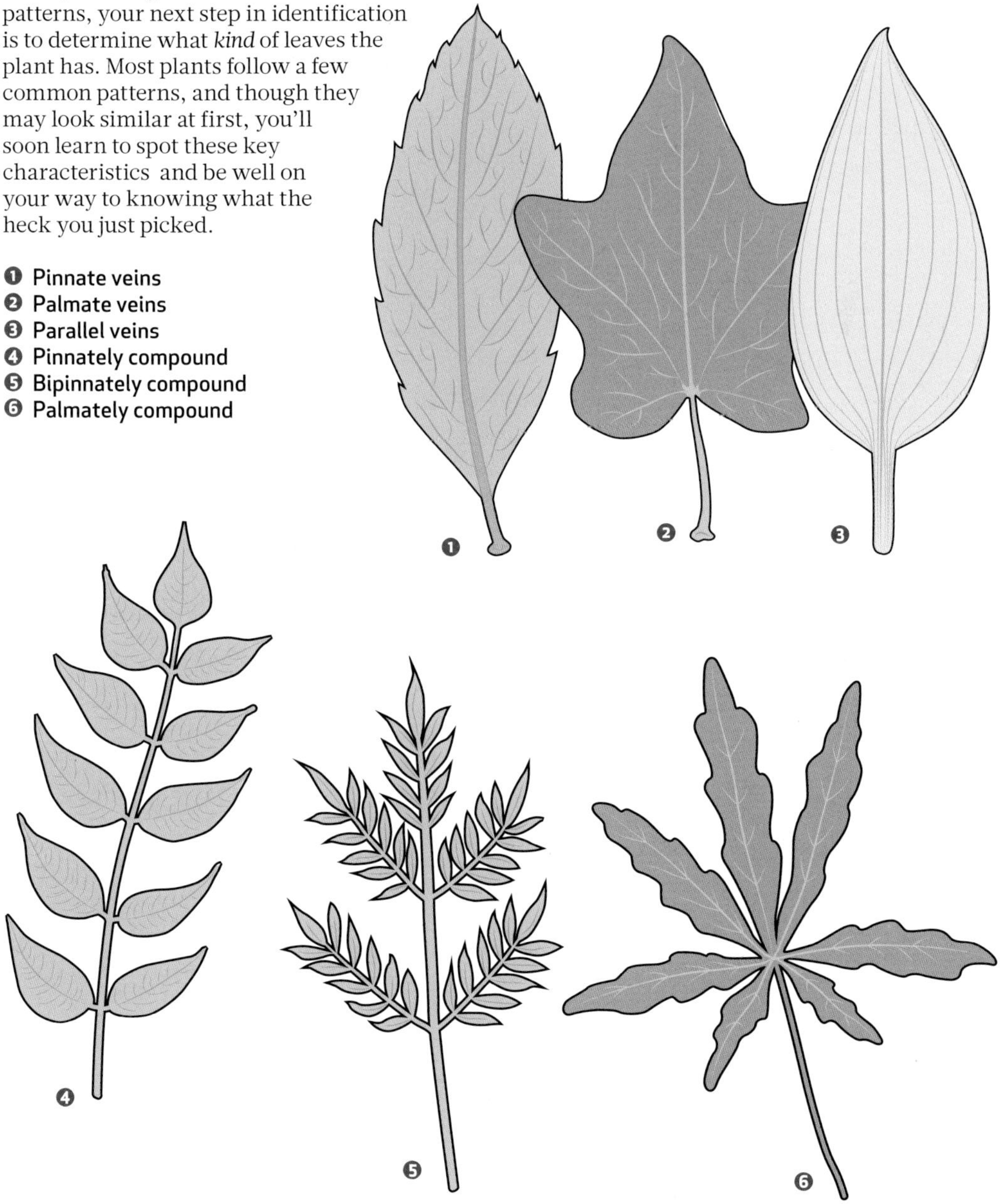

113 SUPERPLANT: DANDELION

BE BLOWN AWAY BY DANDELIONS

The bane of golf courses far and wide, the lowly dandelion (*Taraxacum officinale*) is a familiar lawn and field weed that has a basal leaf pattern, typically with jagged-toothed leaves radiating from the root crown. The flower stems are smooth and hollow, and each one bears a solitary yellow head consisting solely of ray flowers (resembling petals), which later produce a "puffball" seed cluster of numerous single-seeded "parachutes." The plant has a deep taproot, and the leaves are highly variable and may be nearly smooth-edged, toothed, or deeply cut. The plant gets its name from these toothed leaves: *dent-de-lion*, or tooth of the lion. The leaves, stem, and root typically exude a milky white sap when broken. Dandelions grow wild in most of the world, generally in full-sun conditions; they are also cultivated as a green. This common weed, with its edible seeds, crowns, roots, leaves, and flower petals, may well become your new favorite plant.

LEAFY GOODNESS

Young leaves should be eaten raw, before they become too bitter. The blooming flowers can be peeled off their stems (remove all of the green base from them) and eaten in salads, too. The dandelion's leaves and flowers pack a massive dose of vitamins A and C, as well as a strong flavor. The larger (and more bitter) leaves, along with the buds and roots, can be sautéed in a little oil for the best-tasting results. However you choose to prepare your dandelion, you'll give your wimpy taste buds a workout with this bitter yet wholesome green.

FABULOUS FRITTERS

It's been said that deep-frying can turn anything into an edible dish, and it is truly one of the most delicious ways to prepare dandelion. Pick as many blooming flowers as you can, pick off some of the green parts behind the petals, and dredge the flowers in batter. For a salty, savory fritter, use a runny cornmeal batter, and add salt to the fritters after frying them to a golden brown. For a sweeter snack, use funnel cake batter and dust the fried treats with powdered sugar or cinnamon sugar. One more tip: Make a lot of them. They'll disappear fast.

HELPFUL TINDER

Perhaps one of the least-used parts of this ubiquitous weed is its flammable seed down. The seed down acts as a parachute to transport the seeds away from the plant, but in the hands of a fire builder, this fluffy tinder is an explosive fuel. Add it to other tinder and use it to catch fire from matches, lighters, or even sparks.

BREW A ROOT COFFEE

Once you're sure you have safely identified the dandelion, dig up the roots of 10–20 plants. You're looking for roughly 2 lbs (1 kg) of roots for a good-size batch of coffee. Cut the tops off, as they are not needed for the coffee (save them for later, and sauté in butter or oil to make a vitamin-rich cooked green). Here's your recipe for a healthy, caffeine-free coffee alternative.

Preheat your oven to 350°F (177°C) while you wash the dirt off your roots, and cut them into approximately 1/2-inch (12-mm) bits.

Spread the roots on a cookie sheet and bake until they're chocolate-brown and just about to start burning. It usually takes thirty-five minutes or so, but watch the roots closely toward the end so that your hard work doesn't go up in smoke. Once they've cooled, grind with a mortar and pestle or coffee grinder.

Freeze the roasted grounds, or you can store them for a month or two in a breathable container (like a paper bag).

To make your dandelion coffee, pour boiling water into a coffee mug and add 2 tbsp. (30 g) roasted root for every cup (250 ml) of water. Cover the mug with a saucer or some other lid and let the brew steep for ten minutes.

114 FIND THE FUNGUS AMONG US

Mushrooms are some of the most misunderstood organisms on earth. They are part of the fungal kingdom, neither plant nor animal, but sharing traits of each, and they are worth getting to know. Think of the entire organism as a buried apple tree. All of the roots and branches are underground, and the visible part is its fruiting body (the "apples" of the mushroom). These strange fruits inspire loathing in some cultures and love in others, both with good reason. The right mushrooms can make a delicious meal worthy of fine restaurants. The wrong mushrooms, however, can be your last meal, or put you on the fast track to a liver transplant. Pay attention, and use more caution when harvesting mushrooms than with any other plant.

115 AVOID AT ALL COSTS

Mushrooms are some of the most plentiful poisons the wild world boasts. You should become just as familiar with the ones you'd never eat as the ones that you know to be tasty—your life could depend on it.

FALSE MOREL
Gyromitra esculenta

JACK-O'-LANTERN MUSHROOM
Omphalotus illudens

SHOWY FLAMECAP
Gymnopilus junonius

SCALY CHANTERELLE
Gomphus floccosus

FLY AGARIC
Amanita muscaria

DEATHCAP
Amanita phalloides

SICKENER
Russula emetica

DEATH ANGEL
Amanita virosa

116 FOLLOW THE RULES

When working with mushrooms both in the field and in the kitchen, there are some basic rules that will help you avoid many of the hazardous members of the fungal kingdom.

DO	DON'T
Verify you're 100 percent positive about the identification of the mushroom, including the location and season of growth.	Use the mushroom if there is any shadow of doubt in your mind concerning its identity.
Cook your mushrooms—many edible mushrooms are safer cooked than raw.	Eat or taste them raw—and don't consume or cook them with alcohol. Some poisons can do more damage when mixed with alcohol. That chicken marsala can wait.
Cut/bruise the mushroom and watch for any color change in the flesh, which can help with identification, as can a close examination of its structure and odor.	Use mushrooms that are growing out of season. This is a common factor in mushroom poisoning cases. Never eat one that looks right but is growing at the wrong time of year.
Be aware that some edible mushrooms can still cause illness. Use caution with mushroom caps that are scaly or bumpy. More than 50 percent are dangerous.	Eat anything with volva and stem rings (annulus), unless you'd bet your life they are not *Amanitas*. Because you are, in fact, betting your life.

117 MAKE A SPORE PRINT

Mushroom spores can be very useful in making an identification. Start by getting a guidebook that clearly identifies what to look for in a spore print (it's too complicated to go into here). Then, use these steps to make your own identifying spore prints.

STEP 1 Harvest a mushroom you are curious about. Handle it carefully, and assume that any unknown mushroom is deadly.

STEP 2 Wrap each individual mushroom in wax paper or a piece of foil for transport. Plastic bags will make them sweat.

STEP 3 Tape together a piece of white paper and a piece of black, and place the mushroom cap so half is on each color, then invert a disposable cup or bowl over it. Wait several hours.

STEP 4 Remove the cover and the mushroom cap. Observe the color of the spores that were deposited on the paper. (Some may only show up on either the dark or the light side.) Check the color against several guides, and double-check the mushroom's structures against similar mushrooms to ensure that your alleged "edible" mushroom really is safe.

118 CLASSIFY MUSHROOMS

Ready for a culinary adventure? Mushrooms are one of the most coveted wild edibles, but also one of the trickiest to navigate. Pay close attention to details, and you'll have a wild gourmet meal.

COMMON MOREL
Morchella esculenta

SEASON Spring
HABITAT Forests and shady areas
DISTRIBUTION U.S. eastern woodlands

DETAILS Common morels grows in forests, primarily in April and May, and are usually 2–4 inches (5–10 cm) tall. The **tan, gray, or brownish colored head** with irregular pitting can be well camouflaged against leaf litter.

IDENTIFIERS When cut in half, the common morel is **entirely hollow inside**. The cone-shaped head should be fully fused to the stalk at the lower end. If the head is only attached at the top and hangs like a skirt, it's likely a false morel, which can be very poisonous. False morels (the genera *Verpa* and *Gyromitra*) usually grow in the summer and fall—a good time to avoid anything resembling a morel.

USES Several species of morel are edible, though a few notable species are dangerous.

SPORE PRINT Yellowish.

CHANTERELLE
Cantharellus cibarius

SEASON Summer and fall
HABITAT Hardwood and coniferous forests
DISTRIBUTION North America

DETAILS Chanterelles are mushrooms with a golden, **egg-yolk color**, and are some of the best-tasting wild mushrooms. They grow up to 4 inches (10 cm) wide and 3 inches (7.5 cm) tall, with an **overall funnel shape**.

IDENTIFIERS Chanterelles have **thick gills** that extend partially down the stalk. These grow directly from the soil, as opposed to their dangerous look-alikes, the jack-o'-lantern (*Omphalotus illudens*) and the showy flamecap (*Gymnopilus junonius*). These two poisonous species grow from wood, not soil.

USES Edible chanterelle species include red chanterelle (*C. cinnabarinus*), horn of plenty (*C. cornucopioides*), and fragrant smooth chanterelle (*C. lateritius*).

SPORE PRINT Pale yellow.

SULPHUR SHELF
Laetiporus sulphureus

SEASON Summer and fall
HABITAT Forests
DISTRIBUTION North America

DETAILS A large, soft, colorful mushroom (also known as chicken of the woods), sulphur shelf grows on trees and logs in forests, and is easy to spot with its **bright yellow and orange colors**. These **stalkless shelf fungi** grow in clumps on hardwoods and conifers. These clusters can be over 2 inches (5 cm) high and 12 inches (30 cm) across.

IDENTIFIERS Sulphur shelf fruits in late summer and fall. Make certain that the **underside is solid and full of little holes** (pores). If there are gills underneath the shelves, you have a nestcap, which is not known to be edible, although there are no reports of its actually being poisonous, either.

USES Cook the younger, more tender shelves, as the older ones can cause digestive upset.

SPORE PRINT White.

OYSTER MUSHROOM
Pleurotus ostreatus

SEASON Spring and late fall
HABITAT Hardwood and coniferous forests
DISTRIBUTION North America

DETAILS These popular, fan-shaped mushrooms have very short stalks and grow in clumps on rotten wood, stumps, and logs. They can be 2–10 inches (5–25 cm) across and vary from **white to gray in color**, sometimes with a yellowish tint and a brownish top.

IDENTIFIERS Stems are usually attached at the side of the mushroom or offset, though they may be absent. The mushroom has **broad gills** and the **gills are attached to the stalk**.

USES Inspect these mushrooms carefully before cooking, and remove any of the little black beetles that are attracted to this species. Don't be upset about the beetles, though—they are a big help in species identification.

SPORE PRINT White.

KING BOLETE
Boletus edulis

SEASON Summer and fall
HABITAT Forests and shady areas
DISTRIBUTION Throughout North America

DETAILS The king bolete is big, thick, and meaty. It grows in forest soils and may be found scattered through an area or on its own. King boletes may have huge caps, up to 10 inches (25 cm) wide, and an overall height of 10 inches (25 cm). It has **tiny pores underneath the cap**, rather than gills. The **cap is brownish**, and the stalk is whitish to brown in color.

IDENTIFIERS The upper half of the **stalk has a netted appearance**, and the overall stalk is bulbous in shape.

USES There are numerous edible bolete species, but also several poisonous ones. Avoid the bitter bolete (*Tylopilus felleus*), which resembles the king bolete; true to its name, it is extremely bitter. Discard any batch of cooked boletes if they taste bitter.

SPORE PRINT Olive brown.

HEN-OF-THE-WOODS
Grifola frondosus

SEASON Fall
HABITAT Hardwood forests
DISTRIBUTION Southern Canada and U.S. eastern woodlands

DETAILS The **fan-shaped caps** of this mushroom grow in clumps on living and dead standing trees. Larger caps can reach 3 inches (7.5 cm) wide. They have a similar structure to sulphur shelf (*Laetiporus sulphureus*), though the colors are **grayish brown**. The **streaked upper surface** is smooth or a little hairy.

IDENTIFIERS The caps have **white pores on the underside**, which can become yellowed with age.

USES Younger specimens of this mushroom are the best-tasting and most tender choices. Try simmering these mushrooms at low temperatures to tenderize them. They are also good when fried quickly in butter, or for a survival-style feast, skewer a few on a stick for a shish kebab.

SPORE PRINT White.

119 FORAGE FOR TREE NUTS

Tree nuts boast the biggest caloric payout in the wild-food world. Due to their fats, proteins, carbs, vitamins, and minerals, these nuts were a staple food for our ancestors—and still are for many people today.

CHESTNUT
Castanea spp.

SEASON Fall and winter
HABITAT Forests and open ground
DISTRIBUTION Northern Hemisphere

DETAILS The chestnut is a genus of **deciduous hardwood trees and shrubs** in the beech family (Fagaceae). Many species are found through the temperate regions of the Northern Hemisphere. Various species can grow to 33–98 feet (10–30 m) tall. Don't confuse chestnut trees and their nuts with horse chestnuts (genus *Aesculus*), the nuts of which are similar looking—but poisonous.

IDENTIFIERS The **alternate simple leaves** are ovate or lanceolate, with sharply pointed, widely spaced teeth. The nut is contained in a **needle-covered cupule**, 2–4 inches (5–10 cm) in diameter, also known as a "bur." These burs often grow in pairs or clusters, and **each bur can hold one to seven nuts**.

USES The nuts from this tree pack a caloric punch: 3 1/2 ounces (105 g) of chestnut contains 200 calories, vitamins C and B6, and potassium.

BEECH
Fagus spp.

SEASON Fall and winter
HABITAT Forests
DISTRIBUTION Northern Hemisphere

DETAILS Beech trees are **deciduous hardwood trees** found across the Northern Hemisphere. These trees are typically 60–80 feet (18–24 m) tall, with **alternate simple leaves**.

IDENTIFIERS Look for the smooth-barked trees in the eastern woodlands, and look for the **small three-sided seed falling out of a prickly husk** around early October.

USES The nut of a beech tree can be a valuable and delicious wild-food source, but you'll have to be quick to beat the squirrels to them, as they seem to favor these tree nuts above all others. They've always had two-legged competition, however: Native American tribes, such as the Potawatomi, pounded the roasted seeds into flour, and many other cultures have used the oily, sweet nuts for food.

WALNUT
Juglans spp.

SEASON Fall and winter
HABITAT Fields and forest edges
DISTRIBUTION Global

DETAILS Walnut trees are a group of **deciduous hardwood trees** with varying shapes of nuts and **alternate compound leaves**.

IDENTIFIERS These nuts are probably the easiest to identify. Freshly fallen black walnuts (*Juglans nigra*) look like **green tennis balls**. The rough, round husks turn from green to a very dark brown as they lie on the ground throughout autumn.

USES The nutmeats are rich tasting and contain 173 calories an ounce (30 g). They are high in fat, with a fair bit of protein, copper, magnesium, phosphorus, and manganese. The wild animals might even let you get some, primarily because they don't like to chew through those thick, bitter husks—they'll leave them on the ground well into winter. Walnut hulls can be used as a dye, a fish poison, and an antiworm and antiparasite tea.

CHESTNUT ▶

HICKORY
Carya spp.

SEASON Fall and winter
HABITAT Fields and forests
DISTRIBUTION Northern Hemisphere

DETAILS These trees are **deciduous hardwood trees** found in North America and Asia with **alternate compound leaves**.

IDENTIFIERS The nuts have a "double" nut shell. There's a **husk that peels off**, revealing a **nut shell underneath**. And make sure you don't get a poisonous buckeye. They also have a double layered nut shell, but hickory nuts have a **multichambered inner nutshell** (like a walnut), while the bad buckeyes have a solid nutmeat (like an almond).

USES Hickory nuts are the most calorie dense wild-plant food in this book. One ounce (30 g) of nutmeat packs 193 calories, with most of that coming from fat. A majority of hickory nuts taste like their famous relative—the pecan. These sweet and fatty nutmeats are a convenient and useful raw food, picked right out of the shell.

HAZELNUT
Corylus spp.

SEASON Fall
HABITAT Fields, open sunny areas
DISTRIBUTION Northern Hemisphere

DETAILS There are several species of hazelnut trees and shrubs in Europe, Asia, and North America. These are **deciduous shrubs and small trees** with **alternate simple leaves** that are **irregularly toothed**.

IDENTIFIERS The most common species in the United States is the American hazelnut (*Corylus americana*), which grows east of the Mississippi and can reach a height of 10 feet (3 m). It produces **small nuts** that are covered with a **ragged-edged husk**.

USES Just one ounce (30 g) of the flavorful hazelnut contains 170 calories and 4 grams of protein, as well as good doses of vitamin E, thiamin, copper, and manganese. The hazelnut is also known as the cobnut or filbert nut, according to the species. You can eat them raw, or mill into a peanut butter–like spread for confections.

OAK
Quercus spp.

SEASON Fall
HABITAT Forests, deserts, and mountains
DISTRIBUTION Northern Hemisphere

DETAILS There are approximately 600 species of "oak" throughout the world. This list includes **deciduous and evergreen tree** species found in cool climates down to warmer tropical latitudes. North America contains the largest number of oak species, with a range of about 160 species in Mexico alone.

IDENTIFIERS Oaks have **alternate simple leaves** in a wide variety of sizes and shapes. The fruit of the oak tree is a **nut called an acorn, borne in a cuplike "cupule."**

USES One ounce (30 g) of acorn nutmeat, which many of our ancestors ate as a staple food, contains a little over 100 calories. The bitter acid in the nutmeat is easily removed by cracking the nuts into pieces and soaking in repeated baths of warm water, one hour at a time. (See item 138.)

120 HARVEST WILD GREENS

Greens are the backbone of survival foods. Even in the dead of winter, you can find edible greenery growing in protected spots and use them to provide some nourishment.

WATERCRESS
Nasturtium officinale

SEASON Spring through fall
HABITAT Clear running streams
DISTRIBUTION Global

DETAILS Watercress is an aquatic or semiaquatic **perennial plant** native to Europe and Asia. One of the earliest vegetables known to be consumed by humans, its botanic relationship to mustards and radishes is immediately obvious in its mustardy, peppery taste.

IDENTIFIERS Watercress grows in fast, clean streams and springs, with hollow floating stems and **pinnately compound leaves** in an alternate pattern. The small, four-petaled **white flowers** grow in clusters. The leaves and tender stems have a biting, deliciously spicy flavor.

USES Wash thoroughly if you're eating raw watercress, as the clear water it grew from could be full of waterborne pathogens (not harmful to the watercress, but not good for you). Cooked watercress is not as tasty, but is much safer for human consumption.

BITTERCRESS
Cardamine pensylvanica

SEASON Spring
HABITAT Fields, lawns, sunny areas
DISTRIBUTION North America

DETAILS A diminutive **herbaceous biennial**, bittercress (also known as Pennsylvania bittercress) has the familiar **pinnately compound leaves** of other "cresses" in an **alternate pattern**. Native to most of Canada and the United States, it is only found in the springtime.

IDENTIFIERS The smooth leaves are divided into several rounded lobes, each one with one or two lobes, and a large terminal leaflet at the end of the leaf, like most other plants with a "cress" name. Bittercress grows one or more flower stalks, which are purple to green in color. These stems can be anywhere from 4–28 inches (10–71 cm) tall. The **white flowers** are plentiful but tiny, each with four white petals. The fruit is a slender pod about 1 inch (2.5 cm) long.

USES Eat the tender leaves and stems raw as a salad.

WILD MUSTARD
Brassica rapa

SEASON Spring
HABITAT Fields, open sunny areas
DISTRIBUTION Northern Hemisphere

DETAILS This **annual herbaceous field plant** has smooth, succulent, gray-green **simple leaves** with clasping lobes around the stem in an **alternate pattern**. These leaves have many deep lobes and smell of mustard when broken.

IDENTIFIERS The leaves and stems produce a whitish, chalky substance that easily wipes off when touched. Wild mustard has **yellow flowers** with four petals and slender vertical seed pods. Full-grown plants reach heights of 3 feet (1 m), but start as a basal rosette.

USES You can eat the leaves raw when not too bitter, and they make for a good cooked green. You can also grind the small round seeds into a powder and mix with vinegar to make a tangy wild mustard condiment. Related wild mustards in the *Brassica* genus can also be used like field mustard.

WILD LETTUCE
Lactuca spp.

SEASON Spring and summer
HABITAT Fields, open sunny areas
DISTRIBUTION Northern Hemisphere

DETAILS Wild lettuce is a **herbaceous biennial plant**, starting with a basal rosette of lobed and toothed **simple leaves** which give way to a tall flower stalk in the second year of the plant's life. The rosette is common in springtime and often resembles dandelion rosettes. Several species of wild lettuce are native to Europe, yet are also found in North America.

IDENTIFIERS Broken stems and leaves will exude an orange or salmon-hued milky sap, different from dandelion, which has white sap. The leaves can reach 10–12 inches (25–30 cm) in length, and the flower stalks can grow to heights over 8 feet (2.5 m), topped with **yellow composite flowers.**

USES The leaves are best in the spring and have a flavor similar to their cultivated cousin romaine lettuce. Historically, the sap has been used as a sedative.

LADY'S THUMB
Polygonum persicaria

SEASON Spring through fall
HABITAT Fields, open disturbed soil
DISTRIBUTION Northern Hemisphere

DETAILS Lady's thumb (also called redshank) is a native **annual herbaceous plant** of Eurasia and an invasive species in North America. It has an erect yet floppy stem with swollen joints. These joints give rise to the genus name *Polygonum*, which means "many knees."

IDENTIFIERS Lady's thumb grows to a height of 24 inches (60 cm). The leaves are **simple alternate leaves**,which may have a dark V-shaped mark on the surface (or not) and are almost stalk-less.

USES The leaves are the edible part of this plant, and are good raw in salads or as a cooked green. The leaves and stems contain tannins and persicarin, both compounds with anti-inflammatory properties historically used to stop diarrhea. The plant can also prevent infections: Apply the crushed leaves as a field-expedient poultice for wounds.

VIOLETS
Viola spp.

SEASON Spring and summer
HABITAT Fields, lawns, and woods
DISTRIBUTION Global

DETAILS Violets are a diverse group of plants containing almost 600 species. The violets commonly used for wild food are in the genus *Viola*. These are **perennial herbaceous plants**.

IDENTIFIERS Violets are small, usually 4–10 inches (10–25 cm), consisting of heart-shaped **simple leaves** with toothed edges and small flowers, typically with five petals. The flower color is often a quick indicator of species, as there are blue, purple, white, yellow, and combination color violets.

USES You can eat the leaves and flowers of the common blue violet (*Viola papilionacea*) raw as salad leaves or cooked as greens. You can also find candied violets made from fresh flowers (best from the sweet *Viola odorata*) and covered in an egg white and crystallized sugar shell. Violet flowers are also a beautiful addition to baked goods.

SHEEP SORREL
Rumex acetosella

SEASON Spring through fall
HABITAT Fields, open sunny areas
DISTRIBUTION Northern Hemisphere

DETAILS This small plant with unusual spearhead-shaped **simple leaves** grows in fields and gardens. Sheep sorrel is a **perennial herbaceous plant** that has a reddish **alternate branching** stem and grows up to a height of 18 inches (45 cm).

IDENTIFIERS Sheep sorrel leaves are typically about 1 inch (2.5 cm) long and smooth-edged. Each has a pair of lobes at the base that can point outward or down toward the base of the plant.

USES Eat the tender, sour-tasting leaves raw as a salad or steeped in hot water for a sour drink very similar to wood sorrel (*Oxalis* spp.). And like wood sorrel, the sour flavor comes from oxalic acid, so consume in moderation. If regular consumption of either of these plants is followed by urinary gravel (small stones), stop eating—or bigger stones could soon follow.

PLANTAIN
Plantago major

SEASON Spring through fall
HABITAT Lawns and fields
DISTRIBUTION Global

DETAILS The low-growing plantain is a common weed in lawns worldwide. It is an **annual herbaceous plant** that has parallel veined, smooth-edged **simple leaves** that grow in a basal rosette.

IDENTIFIERS Torn leaves often reveal stringy fibers inside the heavy parallel veins. These ripped leaves also have an astringent, cabbagelike odor. The small white flowers grow on slender stalks, which later grow greenish seeds.

USES Add chopped young leaves or green seeds to salads or boil for ten to fifteen minutes as a cooked green. Plantain is one of the best medicinal plants for stings and bites. Crush the leaves into a poultice and keep in place until the pain and swelling are relieved. English plantain (*Plantago lanceolata*) and seaside plantain (*Plantago juncoides*) can be used just like common plantain.

CLEAVERS
Galium aparine

SEASON Spring and summer
HABITAT Fence rows and thickets
DISTRIBUTION Northern Hemisphere

DETAILS Cleavers, which are **herbaceous annuals**, are vinelike woodland and hedgerow plants native to Eurasia and found throughout North America. The plant has a square stem (up to 3 feet or 1 meter in length) covered with tiny barbs that it uses for climbing. The **simple leaves** are narrow, lanceolate to linear, and grow in **whorls** of six to eight.

IDENTIFIERS Cleavers have tiny, star-shaped, white to greenish flowers with four petals.

USES Boil the young shoots and tender plants for fifteen minutes as a cooked green. The cooking water can then be used as a deodorant or drunk as a blood pressure–lowering tonic. Cleavers are related to the coffee bush, and the small, prickly fruits of cleavers can be dried and roasted as a coffee substitute.

CLOVER
Trifolium spp.

SEASON Spring through fall
HABITAT Fields, open ground
DISTRIBUTION Global

DETAILS Clovers (or trefoil) are a genus containing about 300 species of plants in the pea family (Fabaceae). They can be found globally, with most species in the temperate Northern Hemisphere, South America, and Africa. Clovers are small annual, biennial, or short-lived perennial **herbaceous plants**.

IDENTIFIERS Clovers have **alternate leaves** that are trifoliate (three leaflets) and flower heads with many small flowers that create a rounded cluster. Clover flowers can be white, yellow, pink, and many other colors.

USES You can eat clover leaves raw or cooked; the flowers are a great addition to salads and make phenomenal fritters when battered and fried. The most widely used wild edible clovers are white clover (*Trifolium repens*) and red clover (*Trifolium pretense*).

CHICKWEED
Stellaria media

SEASON Spring and summer
HABITAT Lawns and fields
DISTRIBUTION Northern Hemisphere

DETAILS Chickweed is a low-growing **herbaceous annual plant,** native to Europe and often forming a carpet on disturbed grounds of farms and gardens. The small, ovate **simple leaves** grow in an **opposite branching pattern** on the round green stems.

IDENTIFIERS Chickweed's white flowers appear to have ten petals, but actually have five, each partially split. The plant germinates in fall or winter, then forms mats of greenery or vinelike runners in spring.

USES You can eat the tender leaves and stems raw or cooked. Star chickweed (*Stellaria pubera*) is good cooked or raw, and mouse-ear chickweed (*Cerastium vulgatum*) is also good as a cooked green. Chickweed can be used in an anti-itch poultice and can be ingested to relieve constipation.

WOOD SORREL
Oxalis spp.

SEASON Spring through fall
HABITAT Sunny and shady areas
DISTRIBUTION Northern Hemisphere

DETAILS Wood sorrel plants are common **perennial herbaceous plants** found around North America, Europe, and Asia. The plant has heart-shaped leaflets in sets of three, and resembles clover. Stems and leaf stalks are **alternate branching**, and these plants are rarely taller than 6 inches (15 cm).

IDENTIFIERS The flowers are often yellow, though some species are pink or purple, and they all typically have five petals.

USES The leaves, tender stems, and flowers have a refreshing sour taste, and are good in a salad. You can also steep them in hot water, then strain, sweeten, and chill to create a lemonade substitute. Be cautious about overconsumption, as the sour taste is caused by oxalic acid, which is a building block for kidney stones. Stick with a small salad on an irregular basis.

WOOD SORREL & MINER'S LETTUCE ▶

121 FIND BUSHES AND BRAMBLES

Finally, a truism from pop culture TV survival references! There actually are some berries and twigs that you can use for survival food. Here are some of my favorites.

BLACKBERRY

Rubus spp.

SEASON Summer

HABITAT Forest edge, open ground

DISTRIBUTION Northern Hemisphere

DETAILS *Rubus* species are found throughout the Northern Hemisphere. They may grow anywhere, but favor sunny ground and transition areas. Blackberry is a single stemmed **perennial woody plant** that is hairless, often grooved, and has stems that are typically around 6–8 feet (2–2.5 m). It has **alternate branching** with sharp, curved thorns.

IDENTIFIERS The leaves are **pinnately compound** with three or five leaflets that are toothed and hairless, though often thorned.

USES Eat the soft, ripe berries raw or cooked, or dry and steep the leaves in hot water for ten minutes to make a tea that can help treat diarrhea. Blackberry leaf tea can also be used as a mouthwash due to its astringent action.

RASPBERRY

Rubus spp.

SEASON Summer

HABITAT Forest edge, hillsides

DISTRIBUTION Northern Hemisphere

DETAILS The Native American, Asian, and European species of raspberry is now found around the world. It favors moist soil, good drainage, and often grows near or within shaded areas. Raspberry is a **perennial woody plant** that bears biennial stems (canes). During the first year, a new stem (called a primocane) grows to a height of 3–9 feet (1–3 m).

IDENTIFIERS Raspberry is unbranched and bears large **pinnately compound leaves** with three or five leaflets. During the second year, the cane grows several alternate side branches with smaller leaves that are whitish underneath. These side branches produce the berries.

USES The juicy compound berries are red when ripe. Eat them raw or cooked, or dry them for future use. The leaves can be dried and used as a tea similar to blackberry.

MULTIFLORA ROSE

Rosa multiflora

SEASON Summer and fall

HABITAT Fields and fence rows

DISTRIBUTION Northern Hemisphere

DETAILS Native to Asia, multiflora rose can now be found globally. It favors open ground and pastures. This **perennial** species of rose is a **woody plant.**

IDENTIFIERS Rose has finely toothed, **pinnately compound leaves** that can persist into winter, and **alternate branching** with sharp, curved thorns. It has bright red rose hips that are full of pale-yellow seeds.

USES Eat the pulp and skin of the rose hips raw, or steep the entire rose hip to make rose tea. De-thorn the vines by pushing the thorns sideways and then use the vines in basketry. Eat the flowers in summer salads, and the rose hips will be ready to eat in late fall and winter. The tangy, sweet red fruit is a good source of vitamin E—and it's a vitamin C powerhouse, containing seven times your daily allowance.

SMOOTH SUMAC
Rhus glabra

SEASON Fall
HABITAT Open woods and fields
DISTRIBUTION North America

DETAILS Smooth sumac grows in the eastern woodlands of the United States. Related edible species can be found in America, Europe, and Asia. This **perennial woody shrub** can reach heights of 15 feet (4.5 m).

IDENTIFIERS Smooth sumac has **alternate leaves** that are large and **pinnately compound**.

USES Separate the cone-shaped clusters of hard, red, fuzzy seeds from the twigs and soak them in cool water for an hour (or steep in hot water for fifteen minutes, then chill) to make a drink that resembles pink lemonade. Use before the winter rains wash away the flavor, and strain out the berries and hairs. The wood is also suitable for friction fire material. Be aware, as poison sumac (*Rhus vernix*) is a similar-looking shrub with toxic white berries and leaves that can cause an allergic reaction.

BLUEBERRY
Vaccinium spp. and *Gaylussacia* spp.

SEASON Summer
HABITAT Forest and fields
DISTRIBUTION Northern Hemisphere

DETAILS Blueberries and their diverse relatives (cranberries and bilberries) grow in a variety of habitats around the Northern Hemisphere. Blueberries are **perennial woody shrubs** varying in size from the "low bush blueberries" of 4 inches (10 cm), up to the "high bush" of 12 feet (4 m).

IDENTIFIERS The **simple alternate leaves** are ovate to lanceolate, and ½–3 inches (1.2–7.5 cm) long. The small flowers are white, pale pink, or red, and bell-shaped. The berry has a five-pointed "crown," and will turn from pale green to reddish to dark purple when ripened.

USES The berries are excellent raw or cooked and may be dried for storage or medicinal effect. Dried blueberries cure diarrhea (eat 6–10 dried blueberries every hour until the diarrhea subsides) and are said to improve eyesight.

SPICEBUSH
Lindera benzoin

SEASON All year
HABITAT Forests and shady areas
DISTRIBUTION North America

DETAILS Spicebush is an aromatic, **deciduous perennial woody shrub**, native to the eastern half of North America. It grows in damp woods to a height of 10 feet (3 m).

IDENTIFIERS With **simple leaves** and **alternate branching,** the twigs are slender and covered with small raised dots (lenticels).

USES There are many spicy parts of this shrub that you can use for flavoring. Steep the fresh or slowly dried twigs as a tea, or use fresh or dried leaves. The twigs and leaves can be used any time during the season. Peel and dry the skin of the berries to make a spice, and only use the berries when ripe, red, and soft in the early fall. Remember to always put the seeds back in the woods—they are not edible.

122 TRY SOME TASTY TREES

Trees can produce some of the sweetest and most flavorful foraged food. From the sugary syrup of birch and maple, to spruce beer and savory sassafras tea, trees have a lot to offer us.

SPRUCE
Picea spp.

SEASON All year
HABITAT Far northern forests
DISTRIBUTION Northern Hemisphere

DETAILS There are 35 known species of spruce, which is a **coniferous evergreen tree** in the pine family. Spruce is found in the northern temperate and boreal regions. These trees range from 65–200 feet (20–60 m) tall.

IDENTIFIERS **Sharp, square needles** help to distinguish spruce from pine and fir, and the **dangling cones** differentiate from fir. While fir twigs have needles growing from two sides of the twig, creating a flat shape, spruce needles are attached singly to the branches in a spiral pattern.

USES You can eat the spring shoots of spruces, as well or steep the needles in hot water to yield a vitamin C–rich tea. Fresh or dried spruce tips can flavor spruce beer, and the inner bark can be dried and ground into flour. Spruce roots also make a great basketry material.

FIR
Abies spp.

SEASON All year
HABITAT Mountain and forest
DISTRIBUTION Northern Hemisphere

DETAILS Fir is a genus of about 50 species of **coniferous evergreen tree** in the pine family. Found throughout the mountains of North and Central America, Europe, Asia, and northern Africa, fir can reach heights of 30–60 feet (9–18 m).

IDENTIFIERS Fir is differentiated from pines by the attachment of their **needlelike leaves** to the twig by a base that resembles a **little suction cup**. Another quick ID trick is to look at the cones: Firs have **erect cones**, while pine and spruce cones dangle down.

USES The inner (cambium) layer of bark is edible. Shave off the outer bark to reveal this spongy, cream-colored layer, then remove and dry until brittle. You can then grind it into a coarse meal and use as oatmeal or flour.

MAPLE
Acer spp.

SEASON Winter and spring
HABITAT Woodlands and mountains
DISTRIBUTION Northern Hemisphere

DETAILS There are about 125 species of maples around the globe. These **deciduous hardwood trees** are native to Asia, Europe, northern Africa, and North America.

IDENTIFIERS Maple has **opposite branching simple leaves** that are commonly veined and lobed in a **palmate pattern**.

USES The two main food uses of maple are sap and seeds. Collect the sap in late winter and boil down into sugary syrup (see item 215). You should collect the seeds later in the spring from distinctive fruits called samaras—the little "helicopters" that spin their way from the tree to the ground. You can cook the nutlets (seeds) of most species by boiling in water, almost like beans. Not all maples are edible, so check your local species against known edible plants for your region. The wood is also useful for bows, timber, and lumber.

REDBUD
Cercis canadensis

SEASON Spring
HABITAT Woodlands and their edges
DISTRIBUTION Eastern North America

DETAILS The redbud is a small, dark-barked, understory **deciduous hardwood tree** typically 20–30 feet (6–9 m) tall. It is one of the first trees to flower in spring.

IDENTIFIERS Heart-shaped alternate simple leaves grow on slender twigs. Before the leaves emerge, small pink buds appear and open into odd-looking **curved pink flowers**, ½ inch (12 mm) long. To most people, these shapes resemble bunny slippers.

USES The unopened buds and open flowers are a great addition to spring wild salads, and they can be incorporated into baked goods for an interesting color accent. You can harvest the small green seed pods that follow and cook them as a vegetable, but know that they are mildly toxic when raw. The redbud's extremely hard wood can be used for a variety of projects that require strength and flexibility.

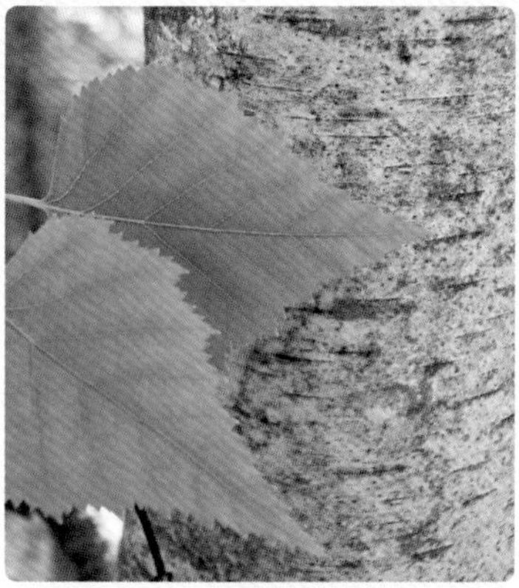

BIRCH
Betula spp.

SEASON Twigs all year, sap late winter
HABITAT Mountainous forests
DISTRIBUTION North America

DETAILS Birch species are typically small to medium-sized **deciduous hardwood trees**, which grow up to 65 feet (20 m) tall and are commonly found in temperate climates.

IDENTIFIERS Birch has **alternate simple leaves** that are toothed and singly or doubly serrated.

USES The black birch is the best one for wild food, as the dark-colored twigs provide good proof of identity. Scrape them and you'll smell a strong **scent of wintergreen** from the methyl salicylate in the bark. In late winter, the sap begins to flow. Tap the larger trees about a month later than the maple sap runs. Collect the abundant sap often, and boil it down into strong, sweet, wintergreen-flavored syrup. You can also steep broken twigs in hot water to make tea.

SASSAFRAS
Sassafras albidum

SEASON All year
HABITAT Forests and thickets
DISTRIBUTION Eastern North America

DETAILS Sassafras is a rough, gray-barked **deciduous hardwood tree** in the laurel family (Lauraceae). This tree can be found in old fields, at the edges of woods, and as an understory tree in woodlands. It has yellowish to greenish twigs with an **alternate branch pattern**.

IDENTIFIERS The most distinctive trait is the **variety of leaf shapes**. Simple oval leaves are common, as well as leaves with one deep sinus (resembling mittens) and leaves with two deep sinuses.

USES The fresh or dried root of sassafras has an intense root beer flavor and makes an excellent tea. You can also steep the twigs for a very different, citrus-flavored tea. Use the dried leaves to thicken soups, and as a traditional gumbo ingredient. The wood is a fair one for friction fire making.

123 SELECT SEEDS FOR GRAINS

Throughout human history, many cultures have relied on wild grains as their primary dietary staple, and this bounty is available today for the knowledgable forager.

CURLY DOCK
Rumex crispus

SEASON Seeds in fall, leaves when available
HABITAT Fields, meadows, open ground
DISTRIBUTION Northern Hemisphere

DETAILS Curly dock, or yellow dock, is a **perennial herbaceous** plant in the buckwheat family native to Europe and Western Asia. Fully grown plants have a reddish stalk about 3 feet (1 m) high.

IDENTIFIERS Curly dock has large **alternate branching simple leaves** growing from a basal rosette. The wavy, "curled" margins resemble a hairless burdock. Greenish flowers grow on top of the stalk, giving way to reddish-brown seed clusters on branching stems.

USES The seed clusters can be ground into flour or cooked as a cereal grain. The cleaned seeds are shiny, caramel-colored, and have three sides (like other buckwheat family members). You can eat the tender leaves raw or cooked, when available, and the root is a large, yellow taproot that has long been a source of medicinal tannic acid.

LAMB'S QUARTERS
Chenopodium album

SEASON Seeds late summer, leaves when available
HABITAT Fields and waste ground
DISTRIBUTION Global

DETAILS Lamb's quarters is a **herbaceous annual** that ranges from small sizes to heights of 6 feet (2 m). It's also known as goosefoot and pigweed.

IDENTIFIERS Each large plant can produce tens of thousands of small, shiny black seeds in late summer. They form in seed heads at the top of the plant, and you can shake them free when ripe. For best results, place a wide bowl under the seed heads and tap with a stick.

USES Eat the **alternate simple leaves** in a salad or cook them for a spinach substitute, when available. Like spinach, you'll need a large amount to make one good-sized serving, as the leaves cook down tremendously. The seeds contain protein, vitamin A, riboflavin, calcium, phosphorus, manganese, and potassium.

AMARANTH
Amaranthus spp.

SEASON Seeds in fall, leaves when available
HABITAT Fields, open sunny areas
DISTRIBUTION Global

DETAILS The *Amaranthus* genus is a group of **annual or short-lived perennial plants**. Amaranth is a common weed around farms and cultivated soils, often growing right in with crops.

IDENTIFIERS Catkin-like bunches of flowers grow in summer or fall, later releasing **small rounded seeds** that can be tan or black. About 60 species are recognized, with flowers and **simple alternate leaves** ranging in color from purples and reds to green or gold.

USES Much like lamb's quarters, the seeds can be used as a grain and the leaves are edible raw or cooked (though better cooked). Amaranth seeds are abundant in vitamins and minerals, and though wild plants of amaranth are often considered weeds, various species and varieties are cultivated as leaf vegetables, grain plants, and ornamentals.

WILD RICE
Zizania spp.

SEASON Fall
HABITAT Marshes and wetlands
DISTRIBUTION North America and China

DETAILS Wild rice is usually found in shallow water less than 3 feet (1 m) deep. There are four species of these **herbaceous annual water grasses**, all of which produce an edible grain.

IDENTIFIERS Wild rice can grow to 9 feet (3 m) tall, with thick, spongy stems. The grasses' leaf blades can reach up to 4 feet (1.2 m) high.

USES Wild rice is not directly related to Asian rice (*Oryza sativa*) and is a little tougher than white rice, with its chewy outer sheath. Wild rice is a good source of B vitamins, iron, potassium, magnesium, phosphorus, and manganese, and 3.5 ounces (105 g) of uncooked wild rice contains 101 calories. This grain is typically harvested in canoes, by paddling under the seed heads and tapping them with a stick so that the rice falls into the open canoe.

WILD OAT
Avena fatua

SEASON Fall
HABITAT Fields and meadows
DISTRIBUTION Northern Hemisphere

DETAILS Wild oat is an **annual herbaceous plant** native to Eurasia and present in most of North America. It goes by many names, such as flaxgrass, oat grass, and wheat oats. Considered a weed in most places, as it competes with crops, wild oat is a **green grass with a hollow stem** that can reach 4 feet (1.2 m) in height. The long grass leaves are generally hairy.

IDENTIFIERS The seeds are inside **hairy spikelets** at the top of the plant, allowing them to stick to feathers, fur, and clothing.

USES Strip the oats from the seed head and thresh them to remove the inedible seed coat. Once this is done, the oats can be rolled, ground into flour, or cooked until they burst.

WILD WHEAT
Triticum spp.

SEASON Fall
HABITAT Fields, open sunny areas
DISTRIBUTION Global

DETAILS Wild wheat is a cereal grain from a **herbaceous annual** grass. It typically grows from 3–4 feet (1–1.2 m) tall and has a similar appearance to wild oats.

IDENTIFIERS Wheat has **grasslike leaves** and bears seed-filled **spikelets** at the top of the plant. Wheat is one of the first known domesticated cereals, grown perhaps as early as 9,000 BCE Ancient species and strains of this wheat can still be found in Europe and Africa, while wild wheat in North America has most likely escaped from cultivation.

USES Thresh the seeds from the inside of the spikelets and grind into flour. Watch out for ergot, which is a toxic purple fungus that grows in the spikelets in place of the actual wheat seeds. Discard any purplish wild wheat collected, as this fungus can be deadly.

124 PICK WILD FRUITS

Wild fruits are the culinary crown jewels of foraging. Nothing is as mouthwatering as a handful of sweet berries, sun-ripened to perfection. Collect 'em quick—they're only around for a short time.

PAW PAW
Asimina triloba

SEASON Late summer
HABITAT Riverbanks and wet areas
DISTRIBUTION Midwest U.S. to the Atlantic

DETAILS The paw paw is a **deciduous tree** in the custard apple family (Annonaceae), found in its native range of the southern, eastern, and midwestern United States and southern Ontario.

IDENTIFIERS Paw paw has large **alternate simple leaves**, and fruits that resemble **chubby bananas** about 2–6 inches (5–15 cm) long and 1–3 inches (2.5–7.5 cm) wide. The fruit is full of **large brown seeds**.

USES These fruits carry 80 calories to the cup (125 g) and contain vitamin C and potassium. The sweet, strange flavor is a little like a banana with hints of mango. Look for them in August on trees near rivers, and pick them when they are fragrant and almost mushy, but before they rot and turn dark. They are best when eaten raw, though they can be cooked in desserts or turned into an interesting dried fruit.

GROUND CHERRY
Physalis spp.

SEASON Summer
HABITAT Fields, open sunny areas
DISTRIBUTION North America

DETAILS Ground cherries are **herbaceous annual plants** that grow a small **fruit in a papery husk**. Some species can grow to 6 feet (2 m) tall, and most resemble the common cherry tomato of the same family. Like tomatoes, most species require abundant light and warm temperatures.

IDENTIFIERS The common ground cherry (*Physalis longifolia*) has a husk covering the berry that has ten veins and can reach lengths up to 1½ inches (4 cm).

USES The small fruits can be used like the tomato (raw in salads or cooked) after they are extracted from the papery husk. Some species have a sweeter taste that works well as a dessert, in fruit preserves, or dried. They also contain pectin and can be made into pie filling or jam.

SEA GRAPE
Coccoloba uvifera

SEASON Late summer, early fall
HABITAT Lawns, fields, and open ground
DISTRIBUTION Global

DETAILS The sea grape is **tropical woody shrub** and a member of the buckwheat family, Polygonaceae. It has stiff, round **alternate simple leaves**, and can be found near tropical coastal beaches throughout eastern North America. The small tree or large shrub is unable to survive frost.

IDENTIFIERS In late summer, the sea grape bears **clusters of grapelike fruit**, each about ¾ inch (19 mm) in diameter. These ripen to a reddish or purple color and contain a large seed that is not edible; only the pulp of the reddish fruits of the sea grape may be eaten.

USES The pulp can be consumed raw, cooked into preserves and jams, or fermented into sea grape wine. In the West Indies and Jamaica, sea grape sap and boiled bark is used to create a reddish brown dye and to tan leather.

SEA GRAPE ▶

PERSIMMON

Diospyros virginiana

SEASON Late summer
HABITAT Fields and forest edges
DISTRIBUTION Eastern U.S.

DETAILS The American persimmon is a **deciduous tree** found in the eastern United States.

IDENTIFIERS Persimmons have **alternate simple leaves** and **small orange fruits**. A related species with larger fruits can be found in Japan and neighboring countries. Watch out for very wrinkled fruits in late October—these are bitter and will give you a strong case of cotton mouth if not yet ripe. Generally, the rougher they look, the sweeter they are.

USES The scientific name of this fruit is *diospyros*, which means "food of the gods"—and it's no exaggeration. The completely ripe, native persimmon fruits are a sticky, sweet treasure trove of flavor. Persimmons have 127 calories and a full day's vitamin C per cup (125 g) of pulp. The wood is also rock hard and makes good mallets and tool handles.

WILD GRAPE

Vitis spp.

SEASON Late summer and fall
HABITAT Forest edges and fence rows
DISTRIBUTION Global

DETAILS Wild grapes are **deciduous woody vines** found throughout the world. Grapes have **alternate simple leaves** that are heavily toothed. More than 20 species of wild grape are found east of the Mississippi, ripening at different times from August through October.

IDENTIFIERS Make sure it's a grape! The Canada moonseed looks like a grape, but it is poisonous. Grapes should have **one to four teardrop-shaped seeds**, while the dangerous moonseed has only one curved and flat seed. The grape vines also have curly tendrils, while the moonseed has no curls.

USES Depending on the species and sugar content, grapes are roughly 100 calories per cup (185 g). Most wild grapes carry decent amounts of vitamins and minerals, and up to a quarter of your daily potassium requirement.

WILD STRAWBERRY

Fragaria spp.

SEASON Summer
HABITAT Woodlands and fields
DISTRIBUTION Northern Hemisphere

DETAILS The wild strawberry is a **perennial herbaceous plant** that grows naturally throughout much of the Northern Hemisphere. There are more than 20 different *Fragaria* species worldwide.

IDENTIFIERS The woodland strawberry (*Fragaria vesca*), is the most common species. Strawberries have **compound leaves with three leaflets**. Look for tan seeds on the surface.

USES Though the wild berries are not high in calories, real wild strawberries are great tasting. One cup of berries will give you more than a full day's supply of vitamin C. Take care to avoid confusion with the Indian strawberry, which is still edible, but completely flavorless. It has red seeds on the surface, rather than tan. When you get a real wild strawberry, you'll know it. It will be very flavorful and sweet and will make your day—or your breakfast.

MALLOW (CHEESEWEED)
Malva spp.

SEASON Summer

HABITAT Sandy soils, dunes, and forests

DISTRIBUTION Southeast U.S.

DETAILS The common mallow (*Malva neglecta*) is also known as in America as the cheeseweed or cheeseplant. This **small herbaceous annual plant** is often considered a weed. There are about 25–30 species in the family Malvaceae, and they are widespread throughout the temperate, subtropical, and tropical regions.

IDENTIFIERS The **white or pink flowers** have five petals and are about ½ inch (12 mm) wide. The small, green fruit resembles a wheel of cheese to many people, hence the plant's nicknames.

USES The crunchy green fruits are good as a trailside snack, fun to put in a salad, and can even be cooked with other wild greens.

CRANBERRY
Vaccinium spp.

SEASON Fall

HABITAT Northern bogs and wetlands

DISTRIBUTION Northern Hemisphere

DETAILS These plants are a group of **evergreen dwarf shrubs or trailing vines** which are closely related to blueberries. Cranberries are found in acidic bogs in the northern regions. They may grow as low, creeping shrubs or grow in vines up to 7 feet (2 m) long.

IDENTIFIERS The **dark pink flowers** have petals that are sharply reflexed (peeled backward). The fruit of the cranberry is a berry that turns from its initial white color to a deep red when fully ripened.

USES The combination of sour and bitter flavors in ripe cranberries discourages most people from eating them raw, although you could. They are much better after cooking and sweetening, such as in cranberry sauce and preserves, but their high vitamin C content is destroyed by the heat of cooking.

AUTUMN OLIVE
Elaeagnus spp.

SEASON Late summer

HABITAT Fields, fence rows, and open areas

DISTRIBUTION Northern Hemisphere

DETAILS Autumn olive grows as a **deciduous shrub or small tree**, typically up to 9–12 feet (3–4 m) tall. The **simple alternate leaves** are covered with minute silvery scales on the top of the leaf and even more on the underside.

IDENTIFIERS The four-lobed, **yellowish-white flowers** give way to small fruits, which are ¼–⅓ inches (6–8 mm) in diameter. The unripe fruit is silvery-scaled and yellow, and it ripens to a red color that is freckled with little brown dots.

USES The ripe fruit starts out very tannic and tart in the beginning of the ripening stage, but eventually increases in sweetness. The red fruits can be eaten raw, cooked into jam or sauce, dehydrated into a dried fruit, and even turned into wine. The seeds are high in protein and can be ingested with the pulp.

MULBERRY
Morus spp.

SEASON Summer
HABITAT Fields and fence rows
DISTRIBUTION Northern Hemisphere

DETAILS Mulberry is a **deciduous tree** that produces sweet berries and strong fiber. The native red mulberry (*Morus rubra*) and several Asian species can be found throughout the United States.

IDENTIFIERS Mulberries have large, heart-shaped, toothed **alternate simple leaves**. These **blackberry-like fruits** dangle from a tree as opposed to growing on a thorny bush.

USES Mulberries provide 85 percent of your daily vitamin C requirement and 14 percent of your daily iron. The berries can be eaten right off the tree, cooked into pies, or turned into sweet wine. Make sure the berries are sweet and ripe, as underripe mulberries can lead to serious reactions (everything from vomiting to hallucinations). You can also use the inner bark of early summer to create very strong cordage fibers.

CHERRY
Prunus spp.

SEASON Summer
HABITAT Forest edges and fields
DISTRIBUTION Northern Hemisphere

DETAILS The cherry tree is a **deciduous tree** consisting of many different species throughout the Northern Hemisphere.

IDENTIFIERS Cherry trees have small-toothed **alternate simple leaves**, and their broken twigs have a strong bitter-sour smell. The black cherry (*Prunus serotina*) is one of the tastier wild cherry species, and bears **reddish-black fruits** that ripen each July.

USES One cup (125 g) of pitted black cherries has 77 calories and a healthy dose of vitamins and minerals. Cherry fruits are great when eaten fresh and still great in pie, jam, and wine. Make sure you spit out the cherry pits—and don't mess around with wilting green cherry leaves. Both are poisonous due to their high levels of cyanide.

HAWTHORN
Crataegus spp.

SEASON Fall
HABITAT Mountains and forests
DISTRIBUTION Northern Hemisphere

DETAILS Hawthorn is a **small deciduous tree or shrub** also called thornapple, May tree, and whitehorn. It belongs to the rose family (Rosaceae) and has many related species. These trees have **alternate simple leaves** and are native to temperate regions of the Northern Hemisphere in Europe, Asia, and North America.

IDENTIFIERS *Crataegus* species usually grow 16–49 feet (5–15 m) tall, with typically thorny branches. These thorns can grow from branches or from the trunk itself, and can reach lengths of 4.5 inches (11.5 cm). Lobed leaves are common, and most species have serrate margins and variable shapes.

USES The red fruits of most hawthorns are tart and look like small crabapples. You can make hawthorn jams, jellies, juices, wine, and liqueur.

◀ HAWTHORN TREE

125 SPOT UNIQUE VEGETABLES

For the survivalist and the wild-food enthusiast, fields and open areas contain a wide range of unique vegetable foods, some with flavors that defy description.

MILKWEED
Asclepias spp.

SEASON Spring and summer
HABITAT Fields, roadsides, and open ground
DISTRIBUTION Global

DETAILS The milkweed plants are **herbaceous perennials**, with **opposite branching simple leaves**. Plants can reach heights over 3 feet (1 m).

IDENTIFIERS They get their name from the **milky white juice** that exudes from any injury.

USES Some milkweeds are quite toxic, but the common milkweed (*Asclepias syriaca*) is an edible wild vegetable. Collect the young shoots (which have downy hairs) when they are around 6 inches (15 cm) long and boil for five minutes. Drain, add boiling water from another vessel, boil another five minutes, drain again, and serve. Treat the young seed pods of early summer likewise for a veggie that tastes like peas. The fiber from the recently deceased stalks makes strong cordage, and the fluff from older seed pods is great fire-starting tinder.

OYSTER PLANT
Tragopogon porrifolius

SEASON Summer
HABITAT Open fields and roadsides
DISTRIBUTION Global

DETAILS Oyster plant (also known as salsify) is a common **herbaceous biennial wildflower**, native to Europe but introduced to North America, Africa, and Australia. The plant can reach a height of up to 4 feet (1.2 m).

IDENTIFIERS With all *Tragopogon* species, the stem is largely unbranched and bears **simple alternate leaves** that resemble grass. Oyster plant exudes a milky juice from the stems, and the **purple flower head** measures about 2 inches (5 cm); each flower has green bracts that are longer than the petals. These plants are hard to spot before flowering, as they blend in with many grasses.

USES Dig up the root for a raw or cooked vegetable that has historically been used as a diuretic, liver cleanser, and tonic, similar to dandelion.

BURDOCK
Arctium spp.

SEASON Spring through fall
HABITAT Open sunny areas
DISTRIBUTION Global

DETAILS This **herbaceous biennial plant** is native to Asia and has been introduced around the world. Burdock is most often known for its 1-inch (2.5-cm) burrs, which tenaciously stick to clothing, fur, and hair. The central stalk of this plant can reach a height of more than 4 feet (1.2 m).

IDENTIFIERS Burdock has large **simple leaves** with wavy margins during the first year. During the second, it has larger, slightly fuzzy leaves with a flower stalk.

USES Collect tender leaves during the first two years of life and boil in changes of water to remove their bitterness (follow the procedure for milkweed). Dig up the very deep roots and also use changes of boiling water to cook. The burrs can be dampened and grown as salad sprouts—and they work as emergency Velcro!

SAW PALMETTO
Serenoa repens

SEASON Fruits in fall, hearts year-round
HABITAT Sandy soils, dunes, forests
DISTRIBUTION Southeast U.S.

DETAILS The saw palmetto is the only species in the genus *Serenoa*. It has sometimes been called *Sabal serrulatum* when associated with alternative medicine. A small, **woody plant**, it typically reaches a height of around 3–6 feet (1–2 m).

IDENTIFIERS The leaves grow in a **palmately compound** arrangement of about 20 leaflets. The petiole (leaf stalk) bears many small sharp teeth or spines, no doubt the source of the "saw" name.

USES The fruit is a large reddish-black berry—an important food source for wildlife and an emergency one for us. But the taste (often likened to bad cheese) leaves something to be desired and makes the berries difficult to eat. Fortunately, the terminal buds contain "heart of palm," which can be cut out and eaten raw or cooked. Just make sure you wear gloves to work with this saw-edged plant.

PURSLANE
Portulaca oleracea

SEASON Spring through fall
HABITAT Virtually anywhere
DISTRIBUTION Global

DETAILS Purslane is an **annual herbaceous** plant in the Portulacaceae family. It has very watery, succulent stems and leaves, and many varieties are cultivated for food. Larger plants reach 16 inches (40 cm) in height.

IDENTIFIERS Purslane has smooth, reddish stems and **alternate simple leaves** clustered at joints and ends. The five-petaled **yellow flowers** can appear throughout the year. Tiny black seeds form in pods that open when the seeds are mature.

USES The leaves, stems, and tender seedpods are edible raw or cooked, and their mild flavor makes a great addition to any wild-food dish. Purslane is often used in soups and cooked like spinach throughout Europe, and the crushed leaves can be used as a poultice to treat insect bites, boils, sores, and stings. Purslane contains calcium, potassium, and vitamin A.

OX-EYE DAISY
Leucanthemum vulgare

SEASON Spring through fall
HABITAT Fields and lawns
DISTRIBUTION Northern Hemisphere

DETAILS The ox-eye daisy (syn. *Chrysanthemum leucanthemum*) is a **herbaceous perennial** widespread throughout Europe and the temperate regions of Asia, and considered an invasive weed in North America, Australia, and New Zealand. This plant is a common sight in grasslands and fields, and flowers are easy to spot on 1–3 foot (30–91 cm) stems.

IDENTIFIERS Blooming from late spring to autumn, the **white flowers** are about 2 inches (5 cm) wide with about 20 white ray florets surrounding a yellow disc.

USES Eat the simple **alternate leaves** raw or cooked, and you can even pickle the unopened flower buds. The taste is complex, with hints of grape, mint, pepper and many other intense flavors. *Leucanthemum* is from the Greek words *leukos* and *anthemon*, meaning "white" and "flower."

126 DIG UP SOME EDIBLE ROOTS

Roots, rhizomes, and tubers are the hidden delicacies of foraging. These buried treasures boast a wealth of calories and other nutritional benefits. Some are even medicinal or energy-boosting.

TOOTHWORT
Dentaria spp.

SEASON Spring
HABITAT Forests and shady areas
DISTRIBUTION Eastern U.S.

DETAILS Toothwort is a small **herbaceous perennial plant** common in the eastern woodlands of North America. This plant grows from a small whitish tuber that looks like a **tiny blond yam**. Toothwort grows to a height of 6–16 inches (15–40 cm).

IDENTIFIERS The plant has **four-petaled flowers** that are typically white or pinkish in color. It has leaves with three long lobe segments and toothed margins.

USES Each plant will have one single tuber, which can be eaten raw or cooked, and has a spicy flavor similar to radishes. Soak the tubers in a spiced vinegar brine to create a crunchy wild pickle, or grate into a paste and blend with dried red pepper flakes to make a "wild horseradish" condiment.

GINSENG
Panax spp.

SEASON Year-round
HABITAT Mountainous woodlands
DISTRIBUTION Northern Hemisphere

DETAILS Ginseng is a **herbaceous perennial plant** that is often hard to locate. It favors rough mountainous forests and is one of the most coveted edible plants. Many species are found across the Northern Hemisphere, the largest of which usually reach a maximum height of 16 inches (40 cm).

IDENTIFIERS All ginsengs have **palmate compound leaves** with three or five leaflets. Each leaflet is finely toothed, and the compound leaf resembles Virginia creeper (*Parthenocissus quinquefolia*) leaves. The **pale yellowish-green or whitish flowers** turn into **bright red berries** in the fall, offering the best chance of spotting this diminutive plant.

USES Brew a ginseng tea or steep in alcohol to take as a tonic. The dried roots can be stored for months before use. You can also eat it raw or simmered in a soup.

RAMP (WILD LEEK)
Allium tricoccum

SEASON Spring
HABITAT Forested mountains
DISTRIBUTION Eastern U.S.

DETAILS Ramps, also called wild leeks, are pungent **herbaceous perennials** from mountainous forest regions of the eastern United States. The green leaves are broad and smooth with a **strong onion scent**. They form clusters and colonies in shady woods, favoring higher elevations.

IDENTIFIERS Ramps grow a very slender flower stalk after the leaves have died back for the year. This flower stalk can be 6–18 inches (15–45 cm) tall and is **topped with a cluster of white flowers**.

USES Ramps are part of traditional meals in the spring mountains and are even the subject of feasts and festivals. Eat the **small white bulbs** and green leaves raw or cooked, in the wide variety of ways onions can be prepared. Ramps are also known for their mild purgative effect, so enjoy in moderation.

WILD GINGER
Asarum canadense

SEASON Year-round
HABITAT Damp woods and riversides
DISTRIBUTION Northern Hemisphere

DETAILS Wild ginger, also known as Canadian snakeroot or Canada wild ginger, is a **herbaceous perennial** native to the broadleaf forests of eastern North America.

IDENTIFIERS The roots are **fleshy rhizomes** (continuously growing underground stems) that are typically greenish in color and shallowly buried. The **leaves are kidney-shaped or heart-shaped** and often grow in pairs, and the flowers are the unusual, with **three hairy sepals that are purplish brown** and tapered tips and bases that fuse together.

USES Use wild ginger root to make a spicy tea, or use the dried root powder as a ginger substitute, but be sure to do so in moderation. Wild ginger smells very similar to true ginger (*Zingiber officinale*), but some studies have shown carcinogens in the root, so use sparingly and with caution.

JERUSALEM ARTICHOKE
Helianthus tuberosus

SEASON Fall
HABITAT Fields, open sunny areas
DISTRIBUTION Northern Hemisphere

DETAILS Neither an artichoke nor from Jerusalem, this sunflower relative is a **herbaceous perennial plant** common in North America. It averages 6–9 feet (2–3 m) tall, with **coarsely toothed opposite leaves**.

IDENTIFIERS Jerusalem artichoke has a slightly sweet tuber that strongly resembles the shape of ginger roots (without the odor). The **large yellow flowers** resemble smaller varieties of sunflower.

USES The roots are the edible part, with 109 calories per cup (125 g) and lots of iron and potassium. They also contain 5–20 percent of your daily allowance of most of the B vitamins. Look for the small sunflower-like bloom in the fall at the top of the tall plants, and dig up the tubers then, as they will be at their largest size and greatest food value. Eat them raw or cooked.

SPRING BEAUTY
Claytonia virginica

SEASON Spring
HABITAT Forests and edge areas
DISTRIBUTION Eastern U.S.

DETAILS This **herbaceous perennial plant** is in the purslane family (Portulacaceae) and about 3–6 inches (7.5–15 cm) tall. The plants consist of a flowering stem with a pair of **opposite grasslike leaves** and some basal leaves, both linear and fleshy, like grass. The stem is light green or slightly reddish green, smooth, and resembles succulents.

IDENTIFIERS Each flower is up to ½ inch (12 mm) across when fully open, and consists of five petals, two green sepals, five stamens with pink anthers, and a pistil with a tripartite style. The petals are white with fine pink stripes varying from pale to bright pink.

USES The **potato-like root,** which you can gather in quantity where abundant, is delicious fresh or cooked like a potato.

SOLOMON'S SEAL
Polygonatum spp.

SEASON Year-round
HABITAT Woodlands
DISTRIBUTION Northern Hemisphere

DETAILS King Solomon's seal, or Solomon's seal, is a genus of flowering **herbaceous perennial plants** in the family Asparagaceae. Most of the 60 species occur in Asia, with a few native to North America.

IDENTIFIERS These plants have an **unbranched arching stem**, which has **broad alternate leaves**. The **greenish flowers** dangle below the stalk and resemble little bells with six lobes. The root bears round scars and is a multijointed rhizome.

USES Eat the leaves, stems, and rhizomes raw or cooked. The roots are most commonly dug in the fall, although they can be found all year. You can also use the rhizomes in teas and tinctures to treat diabetes, hyperglycemia, pain, fever, inflammation, and allergies. Solomon's seal also shows up in Ayurvedic medicine as an aphrodisiac. Your results may vary.

INDIAN CUCUMBER ROOT
Medeola virginiana

SEASON Summer and fall
HABITAT Shady moist areas
DISTRIBUTION Eastern U.S.

DETAILS Indian cucumber root is a small **herbaceous perennial plant** in the lily family (Liliaceae), found in damp forested areas and riverine woodlands.

IDENTIFIERS The slender upright stem bears one to three **sets of leaves in whorls**, typically as tall as 1–2 feet (30–60 cm). Most whorls have five to nine leaves, with the uppermost whorl bearing the fewest leaves and **greenish-yellow flowers** that give way to dark purple berries. A small white tuber is buried just below the base of the plant stalk and resembles a white yam.

USES This tuber is sweet, juicy, crunchy, and actually tastes of cucumber. Most likely, you'll eat it raw, though you can also pickle it or eat it as a cooked vegetable. Gather only where abundant, as these plants are increasingly rare in many places.

TROUT LILY
Erythronium americanum

SEASON Spring
HABITAT Shady moist areas
DISTRIBUTION Eastern U.S.

DETAILS Trout lilies are **herbaceous perennials** found in shady areas near water. The banks of trout streams are likely places to look, probably yielding the name (though their gray, green, and brown mottled leaves could also resemble the coloring of brook trout).

IDENTIFIERS The **mottled green and brown spotted leaves** are the most obvious identifying feature. The trout lily also has a **single yellow flower with six petals**. The **oval leaves come in pairs** and are 3–8 inches (7.5–20 cm) long. The root is a **small bulb** resembling an onion, but lacking the characteristic odor.

USES The leaves, flowers, and bulbs can be eaten raw or cooked. Trout lilies can cause mild stomach upset in sensitive people, so limit your consumption until you've determined your body's reaction to the plant.

ARROWHEAD
Sagittaria latifolia

SEASON Fall
HABITAT Wetlands
DISTRIBUTION Northern Hemisphere

DETAILS Arrowhead (or duck potato, Indian potato, or wapato), is a **herbaceous aquatic perennial** that grows in colonies in shallow wetlands. Arrowhead stems can be 6–30 feet (2–9 m) in length, depending on the water depth.

IDENTIFIERS The leaves are **arrowhead shaped** and the roots are white, producing **whitish tubers with a purplish skin** in the mud under the water.

USES The edible tubers were used extensively by the native peoples of North America. Arrowhead is traditionally harvested by using a long wooden tool, such as a hoe or pick, to snag the roots. Once detached, the tubers usually float. You can eat them raw or cooked to enjoy a flavor reminiscent of potatoes and chestnuts. You can also slice and dry the tubers, then grind into flour.

WILD CARROT
Daucus carota

SEASON Year-round
HABITAT Fields, open sunny areas
DISTRIBUTION Northern Hemisphere

DETAILS The wild carrot is a **herbaceous biennial plant** in the family Apiaceae. Native to Europe, it lives for two years and is also known as bird's nest, bishop's lace, and Queen Anne's lace. The domesticated carrot is descended from this wild forebear.

IDENTIFIERS The **leaf stalks and flower stalks are hairy** and the **flowers are complex white umbels**. The plant has **compound alternate leaves**, referred to as dissected (heavily divided). The taproot is carrot-scented when bruised.

USES Eat the roots raw or cooked during the first year of the plant's life. For the woodier second-year roots, add to soups as a flavoring (remove before serving). Be extremely cautious of the similar looking poison hemlock (*Conium maculatum*)—it lacks hairs and has an unpleasant chemical scent.

CHICORY
Cichorium intybus

SEASON Year-round
HABITAT Fields, open sunny areas
DISTRIBUTION Northern Hemisphere

DETAILS Chicory is a **herbaceous perennial plant** that is native to Europe and now naturalized across the hemisphere.

IDENTIFIERS The **basal rosette leaves** are similar to dandelion leaves, and the flower stalk has smaller **alternate branching leaves**. The **blue composite flowers** have ragged square edges to the rays. This plant may live for several years, coming back from a taproot or cluster of taproots.

USES Eat the leaves and flowers raw or cooked, and roast the roots to make a coffee substitute. Preheat your oven to 350°F (176°C), while you wash the roots and cut them into small bits. Spread on a cookie sheet and bake until chocolate brown. Pour boiling water into a coffee mug and add 1 tbsp. (7 g) of roasted chicory root for every cup (250 ml) of water used. Let the brew steep for ten minutes.

127 SUPERPLANT: CATTAIL

FIND SOMETHING GOOD IN THE SWAMP

In America, the common cattail (*Typha latifolia*) is a tall, grasslike marsh plant that often grows in dense stands in wetland areas and drainages. It has blade-shaped, erect leaves and stiff stems topped with a sausagelike brown seed head. There are many edible and useful parts of this plant, but make certain you gather it from unpolluted waters. Cattail is notorious for soaking up toxins and heavy metals in polluted areas. Man-made swamps of cattail are even used as a final filtration bed in some greener wastewater treatment facilities. Various species of cattail (*Typha* spp.) are found worldwide.

CAT ON THE COB

In early summer, you'll briefly have access to two different and bizarre cattail foods: the unopened pollen spike and the pollen itself later, when those spikes emerge. Both of these are protein packed and edible after a little cooking. Find the unopened spikes by feeling the green center spike of cattails that are nearing full height. You should be able to feel a distinct difference between the bigger seed head (in the bottom position, atop the stalk) and the skinnier pollen spike at the very top of the stalk. Cut this upper spike free from the plant, keeping the leaf wrapping intact. Boil these spikes whole for ten minutes in salted water, peel back the husks, and eat them like corn on the cob. Once the spikes have emerged, you can collect the sulfur-yellow pollen by tapping the pollen spike into a large bowl. Sift this powder to filter out any small bugs, and add it to flour to boost the protein.

INSECT REPELLENT

Baffle the bugs of the cattail swamp! The stinking smoke of smoldering cattails can act as a good bug repellent. Dead, dried cattail heads work well and can be found throughout the year. Collect a dry, brown seed head and light one end with a small fire. It will usually smoke without going up in flames completely. Place the smoking cattail punk on a fire-safe surface upwind from your position, and the bug-repelling smoke will waft over you for up to a half hour. This is also a handy way to transport a fire from one place to another.

TENDER SHOOTS

In April, you can survey the cattail swamps for cattail shoots. These fast-growing shoots have an oval cross section, and have bright green leaves with whitish bases, like onions. Start collecting when they are $1\frac{1}{2}$ feet (46 cm) high. Grip each stalk firmly, as low as you can reach on the plant. Squeeze it hard, pull upward, and it should break free with a popping sound. Collect several dozen of these and boil the whitish ends in water for ten minutes. Eat them by biting down on the white section and pulling the rest between your teeth. Anything tender is the edible part, anything fibrous can go back in the swamp.

DIG UP WINTER SPROUTS

The horn-shaped sprouts on cattail rootstocks can be washed and cooked up as an unusual vegetable. Never eat the sprouts raw—even when gathered from clean waters, and even if someone tells you they're fine. You never know what pathogens are in the water until it's too late. Cook these little pointy sprouts thoroughly and enjoy their rare taste, something of a mix between cucumber and potato. Look for them especially at the base of last year's dead cattail plants.

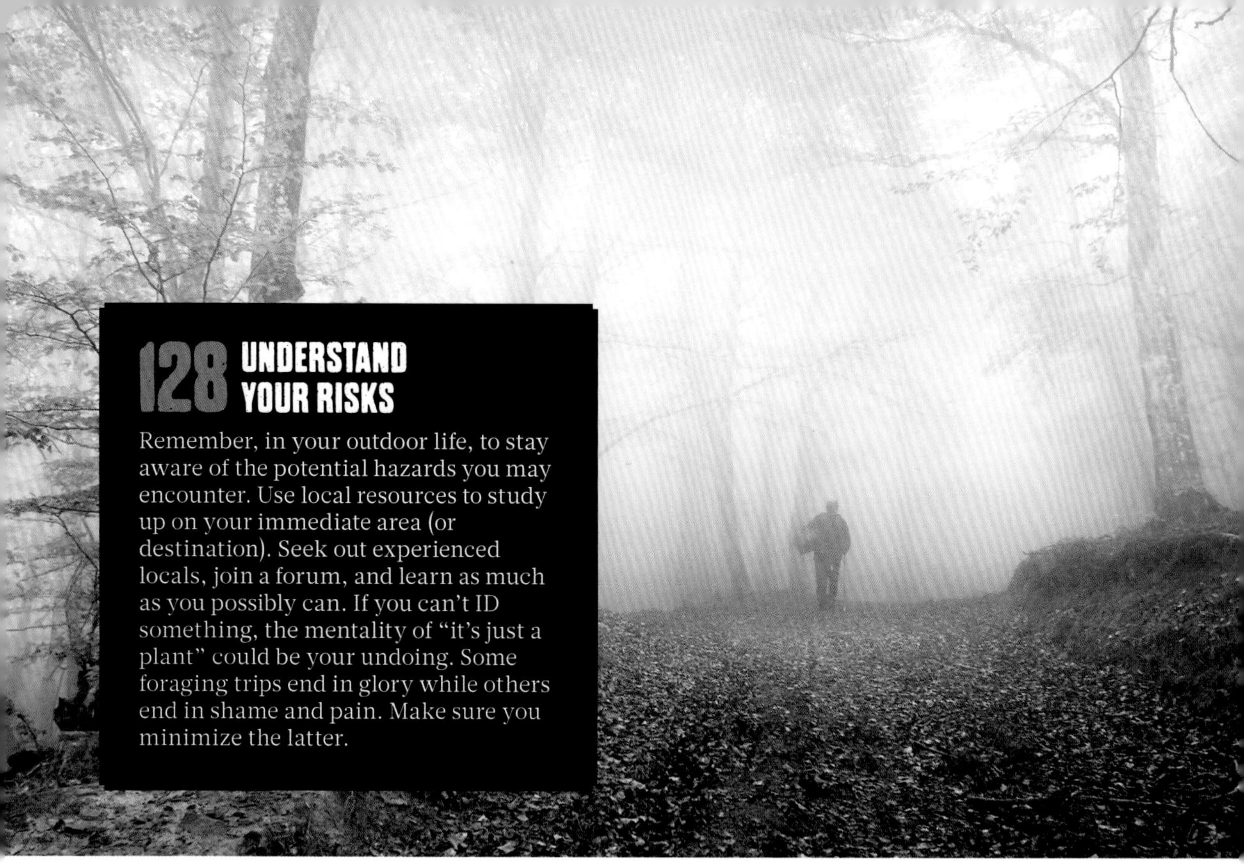

128 UNDERSTAND YOUR RISKS

Remember, in your outdoor life, to stay aware of the potential hazards you may encounter. Use local resources to study up on your immediate area (or destination). Seek out experienced locals, join a forum, and learn as much as you possibly can. If you can't ID something, the mentality of "it's just a plant" could be your undoing. Some foraging trips end in glory while others end in shame and pain. Make sure you minimize the latter.

129 SPOT THE CHAMELEON

Poison ivy (*Toxicodendron radicans*) is one of the greatest plant chameleons out there. This notorious trickster can appear to be a small herbaceous plant when young, a small tree or carpet of vines when several years old, and a massive hairy vine after a decade's growth.

Contact with any part of this plant will cause a severe rash for most people. Burning any part of it will send its irritant oils airborne, which can cause even more harm, especially if inhaled. Poison ivy contains a phenolic substance called urushiol, which is responsible for roughly two million contact dermatitis cases in the United States each year. Remember the old saying, "leaves of three, let them be," and commit the pictures below to memory.

Young poison ivy leaves

Poison ivy resembling a young tree

Older poison ivy vine with hairs

130 STAY HANDS FREE

Not all plants are helpless—they can, in fact, bite back. Many have defensive adaptations, from irritating oils to sharp thorns. Be aware of the following botanical armaments and naturally occurring defense mechanisms.

DEFENSE	EFFECTS	WATCH OUT FOR	
OILS	Oils from many common (and well-known) plants can produce a severe rash		Poison ivy (left), poison sumac, poison oak, wild parsnip, trumpet creeper
NEEDLES	Punctures from needles can be deep and harmful		Cacti (left), evergreens, ocotillo or desert coral
THORNS	Thorns will scratch and puncture skin		Blackberry (left), aloe, thistle, citrus trees, prickly gooseberry
SPINES	Some plants have spines that deliver painful stings		Stinging nettle (left) or common nettle, fever tree
LATEX	A saplike milky fluid called latex will irritate eyes and skin, causing inflammation and pain		Eyebane (left), also known as spotted spurge; poinsettia

131 BE ALLERGY ALERT

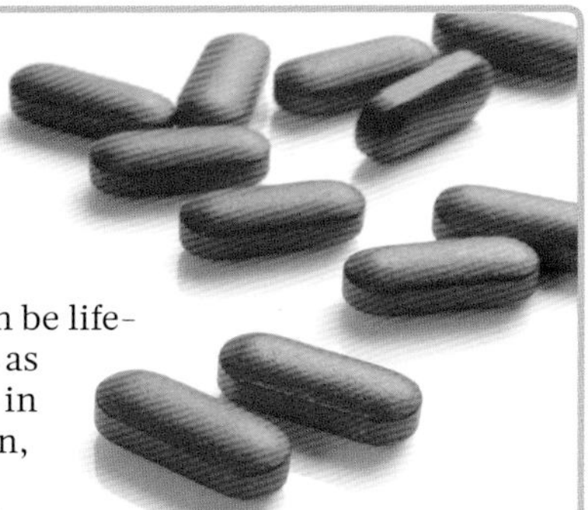

Although most common edible plants are widely tolerated, you never know who might be sensitive to them. An allergic reaction can range from nausea or digestive upset to rashes, hives, or other skin irritation. In the worst cases, allergies can be life-threatening. If you have food allergies, be especially cautious as you try new wild edible plant foods, following the guidelines in item 106. If you think you might be having an allergic reaction, seek medical help immediately. If the reaction is severe (particularly if breathing becomes difficult) and you can't get medical treatment quickly, taking oral antihistamines such as Benedryl can literally be a lifesaver. Many experts recommend carrying an antihistamine you know works for you, just in case you run into something you didn't know you were allergic to.

132 DON'T BE FOOLED

One of the trickiest parts of foraging is avoiding the dangerous plants that look enticing. Berries are usually the worst culprit, followed by other fruits and nuts. Keep these off your menu.

POKEWEED BERRIES
Cause digestive distress and death

BUCKEYE NUTS
Can cause cardiac arrest

NIGHTSHADE BERRIES
Lead to respiratory troubles, coma, or death

YEW BERRIES
Cause cardiac and respiratory failure

HORSE CHESTNUT
Can cause digestive upset but is rarely fatal

HORSE NETTLE FRUIT
Potentially fatal

WHITE BANEBERRY FRUIT
Causes severe digestive upset

VIRGINIA CREEPER BERRIES
Potentially fatal

133 ACT QUICKLY

If you suspect poisoning, you'll need to act fast. While most poisonings merely cause digestive distress, you don't want to take any chances in case worse symptoms develop. A quick response to toxins will minimize the damage they can cause and perhaps even save a life.

IF MEDICAL CARE IS AVAILABLE

Call 911 immediately if you suspect poisoning. Give them the name of the plant or the best description you can muster. Explain what plant part was eaten and how much of it. Provide the time and manner of consumption, as well as the age and weight of the victim. Finally, describe the poisoning symptoms that you observe. Wait for an ambulance or take a trip to the doctor as directed.

IF MEDICAL CARE IS NOT AVAILABLE

In this scarier scenario, you're on your own. Have the victim drink several glasses of water and induce vomiting. This can be done by sticking a finger or twig down the throat or taking an emetic (like ipecac syrup). The victim should vomit several times, until the stomach is clear. Then monitor for symptoms of shock or other serious issues. Get to skilled medical care as soon as possible.

134 PICK YOUR POISON

While coming into contact with plant toxins and irritants can be, well, irritating, consuming plant toxins is generally the worst thing you can do. While some toxins are mild, causing nothing more than a stomachache, other toxins can be fatal. And if that isn't bad enough, some plants can even harbor multiple toxins. Make sure you don't put these poisons on your plate.

ALCOHOLS Plant alcohols can cause some of the most severe poisonings, even leading to death. For example, water hemlock contains the alcohol cicutoxin, which can be fatal even in small amounts.

ALKALOIDS Although this category includes some popular chemicals (like caffeine), they can also do a world of harm. Alkaloids are the largest group of toxins, and their effects range from indigestion to death.

AMINES These dangerous nitrogenous compounds (derivatives of ammonia) can be found in American mistletoe.

GLYCOSIDES When consumed, glycoside compounds convert into sugars and nonsugar residue (the poisonous part). Cardiac glycosides, like the ones found in dogbane, can cause cardiac arrest. The cyanogenic glycosides found in cherry leaves and pits can act like cyanide.

OXALATES This group of toxins has a corrosive effect on animal tissues. Calcium oxalate is one of the most common forms, and it's found in many plants. These small, insoluble crystals create burning and stinging sensations on mucous membranes and can lead to kidney stones.

POLYPEPTIDES These protein building blocks can be deadly in amanita mushrooms. They include toxins like amatoxin and phallotoxin—fatal poisons that can destroy the liver and kidneys.

IT COULD HAPPEN
135 MUSHROOM MADNESS
MY FAMILY WAS CAMPING IN A REMOTE WILDERNESS AREA . . .
AND BEFORE I KNEW IT, HE HAD A MYSTERIOUS MUSHROOM IN HIS HAND.
I JUMPED INTO ACTION!
WE WATCHED HIM CAREFULLY FOR SIGNS OF ILLNESS.
TO BE SURE, WE DECIDED TO FIGURE OUT FOR CERTAIN WHAT KIND OF MUSHROOM THIS WAS.

I GUESS I LET LITTLE HENRY WANDER OFF . . .
BUT WHO KNOWS IF THAT WAS THE FIRST ONE HE FOUND . . .
ONE SUCCESSFUL SPORE PRINT LATER, WE COULD ALL GET BACK TO RELAXING!

136 GO NUTS FOR ACORNS

Want a food that's high in protein, fat, and carbohydrates? Look no farther than your nearest oak tree. That's right, acorns are a wild-food powerhouse that can be found all across the Northern Hemisphere. Ancient peoples used these hardy nuts as a staple food.

Acorns vary in size and appearance and may even resemble other tree nuts; check for a solid nutmeat surrounded by a thin shell. This shell grows inside a cap, which may or may not remain intact. The caps can be flat, with the majority of the nut sticking out of them, or may surround most of the nut.

All acorns are technically edible, but some contain bitter tannic acid, which needs to be leached away (see item 138). Tannic acid does provide some useful medicinal benefits when used topically or as a mouthwash, but consuming it can lead to illness. Bitterness can vary from nut to nut and tree to tree, and according to different habitats and species.

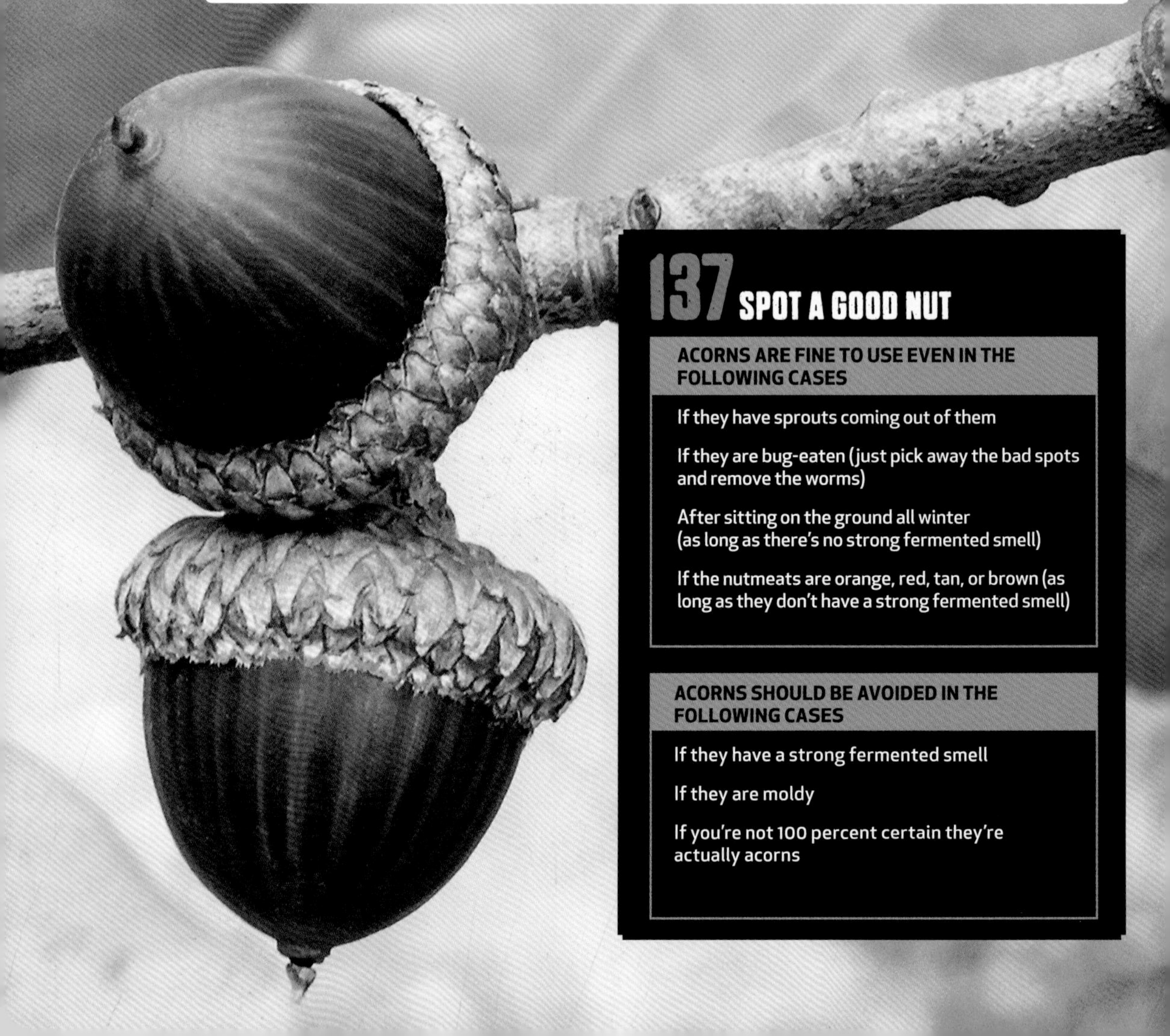

137 SPOT A GOOD NUT

ACORNS ARE FINE TO USE EVEN IN THE FOLLOWING CASES

If they have sprouts coming out of them

If they are bug-eaten (just pick away the bad spots and remove the worms)

After sitting on the ground all winter (as long as there's no strong fermented smell)

If the nutmeats are orange, red, tan, or brown (as long as they don't have a strong fermented smell)

ACORNS SHOULD BE AVOIDED IN THE FOLLOWING CASES

If they have a strong fermented smell

If they are moldy

If you're not 100 percent certain they're actually acorns

138 PROCESS YOUR ACORN BOUNTY

To make acorn flour, first you're going to want to leach out the bitterness. Some people like to boil them, but I find that really doesn't get all the tannic acid flavor out. Also, boiling can destroy some beneficial starches. Instead, I recommend leaching the nuts in baths of warm and cold water.

COLLECT Gather the acorns by hand or using tools to rake or shovel them (A). In short grass, they can be scooped with a "bedding fork," which is like a pitchfork with two dozen tines. Or lay out tarps under an oak, shake the branches (or just wait a few days), and collect the fallen soldiers.

PREP Remove any attached caps immediately (in case of worms), crack the nut's thin shell, and remove the nutmeat (B). You can now leach, dry, or freeze the nut. You can also roast them inside their shells to make tough nuts easier to crack—or just for a new flavor.

LEACH Taste-test by chewing a small piece. If it's not too bitter, you probably have a white oak acorn, which can be ground into flour once it dries. If it's bitter, soak the nutmeats in alternating warm and cold water (C). Every hour or so, test to see if they're still bitter. If so, change the water and keep soaking. You can also submerge them in a bag or basket in a stream, but in this case you'll need to cook the acorn meat before tasting. This may take hours or even days depending on the tannic acid content.

GRIND Dry the nutmeat until you are able to grind it without forming a paste (D). The resulting flour or meal can be used immediately, frozen for future use, or thoroughly dried and stored in an air-permeable cloth bag or wood vessel in a very dry location. If you store it, inspect it weekly for mold or bugs—and know that freezing is the best storage method for acorn flour.

139 CASE STUDY: HUGH GLASS

If you've ever doubted that the American frontier was a rough place, then a story like this one—in which trapper, scout, and all-around mountain man Hugh Glass survived on wild plants after a bear attack—should set you straight. His month-and-a-half-long nightmare started when he woke up after being left for dead by fellow trappers—and then things somehow got even worse.

WHO HUGH GLASS

WHAT LEFT FOR DEAD AFTER A BEAR ATTACK

WHERE MISSOURI TERRITORY

WHEN 1823

HOW LONG HE SURVIVED SIX WEEKS

HIS STORY Hugh Glass was a mountain man on a fur-trapping expedition in August 1823. The expedition planned to proceed up the valley of the Grand River in present-day South Dakota, but when Glass accidentally surprised a mother grizzly bear with her two cubs, he was massively injured. He managed to kill the bear with help from his trapping partners, John Fitzgerald and Jim Bridger, but was left badly mauled and unconscious. The expedition leader, Andrew Henry, was convinced that Glass would not survive his injuries.

Henry asked for two volunteers to stay with Glass until he died, and then bury him. Bridger (then 19 years old) and Fitzgerald stepped forward and began digging his grave, but instead of waiting, they left him alive and later incorrectly reported to Henry that Glass had died.

HOW HE DID IT Glass regained consciousness with a broken leg, cuts on his back exposing bare ribs, all his wounds festering, and abandoned without weapons or equipment. He was more than 200 miles (320 km) from the nearest settlement, at Fort Kiowa on the Missouri. He set his own broken leg, wrapped himself in the bear hide his companions had placed over him as a shroud, and began crawling. To prevent gangrene, Glass lay down with his wounded back on a rotting log and let maggots eat the dead flesh. Glass survived mostly on wild berries and roots. It took him six weeks to reach the Cheyenne River. He then fashioned a crude raft and navigated by referencing the prominent Thunder Butte landmark. Aided by friendly Native Americans who sewed a bear hide to his back to cover the exposed wounds, Glass eventually reached the safety of Fort Kiowa. After a long recuperation, Glass set out to track down and avenge himself against Bridger and Fitzgerald. When he found Bridger, on the Yellowstone near the mouth of the Bighorn River, Glass spared him, purportedly because of Bridger's youth. When he found Fitzgerald, he had joined the United States Army, so Glass restrained himself—killing a U.S. soldier was punishable by death. He did, however, recover his "borrowed" rifle.

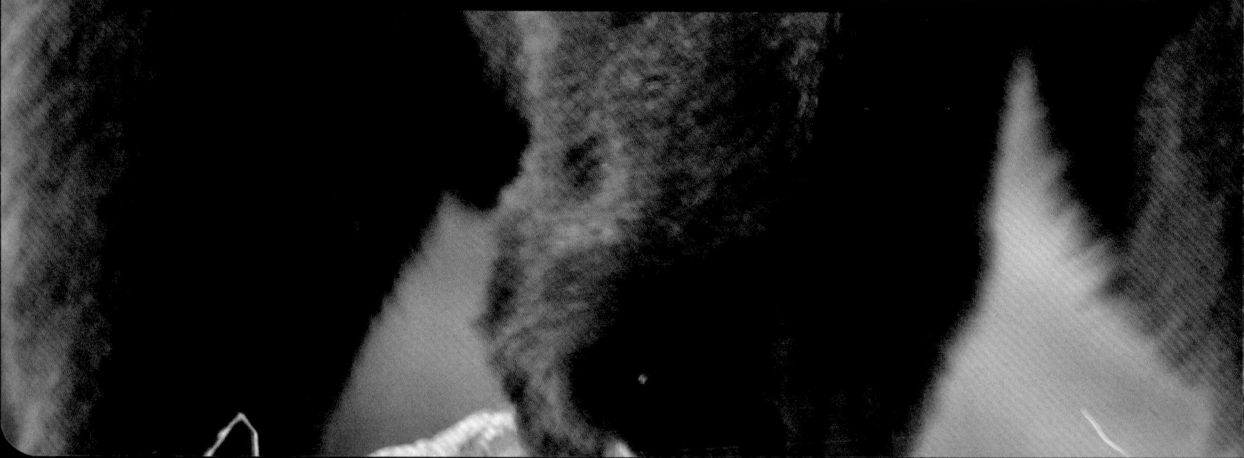

COULD YOU DO IT?

How in the world could you survive being critically wounded, bereft of equipment, and left for dead in the wilderness? It sounds like a recipe for certain death, and yet Glass managed to beat these unbelievable odds. Not only did he shelter himself, collect food, and do his best to nurse his wounds, he also had to stay vigilant for unfriendly locals, who might not have welcomed a trespasser on their lands. Here's how you might be able to pull off this feat of extreme survival.

SHELTER With the bear-hide death shroud, you might be able to stay warm at night without too much work, though it's not much of a shelter if the weather turns foul.

WATER Before European cattle brought giardia and other pathogens to frontier waterways, the creeks and streams provided cleaner water. Today, under the circumstances of Hugh Glass's story, your best bet would be to locate the springs that fed the local watercourses. Drinking directly from springs is the best way to get safe water without equipment or fire.

FOOD You can survive off roots and berries—for a while, anyway. In the late summer in the American frontier, you can find paw-paw fruit, Jerusalem artichoke tubers, wild cherries, Indian currants, and many other wild edible plants.

MOTIVATION Apparently, revenge is a powerful motivational tool. It kept Glass going, despite massive, infected wounds and a lack of survival gear. Considering the circumstances, the two men who were the focus of that revenge were extremely lucky to have been spared.

140 DINE OUT IN THE CONCRETE JUNGLE

Eat the weeds from city sidewalks? Sure, why not? Urban foraging has grown over the past few years, from a few folks doing plant walks in city parks to a career path for urban harvesters who sell to fancy restaurants. In fact, every city I've ever visited boasted an amazing array of wild edibles. Tough weeds spring up through the cracks in the sidewalk and in green spaces throughout every modern metropolis. As long as you exercise a little reasonable caution, you can treat yourself to a fancy meal made of city weeds.

Concrete and asphalt aren't all that harmful to have around your wild edible plants, but the things that go along with these hard surfaces can be a problem. Pollution is rampant in cities; cars release everything from vehicle exhaust to motor oil and antifreeze—none of which are good for plants or people. Cities that contain industrial activity can be even worse, with factories and refineries belching out filth to rain down on the locals. To avoid the heavy metals and pollutants of the city, watch out for the following.

URBAN HAZARDS

Sites near industrial areas

Ditches and waterways

Downhill and drainage areas of parking lots

Swampy areas downhill from the city or inside the city

Vacant lots or areas with signs of dumping activity

141 PARK IT

The idea of picking edibles at the park may not get your mouth watering, especially when you think about the reason dog owners take their walks there. But once you get off the manicured grass, you'll find wild edibles in abundance—I see them on the edges of every park I visit.

If you're worried about pet droppings or potential pesticides, just wash your harvest as soon as you get home. For even more insurance against pollution, wash the plants and then cook them. I guarantee that there are fewer pesticides and chemicals on your foraged greens than on the conventionally grown batch at the grocery store.

142 CRUISE THE STREETS

Wild fruit and nut trees are surprisingly common in residential areas. City planners love the idea of stately oaks—later, those oaks yield a bounty of acorns to local urbanites. Wild cherries and wild grapes often grow up along fences and walls thanks to the birds that perch there and deposit the seeds. A friend of mine makes unparalleled meals and beverages from edibles that he collects entirely within his residential section of Baltimore, Maryland. His wild cherries soaked in brandy are particularly delicious. Grab a friend and a collecting bag, and take a walk—you never know what you'll find.

143 MEET TEN WILD WORLD TRAVELERS

It's always good to run into a familiar face when you're far from home. It might be even better to run into a familiar root or flower. Many edible plants occur in the wild all over the globe. Some were carried to new continents because of their valuable edible and medicinal properties, while others may have inadvertently tagged along with travelers, setting up populations as weeds in new lands. However the plants may have spread, familiar edibles can be found all over. Don't be surprised if you start seeing these ten edible plants no matter where you're traveling.

DANDELION
Taraxacum officinale
Native to Europe, the dandelion's flowers, leaves, and roots are all edible. (See item 113.)

SPEARMINT
Mentha spicata
Native to Europe, spearmint leaves are edible and medicinal.

BURDOCK
Arctium minus
Native to Asia, burdock has large, edible roots and leaves. (See item 125.)

PURSLANE
Portulaca oleracea
Native to Asia, purslane makes a tasty salad green and pickle. (See item 125.)

PLANTAIN
Plantago major
Native to Europe, plantain has edible leaves that also have medicinal properties. (See item 120.)

CATNIP
Nepeta cataria
Native to Eurasia, catnip is a strong mint that can be used for tea and in medicines.

CHICORY
Cichorium intybus
Native to Europe, chicory leaves make a great salad and the roots can be used for coffee. (See item 126.)

WATERCRESS
Nasturtium officinale
Native to Europe, watercress leaves and stems make for a delicious salad. (See item 120.)

YARROW
Achillea millefolium
Native to Europe, yarrow leaves can be used to make a tea and several medicines. (See item 182.)

WILD CARROT
Daucus carota
Native to Europe, this wild edible root is the origin of today's carrot. (See item 126.)

LIVING WILD

To truly live wild, you'll have to combine all of your food-gathering skills and survival techniques and then take them to the next level. Becoming self-reliant requires the same diverse and colorful patchwork of skills that many of our ancestors possessed. Think of this chapter as a living history lesson focused on the value of adaptability.

Like all smart survival strategies, living wild starts off with preparation. Getting lost in the woods is no joke—but whether you're trying to survive three days or indefinitely, whether you're adding some wild greens to your balcony or completely getting back to the land, you need to know what it's going to take.

You can use the information in this chapter to stock a survival pantry, become a gourmet camp cook and fire expert, grow a survival garden to feed your family, preserve your goods for the long haul, and learn to make wild medicines with the natural plants growing all around you. In a survival situation, your fire-building and camping kit will help get you out alive—but to me, these skills go deeper: They're about quality of life.

I can't imagine letting February go by without making maple syrup or going without my favorite homemade medicine any time of year. These skills have changed my life—and my way of thinking—for the better, and I hope they do the same for you.

144 SURVIVE THREE DAYS IN THE WILD

Could you make it on your own in the woods for three days? With the wild-food knowledge you've gained so far, you're well on your way. But there's more to surviving than just staying fed. Here's what else to consider:

Make sure you understand the survival priorities: shelter, water, fire, and food. You also need to know how to find your way back to civilization—or signal for help if you're unable to move. You'll need to maintain your morale, take care of any injuries, and stay safe from harm.

No matter how your wilderness trial (or adventure) unfolds, you will need the skills to turn nothing into something. Follow the priorities of survival as we work our way through an outdoor excursion gone wrong.

START WITH AN ADVANTAGE

A survival kit should be part of your gear no matter what you're doing outside. This kit can give you the items to provide for your basic needs, and it may even give you the tools (like signaling gear) to get out of your predicament on the first day. Pack the following items in a kit and keep it close.

- ☐ A space blanket and a large garbage bag, for shelter and catching rain
- ☐ A metal cup or bowl to boil water for disinfection
- ☐ A compass to help you find your way and guide you in a straight line
- ☐ Multiple fire starters: a lighter, waterproof matches, and a ferrocerium rod are good choices
- ☐ Signal gear: a whistle, for an audible signal day or night; a mirror for a visual signal on sunny days
- ☐ First-aid gear: a small medical pack can be very handy
- ☐ A fishing kit: monofilament and hooks, to provide food and help pass the time

GET SHELTER

Your top survival priority the instant you realize you're lost is shelter. Use the space blanket from your survival kit to stay warm or turn the trash bag into a sleeping bag by filling it with leaves. Build a small (barely bigger than your body), insulated "nest" from materials like sticks, grass, and leaves. If your clothes are inadequate, stuff them with leaves, grasses, or any other material that can trap your body heat.

FIND A DRINK

You'll need to source some water on the first day, too. Lay a trash bag in a hole to catch water from precipitation and look for natural springs—a common way to get reasonably safe drinking water without any tools or materials. Don't drink any water without disinfecting it—use your kit's metal container to boil it, or look for bottles and cans that can be used as boiling vessels.

START A FIRE

By the end of the first day, that fire-starting gear in your survival kit will be worth its weight in gold. But many fire-starting methods can be inadequate in wet or windy weather, so be sure your kit is stocked with some tinder or fuel. Cotton balls, dryer lint, curls of birch bark, and even greasy snacks can help build the flame. Fire is also a great way to signal for help.

SCROUNGE A MEAL

You'll spend most of the second and third days looking for food—when you're not signaling for help. If you're unsure about the edible plants, stick to animal foods. Freshwater fish, worms, crickets, and other critters are safe to eat—just cook them thoroughly, in case they have parasites or pathogens. Stay strong and focus on calorie-dense foods like fatty animals, tree nuts, and organ meats.

KEEP IT POSITIVE

A positive attitude and a generous streak of mental toughness can be literal lifesavers, especially under dire circumstances. The nights are usually the worst time during emergencies: It's just you and your thoughts. Find little ways to maintain your morale and remain motivated to survive. Think of family, friends, and loved ones, and fight to stay alive—not just for yourself but for them.

SIGNAL FOR HELP

The skill of signaling is your ticket home. The whistle from your survival kit can signal your distress to others, day or night, as long as you have breath to blow it, and a mirror can give you a signal range much farther than the sound of the whistle can carry. Don't forget about the power of a smoky fire, either.

STAY SAFE

You may face dangers in the wilderness, so arm yourself for survival as best you can. Carry a spear, club, knife, or whatever you can find, in case you need to defend yourself. Consider all of the sources of harm that could befall you, and make plans to avoid becoming one of their victims.

145 FOLLOW THE SIGNS

Water is one of your top survival priorities, but where to find it? Start by walking downhill, looking for natural drainages where water will flow. You can also use vegetation as an indicator, looking for reeds, cattails, sedges, and other aquatic vegetation. Listen, too, for aquatic animals like water birds and bullfrogs, and observe where the big animals are going to quench their thirst. Remember that rain, snow, sleet, hail, and dew can all be potential water sources. Always melt any frozen water source before drinking, and treat it as if it could be contaminated.

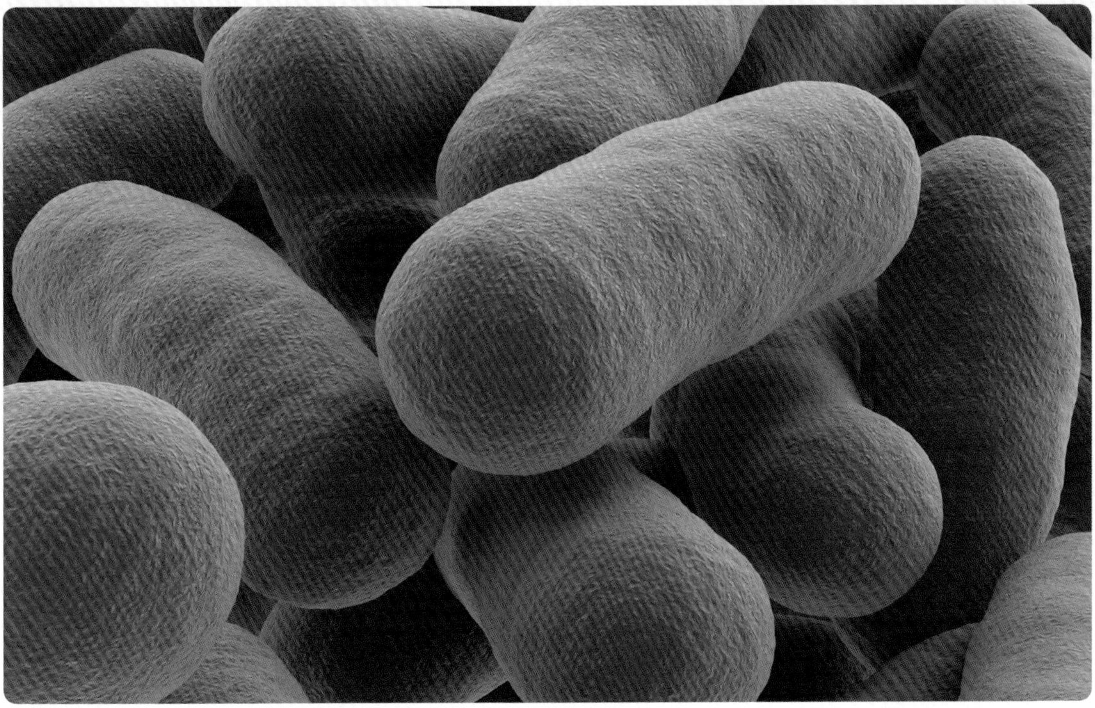

146 KILL THE VARMINTS

You can disinfect your drinking water safely and effectively with common household chemicals. Just be aware that this type of chemical disinfection doesn't remove salt, toxins, or radiation—it just kills the living pathogens that could make you sick. Here are some simple and effective methods for doing this.

CHLORINE BLEACH Add 2–4 drops of ordinary chlorine bleach per quart (1 l) of water. Use 2 drops if the water is warm and clear. Go to 4 drops if it is very cold or murky. Put the bottle lid back on, and shake the container. Then turn the bottle upside down and unscrew the cap a turn or two. Let a small amount of water flow out to clean the bottle threads and cap. Screw the lid back on tight, and wipe the exterior of the bottle to disinfect all surfaces. Let it sit for an hour in a dark place before drinking.

TINCTURE OF IODINE Use 5–10 drops of tincture of iodine 2% per quart (1 l) of water. Flush the threads, wipe down the bottle, and allow it to sit in the shade for one hour. Use 5 drops tincture of iodine for clear warm water and up to 10 drops for cold or cloudy water.

POVIDONE IODINE You'll need 8–16 drops per quart (1 l) of water with povidone iodine. Add 8 drops for pleasant-looking water and 16 drops for swamp water. Clean the bottle threads and then wait an hour, as you would with the other methods.

147 USE A QUALITY FILTER

One of the best investments in survival and outdoor gear is a top-of-the-line water filter. There are many great ones on the market that have a filter element to screen out larger organisms and a disinfecting element to kill smaller biologicals that could try to weasel their way through the filter. Pick a model that can be cleaned in the field, offers a long life and high-filtering capacity (thousands of liters, not hundreds), and has received rave reviews.

148 BUILD A WATER STILL

The most complete disinfection solution is water distillation. When water is heated into steam, the steam can then be captured to create pure water. Distillation won't remove all possible contaminants, like volatile oils and certain organic compounds, but most heavy particles will stay behind—including radioactive fallout. A quick way to make a steam distiller is by using a pressure canner and some small-diameter copper tubing.

SET IT UP Locate a canner and about 4 feet (1.2 m) of 1/4-inch (6-mm) copper line. Set your canner pot on your stove top, over a camping stove, or over an improvised cinder block fireplace. Fill your canner pot two-thirds full with the questionable water (salt water, muddy water, virtually any water except any tainted by fuels, which evaporate at low temperatures). Screw on the canner lid.

ADD THE COIL Make the coil, also known as the worm, from copper line coiled in a downward spiral. Use a stick or some other support for the coil to avoid stress on the joint at the canner's steam vent. Ream out one end of the copper tubing and force it down over the steam fitting on top of the canner lid if it's smaller than the steam vent. Compress the line if it is bigger than the vent. Tie this joint with rags or dope it with a paste of flour and water once everything is in position.

BURN THE FLAME Whether a stove or a campfire powers your still, you'll have to play with the size of the fire for best results. If you run it too hot, you'll just blow steam out the coil. If you run it too cool, nothing will happen. Start out with a small amount of heat and work up if needed. Once the pot gets close to boiling, water should start to pour out of the coil. The surrounding air will cool the copper, and the steam will condense into distilled, drinkable water.

149 FIRE IT UP

Boiling your water kills 100 percent of unwelcome living organisms—it's not fancy, but it works. Make sure you have a heat-safe receptacle; place glass bottles on the edge of the fire to avoid breakage, and never use galvanized metal. Let it boil for ten full minutes, starting your count when the first big bubbles jump to the water's surface.

150 LIGHT YOUR FIRE

Fire is one of the most versatile forces that humans have ever harnessed and a vital part of survival. Don't forget to learn the old-school skills of fire building; you may not always have a lighter on hand, and you may need your flame to last. Study how to make fire in the worst weather, harsh conditions, and with unusual materials so you don't get caught in the cold.

151 SELECT THE RIGHT TINDER

Your first step in fire building is finding natural tinder—the dead, dry, plant-based materials that can turn a coal, spark, or small flame into fire. Tinder and an ignition source are the foundations of fire making, and all of the tinder used should have several things in common.

DEAD Tinder should be dead but not rotten plant-based materials. Rotten plants usually lose much of their fuel value as they decompose, and though there are always exceptions, you should concentrate on the dead stuff.

DRY It should be as dry as possible. In rainy weather this may mean finding a few scraps at a time, even one leaf at a time, and keeping that tinder dry while you search for more.

FLUFFY It should be light, airy, and have a lot of surface area for its mass. In other words, it needs to be fluffy. Materials that are not fluffy should be processed in some way to increase their surface area so they can reach their combustion temperature as quickly as possible.

152 KNOW YOUR SOURCES

The following are just a few of the many sources of tinder that you can find in the outdoors. Use them individually or blend them together for even better results.

TINDER MATERIALS

- ☐ Grasses
- ☐ Ferns
- ☐ Evergreen needles
- ☐ Tree leaves
- ☐ Fibrous inner tree bark
- ☐ Weed tops and seed down
- ☐ Fine wood shavings
- ☐ Coconut and palm fiber

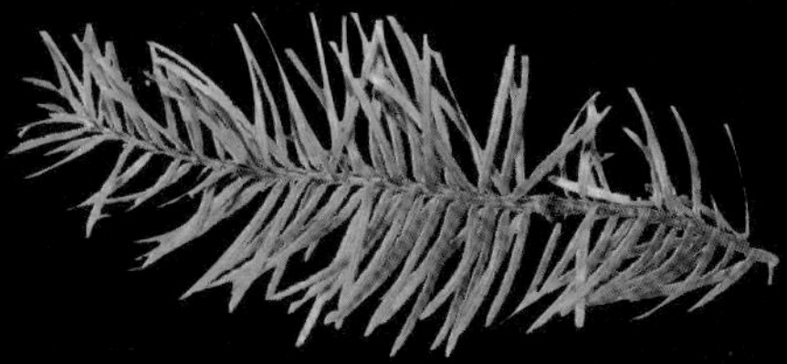

153 STOCK UP ON KINDLING

Kindling, obtained from dead twigs and vines, wood splinters, and bark, feeds the flames sparked with tinder and provides the heat to burn firewood. Here's what to keep in mind.

DRYNESS Like tinder, kindling should be as dry as possible.

VARIETY Collect plenty of different sizes—everything from the bits that look like pieces of wire to the twigs and branches that could almost be considered firewood.

VOLUME It is very important to pack the kindling pieces tightly together. Most dry-weather fire-making failures are due to failing in this regard, so gather a lot.

154 BUILD A TEEPEE

The teepee shape is a perfect architectural style for setting up your fire. It can be set up one stick at a time (laborious) or formed into a cone as you collect the materials (easier!).

Place a slab of dead bark on the ground if conditions are really wet; otherwise, just use a good foundation of tinder to buffer your fire from dampness and cold. Use a lot more kindling than you think necessary, and remember that a good length for the slender pieces is around 10 inches (25 cm).

Light the teepee on the side that any breeze is coming from, to feed air in and drive the fire into the fuel. Light the tinder with whatever fire-starting method you have available, and the rest will soon be aflame.

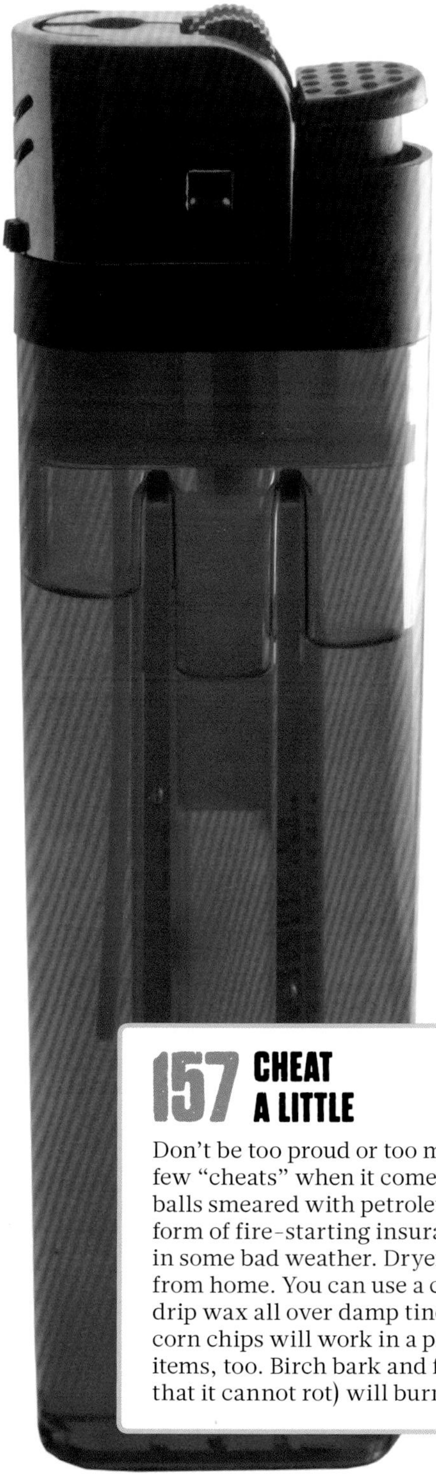

155 FEEL THE SPARK

There are dozens of methods you can use to spark your fire, but as in so many things in life, the tried-and-true ways are the best.

A butane lighter is generally your best bet, as it will ignite any flammable materials. Matches aren't bad, either, though you only get a few dozen in a box and they are vulnerable to moisture. Ferrocerium rods (spark rods) are a durable choice, but they won't light all materials equally easily.

You can also learn and practice friction fire building skills, though these can be very tricky in wet weather or if you're injured.

My top recommendation is to carry several butane lighters. That way, you'll be prepared even if you lose one—or two.

156 PICK THE RIGHT SPOT

Choosing a location for your fire is a very important fire skill, not only to make the most of the fire's heat and light but also for safety. Pick a spot that is at least 14 feet (4 m) away from your shelter, and make sure it is downwind, as drifting sparks can create a hazard. Try to set up in a place out of the wind, while avoiding the natural fire hazards of dried grasses and brush. Don't build fires next to rotten stumps or dead trees, either—the rotten wood or roots can smolder for a long time, starting a forest fire days later.

157 CHEAT A LITTLE

Don't be too proud or too much of a purist to accept a few "cheats" when it comes to fire building. Cotton balls smeared with petroleum jelly are an excellent form of fire-starting insurance, should you get caught in some bad weather. Dryer lint is another helpful item from home. You can use a candle nub to light a fire, or drip wax all over damp tinder to give it a boost. Even corn chips will work in a pinch. Nature has some helpful items, too. Birch bark and fatwood (pine so full of pitch that it cannot rot) will burn even when soaking wet.

159 SET UP A GRIDDLE

Who wouldn't want to wake up to the aroma of bacon cooking? You can achieve this heavenly morning ritual even in the great outdoors—just fashion a griddle.

Start with a flat stone that will work for frying. It should be able to handle high heat and not be too gritty or rough, as the food will stick to it.

Prop the griddle on a stand of rocks or have it straddle a trench in the dirt with the fire underneath. Maintain a coal bed by feeding it plenty of twigs and sticks. You can cook virtually anything to perfection—meat, vegetables, fry bread, etc. Just remember a few of these pointers.

GRIDDLE TIPS

Maintain constant flames beneath your cooking surface for even heating.

Find a rock with a slight depression in the surface—it will hold oil for frying.

Test unfamiliar rocks by placing one in a large fire and moving far away. If it pops or crumbles, find a new type.

Never collect rocks from a wet location, as trapped steam can make them explode when heated.

When finished cooking, let the griddle slowly cool down on its own. Don't try to wash it until it's cold.

158 COOK LIKE A CHAMP IN CAMP

Even if you're not a pro chef at home, you can cook some phenomenal meals out in the woods. Some of the best food I have ever eaten has been prepared simply and cooked over an open fire—by far the fastest and most direct way to cook solid foods.

Just stick your meal-to-be onto spits or skewers. Metal ones can be reused again and again, or you can make them from green living wood for a single use—just make sure your skewers are from a nontoxic species.

Using live wood for skewers is a very handy trick, as the moisture-filled sticks resist burning. This method can be used on a small scale, like roasting a marshmallow on the end of a stick, or you can fashion a spit that will help roast an entire animal. If you decide to cook something on the big side (say, chicken-size or larger), make a spit that has a side spike or prong of some kind. When the roast, bird, or carcass is impaled on the spit, this prong will stabilize the food as the spit turns.

160 BUILD A STONE OVEN

A stone oven is great for meats, vegetables, and baked goods and can be used repeatedly by simply rebuilding the fire. Just about any tight pile of durable rocks with a hole in the middle can work—the fire's heat builds up in the stones and then radiates out. There are two types of stone ovens: internally fired, which is made of very large stones around a fire; and externally fired, which involves maintaining a fire all the way around and on top of an oven made of thinner slabs. I have made crispy pizza with an externally fired oven, and I've made juicy roasts and desserts with an internally fired oven.

STEP 1 Collect rocks that can handle high heat (the rougher, the better). Look for an existing flat stone in the ground for an internally fired oven base, or place one in a good location.

STEP 2 Build three stone walls and fill in the gaps with clay, if you can.

STEP 3 Form the top using one or several large, wide rocks and caulk with clay. If the oven is internally fired, it's best to leave an opening near the top to act as a chimney during firing.

STEP 4 Select a large, flat rock to be your door, which should cover the oven opening and be located opposite the chimney hole.

Once built, the oven can be fired right away. For an internally fired oven, burn your fire for 1½ to 2 hours, sweep out the ash and coals, place the food inside, shut the door, and seal the chimney as tightly as possible.

If you've built an externally fired oven, you can place the food inside before or during the firing. Tightly seal the door and cover the oven with coals and fire. The food will need to be turned to cook the bottom, unless you placed it on a hot flat stone inside the oven or built an elevated oven with a fire underneath (like building a stone oven on top of a stone griddle).

IT COULD HAPPEN
161 A ROCKING DINNER
ON A CAMPING TRIP WITH MY GIRLFRIEND, I DECIDED TO SHOW OFF MY CAMP-COOKING SKILLS BY BUILDING A STONE OVEN.
EVERYTHING WAS GOING FINE, UNTIL . . .
BRAM
LUCKILY, WE ALL AVOIDED INJURY, AND THERE WERE SOME GRANITE HUNKS NEARBY.

I GATHERED A BUNCH OF NICE, SMOOTH ROCKS . . .
SET THEM UP . . .
AND LIT THE FIRE.
TURNS OUT, SMOOTH ROCKS PROBABLY COME FROM WATERWAYS AND WATER IN THE ROCKS . . .
WELL, WE LEARNED WHAT HAPPENS THEN.
OUR NEXT OVEN TURNED OUT MUCH BETTER.

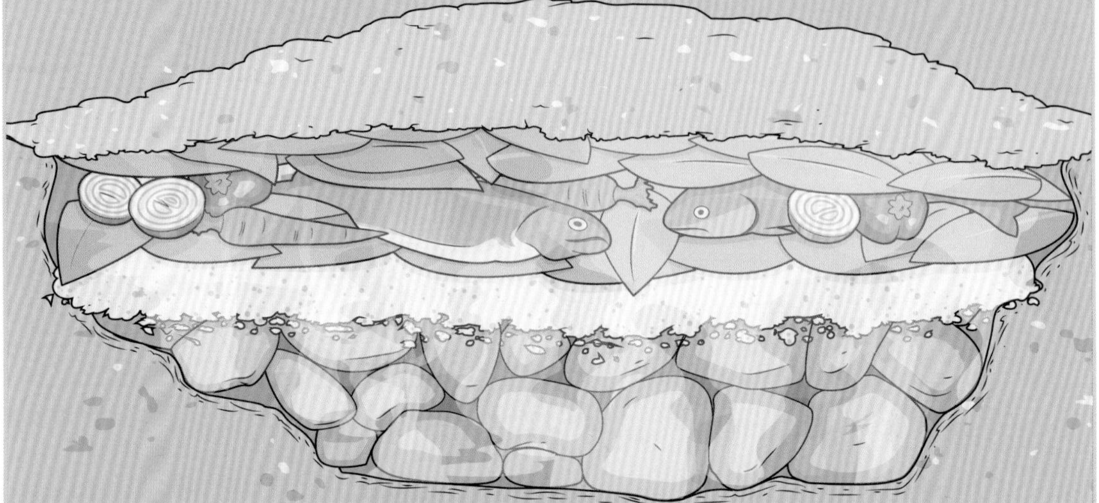

162 MAKE A STEAM PIT

This elaborate cooking method is worth the trouble because it makes great-tasting food that stays hot for hours. The steam pit is a hole in the ground (or a raised mound) with hot rocks at the bottom covered with dirt or sand. You then sandwich-wrap food between two layers of green vegetation and cover with dirt and/or tarps to seal in the steam. This technique is used all over the globe, often for feasts and special occasions.

STEP 1 Start by digging a pit in the soil or collecting loose soil and sand for a mound. The pit can be any depth, width, or shape, and it can be dug in dirt, clay, or sand.

STEP 2 Collect a pile of rocks that are capable of handling a lot of heat. Make sure you have enough to fill the bottom of the pit—you can even place them in there like a puzzle to see where the stones fit best.

STEP 3 You now have a choice of leaving the stones in the pit and building the fire on top of them, or taking the rocks out of the pit and placing them in a big fire. Either way, the stones should be heated for two hours. If you heat the rocks in the pit, you must scoop the remaining wood, charcoal, coals, and ash out of the pit when the rocks are hot enough, to avoid imbuing your food with an unpleasant flavor. If you heat the stones outside the pit, use a shovel or a large greenwood pole to roll or push the rocks into the pit.

STEP 4 Gather your green vegetation during the rock-firing time. Good steam-pit vegetation is green grass, seaweed, pine boughs full of green needles, or any other abundant nontoxic green plant material. To build a steam pit in winter, you'll probably have to go with pine boughs, as your choices will be limited.

STEP 5 Once the pit has nothing but hot rocks in it, apply a small amount of damp soil or sand to insulate the hot stones. Add some green vegetation, and then place your food in a single layer on top. Root vegetables and seafood are great when cooked in this manner. Wrap tender foods with large, edible leaves (like burdock) to prevent them from falling apart.

STEP 6 Bury the food with your remaining vegetation. Cover it with a tarp and/or soil. Come back three or more hours later, dig up your food, and enjoy.

163 COOK IN A DUTCH OVEN

These wide cast-iron pots are the most versatile cooking implements you can buy. Dutch ovens serve as a pot, griddle, and pan all in one. And they can also act like an oven, baking everything from bread to cookies. The only drawbacks may be the weight and the price, as Dutch ovens can be heavy on both counts.

BAKING To bake in the Dutch oven, build up a large bed of coals in a fire. Set the oven into the coals and place coals on top of the lid. Try to follow the average cooking times for the food you are preparing, and replace the coals on top of the lid as they burn down.

BOILING You'll need flames underneath the oven to boil successfully. Hang the attached bail (handle) from a chain or dangle it from a tree. You can also thread a greenwood pole through the bail and support the pole with posts or convenient forks in small trees.

164 CASE STUDY: THE LYKOV FAMILY

How long could you last if you had to live off nature instead of a paycheck? Tough frontiersmen and women of yesteryear lived out their days in the wilderness, where self-sufficiency was not a matter of choice. Could a person today survive indefinitely if he or she were stranded in a remote region? Incredible survival stories abound, but there is one in particular that is a powerful testament to the human capacity to survive in the wild.

WHO THE LYKOV FAMILY

WHAT ESCAPING RELIGIOUS PERSECUTION IN RUSSIA

WHERE THE SIBERIAN WILDERNESS

WHEN 1936

HOW LONG THEY SURVIVED OVER 40 YEARS

THEIR STORY In 1936, a Russian family of four fled into the Siberian wilderness to escape religious persecution. Taking a few homesteading supplies and some seeds, Karp Lykov, his wife, Akulina, their nine-year-old son, and their two-year-old daughter retreated into the forests. They built a succession of primitive huts as they traveled, until reaching a habitable spot near the Mongolian border. The couple had no contact with the outside world and became completely self-sufficient.

They had two more children, born in the wilderness, who had never seen a person outside their family until a geology team found their home in 1978.

HOW THEY DID IT For sustenance, the family of six spent their days hunting, trapping, and farming by saving seeds each year to replant next season. The Lykovs had brought a crude spinning wheel, and they grew hemp to produce the fiber for their clothing. Their staple food was potato patties mixed with hemp seeds and ground rye. They lived this way, deep in the forests, for over 40 years.

The unending issues of nourishment and vulnerability to injury and illness are the main critical factors for indefinite survival. That's assuming you maintain your motivation when things get tough—which they invariably will. The Lykov family survived in no small part due to their devotion to God and to each other. They also grew as much food as the land allowed and rationed it carefully. Each winter, the family would creep close to starvation, but they still held a council meeting to determine whether they should save their seeds to replant or eat them all. Each year, the family made the hard decision to save their seed stock for the next season—even though one winter, it cost the mother her life.

COULD YOU DO IT?

The technical aspects of long-term survival are quite complex. Depending on the place you take up residence, you may require some very specialized tools or techniques to grow, collect, and catch enough food. But first, you've got to survive the short-term.

SHELTER This is your most immediate need in survival scenarios, and over time, your shelter becomes your home. Generally, traditional native cultures of any area devised the best shelter style based on the available building materials, weather, and hazards of the area. Cone-shaped homes (or roofs) have been a global favorite, and angular buildings with angled roofs are also of ancient origin. Find out what native people did for shelter in your area, and let your resources, tools, and building skills lead the way.

WATER Staying safely hydrated is both a short- and long-term survival priority. The Lykov family was fortunate to find abundant springs and clean water in the Siberian wilderness, but not all homesteaders are so lucky. Without fresh water, boiling is your best bet—and even if you don't have a fire-safe container, you can heat rocks and use them to boil water in a wooden or bark bowl.

FIRE What happens when you run out of matches? You'll either have to keep your fire burning constantly (which was done in the past), or you'll need long-lasting or replaceable fire-starting gear. Flint and steel kits contain one part that lasts a long time (the high carbon steel striker can last for decades), and the remaining parts (like flint and char) are replaceable. Friction fire is another fire-building technique that can keep you surviving over the long haul.

FOOD Food will play a critical role in a survival scenario of any length. The Lykov's farmed and foraged for their staples, and wherever you go, you can look to the native peoples for guidance on the best local wild foods and ways to live off those resources.

ATTITUDE The Lykov family had each other and their faith to provide mental and emotional support during their struggle to survive day-to-day. But what would happen if you were alone, struggling against crushing loneliness and isolation? Should you find yourself in this situation, try treating animals like pets so you have something to communicate with. Faith in a higher power can also sustain you. To make it through each day, you'll need something bigger than yourself, something worth fighting for, and something more important than mere survival.

165 FLAKE A STONE SPEAR

Stone spear points date back millennia, but don't think of them as backward or ineffective just because they're old. A famous test in the 1970s proved that stone-tipped spears could even punch through elephant hide, piercing vital organs (don't worry, the elephant had already died of natural causes prior to the test!).

You can use traditional methods to create a stone spearhead or a shorter-handled stone knife. All you need is a high quality stone piece that is larger than your intended project, and the tools for stone working—plus some practice and patience. Here's the technique for using direct percussion to create the rough shape of your blade, then finishing it off by pressure flaking with a pointed tool.

STEP 1 Select a piece of flinty rock about the size of a sandwich. This will be the rock you're breaking into a point. Select another rock that's round, rough, and a little bigger than a large egg to serve as your hammer. With a wax pencil or marker, draw a line around the circumference of the first rock (imagine a line where you'd cut a bagel). This is known as the midline and it will indicate the center mass of the rock.

STEP 2 Wearing gloves and goggles, hit the thinnest edge of the "sandwich" rock with your hammer stone. Hit just slightly above the midline and right on the edge. Follow through with the strike, like driving in a nail with a hammer. If you picked a good stone for your spearhead and you hit it hard, you should knock a flake of stone from the underside of the rock.

STEP 3 Work your way completely around the stone, striking flakes to create a sharp edge. Alternate the sides of the rock you are striking.

STEP 4 Once you have removed flakes of stone all the way around, work further down with gentler hammer strikes. Strike in spots that have a pronounced ridge underneath the rock, as the force of your strike will travel along these ridges.

STEP 5 Final shaping is too delicate to perform with jolting percussion strikes, so now it's time to turn to pressure flaking—flaking the edge of the stone with a hard, pointed tool. A traditional choice is a broken deer antler tine; a copper nail driven into the end of a short stick also works. Wear a thick leather glove or pad your palm with pieces of leather, and press hard on the stone edge with your tool to chip it. With a fair bit of practice, you'll be able to remove long flakes and give your stone tool a uniform shape. For arrowheads and spears, chip in notches at the base of the point.

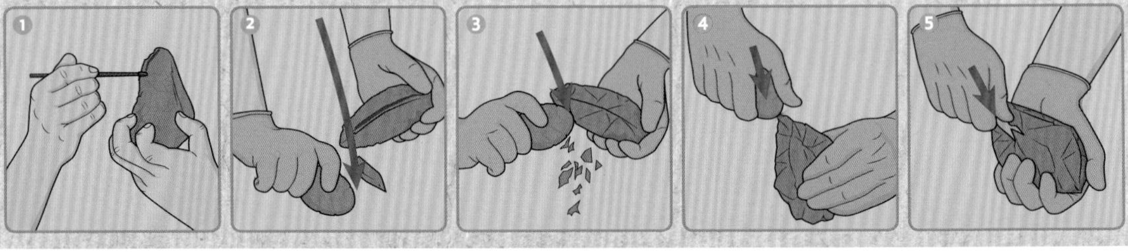

166 ROCK OUT WITH PERCUSSION

If you need some sharp, expedient blades (like for butchering), the easiest way to get them is via a method called bipolar percussion. In this method, you rest the stone you are trying to break on a large stone and strike it hard with a hammer rock. It's like being a blacksmith—the big rock is your anvil, providing unyielding resistance behind the breaking rock.

Stand your breaking rock on its tallest axis—this will allow the shock waves from the hammer stone to move through the rock via its most efficient path. For your hammer, use a large, flat stone that's four to five times larger than the rock you are trying to break. If you're lucky, you'll fracture off some thin, wickedly sharp stone blades within a few strikes.

For any stone tool work, make sure you wear gloves (preferably leather) and glasses or goggles to protect yourself from flying stone chips.

167 TEST YOUR LOCAL STONE

Razor-edged rocks are as close as your local creek, if you're in the right area and know how to break them. Not all rocks produce a good cutting edge when they break, and many have interiors that won't work for your purposes, so test your stones by delivering a quick tap with a hammer stone to break off a piece. This will show you the rock's interior and how it breaks, which is everything you need to know.

You don't need to be a geologist to sort it all out: Flint, chert, jasper, chalcedony, quartz, and obsidian can all break to make sharp cutting tools. Just try out different types of local rock to see what works.

168 KNOW YOUR KNOTS

There is essentially a knot for every outdoor occasion. Whether it be a simple overhand or the more complicated utility knots shown here, knowing basic rope twists in a survival situation can literally save your life. Don't let these knots intimidate you—you'll get the hang of them after a few tries, and because a picture is worth a thousand words, let the illustrations guide you through your practice.

TRUCKER'S HITCH This versatile knot is great for tying down heavy loads for transporting. The combination of knots allows a line to be pulled very tight using the pulley effect of the loop in the middle line. Use it to tie your canoe or kayak to a roof rack or to secure heavy loads in place.

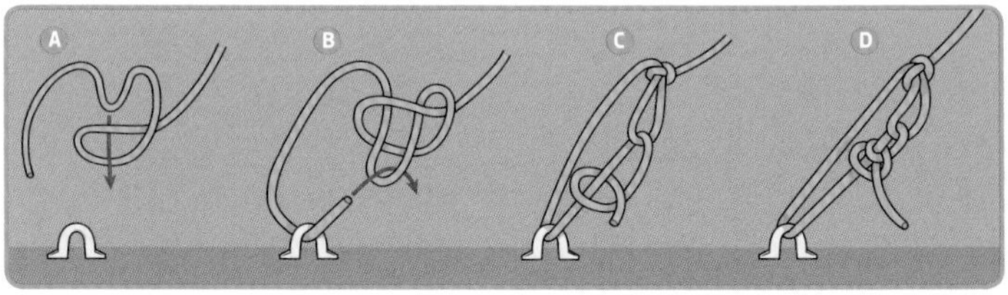

HOW TO TIE Begin by loosely looping your rope as shown (A), leaving the tail end free. Then feed the tail end through your anchor point and then through the loop you made in the first step (B). Next, loop the free end into a half-hitch knot (C). Finally, for extra security, tighten all knot points (D).

HEAVING LINE KNOT There are plenty of times when you might need to throw a rope, and you need a knot that provides enough mass to do the job. A standard heaving line knot doesn't quite add enough weight and mass, but this supercharged version does.

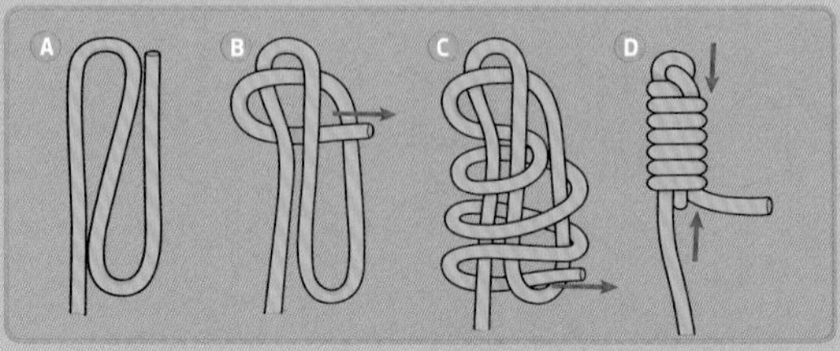

HOW TO TIE Make two bights in the end of the rope (A)—this results in three "rungs" of rope next to one another. Leave plenty of line in the working end for the wraps.

Next, weave the working end under the middle rung and over the bottom rung, then loop it around the back of the knot to bring it between the top and middle rungs (B). Now wrap all three rungs six to nine times (C). On the last wrap, thread the working end through the remaining loop and tighten (D).

CONSTRICTOR KNOT Easy to tie and extremely reliable, the constrictor knot exerts a ratchetlike grip on any curved surface, such as a post, rail, tree, or human appendage. You can use it to close the mouths of gear bags, secure a rod tube to a backpack, or fashion a string leash for your eyeglasses. To hang camp tools, file a rough groove in each tool's handle, tie a constrictor hitch around it, and then knot together the ends of the cord. The only caveat: It is not easily untied. Then again, it won't come undone accidentally, either.

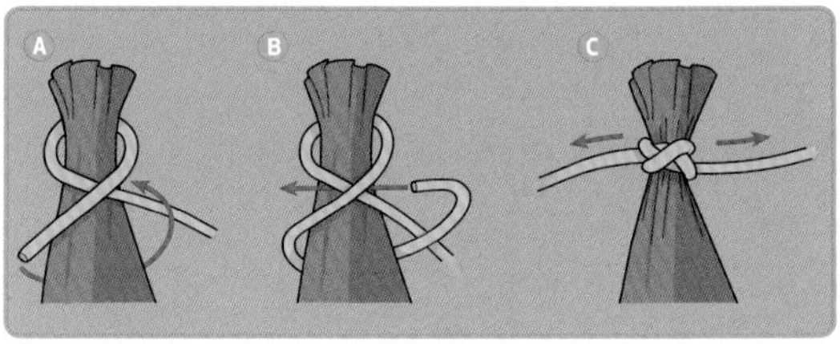

HOW TO TIE Make a simple loop, crossing the working end of the rope over the other (A). Next, circle the working end behind the item you're tying up, then pass it under the standing end and under your "X" (B). Then pull both ends to constrict (C).

BUTTERFLY LOOP Use this loop to hang gear, as a ladder step, or as a canoe bridle to tow a canoe behind a boat.

HOW TO TIE Hang a rope from your hand and coil it twice to form three coils (A). Move the right coil over the middle coil to the left, so that the center coil becomes the right coil, then move this coil to the left over the top of the other two coils (B). Take the coil you just moved to the left and pass it back to the right, under the remaining coils, to form a loop (C). Pinch this loop against your palm, using your thumb to hold it. Slide your hand to the right, pulling this loop (D). Tighten the knot by pulling both ends of the rope (E).

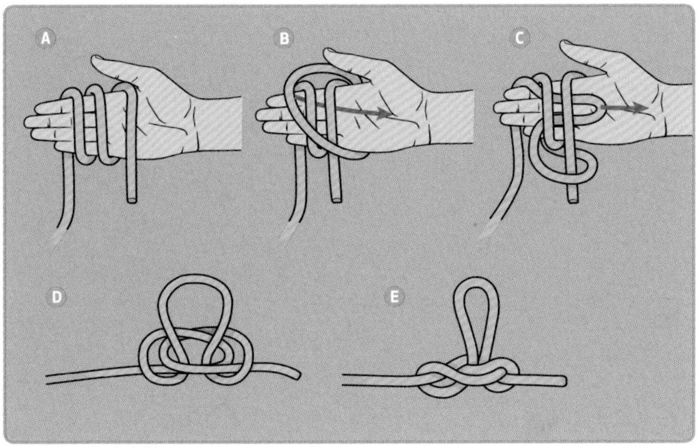

HUNTER'S BEND Unlike most knots, the hunter's bend is relatively new, invented only in the 20th century. It's perfect for joining two ropes, of either equal or dissimilar diameters, which makes it perfect for survival situations when odd scraps of cordage might be all you have at hand. And it's a great knot to use with slick synthetic ropes.

HOW TO TIE Lay the two lines side by side, with tag ends in opposite directions (A). Loop the lines, making sure neither rope twists on top of the other (B). Bring the front working end around behind the loops and up through the center (C). Push the rear working end through the middle of both loops (D). Seat the knot by holding the standing parts firmly and pulling both working ends. Pull the standing parts in opposite directions to set the knot (E).

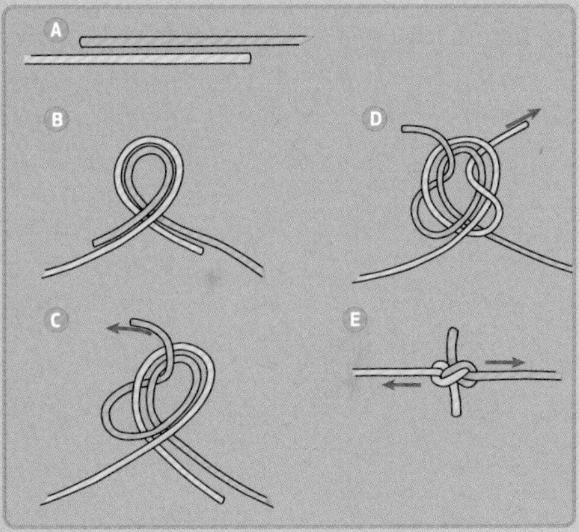

DOUBLE FISHERMAN'S KNOT This useful knot joins two ropes together with a streamlined bend that has just enough bulk to provide a good grip. Often used in climbing and for search and rescue, it's also handy for doing minor repairs on your gear, as you can combine ropes of different widths. If you combine it with old fly lines, for example, you can replace broken zipper pulls or construct sunglass tethers. With 6mm or 7mm rock-climbing cord, it makes awesome grab handles for duffels, canoes, and coolers.

You can triple or quadruple the knot to make it more secure—simply repeat the process and alternate the ropes looped and pulled. As with many of these intricate knots, however, they are nearly impossible to undo.

HOW TO TIE Lay the two ropes down, with tag ends in opposite directions. Tie a double overhand knot with one rope around the second (A).

Pull the tag end of each rope through the knot on the opposite side of the other (B). Using the tag end of the second rope, tie a double overhand knot around the first (C). Tighten until snug (D).

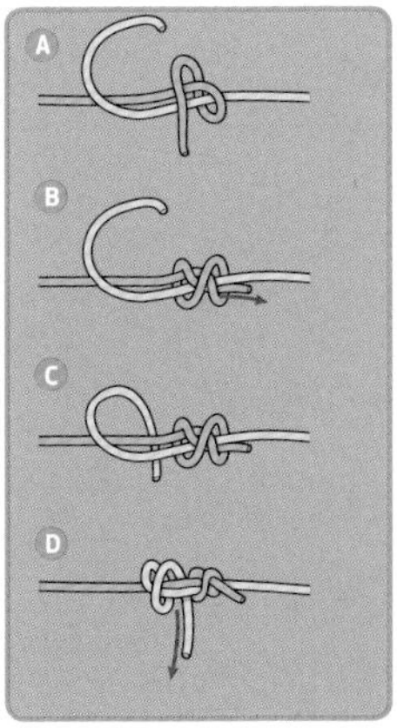

169 EAT YOUR WAY THROUGH THE SEASONS

Some tenacious wild edible plants and hardy animals can be found every single day of the year, but most wild foods, from both the plant and animal kingdoms, have a shorter window of harvesting opportunity.

Spring and fall are usually the busiest times of the year, but every month yields certain seasonal treats and delicious fare. To make the most of this annual bounty, stay vigilant to the changes that each month brings—and keep an eye on your calendar so you don't miss your favorites.

JANUARY

SYRUP Start testing your maple, sycamore, birch, and hickory trees in the middle of the month to catch the beginning of the sap run for syrup.

PINE Shave off some inner pine bark (guilt-free, after ice storms knock down limbs and branches) to dry and grind into flour. Don't worry about the bark spoiling—winter is nature's refrigerator.

FISH Hunting and trapping seasons come to an end. Anybody up for ice fishing?

FEBRUARY

SYRUP Tap your syrup trees, collect the sap, and boil it down. Start brewing maple ale for spring drinking and vinting maple wine for summer and fall.

GREENS Collect early spring greens such as wild onion. Make pine needle tea for your daily dose of vitamin C.

FISH Prepare your fishing tackle; fly fishing season is about to begin.

MARCH

GREENS Spring salad greens start to emerge from winter slumber.

CATTAIL Brave the swamp water to find tender cattail sprouts.

TURKEY The first spring turkey seasons open.

SHEDS You may start noticing shed antlers from deer and elk—keep these spots in mind for the future.

APRIL

FLOWERS Harvest edible flowers such as redbud, dandelion, and violet. Look for knotweed shoots and new tips of greenbrier.

FISH Trout season typically opens April 1.

VEGETABLES Dig for toothwort tubers, spring beauty corms, and ramp bulbs. Boil starchy cattail shoots.

MORELS Keep an eye out for morel mushrooms.

POLLEN Gather pine pollen by shaking the twig tips over a bowl (add to flour for a protein boost).

MAY

FISH Enjoy fishing trips, crabbing, and clam digging as the water warms up. Watch for the shad runs in the rivers of the eastern United States.

GREENS Collect late spring flowers, salads, vegetables, and roots.

CHICORY Find the blue flowers of chicory, and roast the roots into a caffeine-free coffee substitute.

JUNE

FRUITS Watch closely for early berries like blueberry and black raspberry, especially toward the end of the month.

VEGETABLES Find young milkweed pods and boil them in changes of water for a dish similar to peas.

CATTAIL Look for cattail pollen spikes to reach their full height. Cut them off just before they open for a "corn-on-the-cob" vegetable, or let them open and collect the pollen as you would with pine.

JULY

FRUITS Blackberries, red raspberries, and wild cherries come into season.

TEAS Cut and dry the leaves for your year's tea supply. Spicebush, blackberry, mint, yarrow, and wintergreen can make for a good tea collection.

TREES Dry sassafras leaves and grind them into a powder to thicken your soups and stews.

FISH Stay alert to summer salmon and grunion runs of the American west coast.

AUGUST

FRUITS Paw paw fruit ripens about two weeks after the blackberries, red raspberries, and wild cherries are finished.

GRAINS Shake amaranth and lamb's quarters seeds from their heads and grind them into grain.

GAME Start scouting your familiar hunting areas for deer sign.

SEPTEMBER

NUTS Tree nuts begin to drop in late September, heralding the coming of fall. Collect the hickory nuts, beechnuts, and other sweet seeds before the animals get them all. The bitter acorns and thick-husked walnuts can wait a few weeks—they're lower on every creature's list.

GAME Plan your hunts for deer and other big game. Many bow seasons and western big-game seasons open in September.

OCTOBER

GAME BIRDS Upland bird and waterfowl seasons open.

FRUITS Collect ripening berries like spicebush, barberry, and rose before migrating birds eat them.

MUSHROOMS Look for fall mushrooms after rain. The yellow and orange of sulphur shelf is easy to spot against the wet forest logs—until the leaves start to turn.

FISH Trout fishing resumes once the mountain rivers have cooled.

NOVEMBER

FRUITS Look for persimmons ripening into gooey messes on their trees. Perfectly ripe persimmons are soft and wrinkled—they should go beyond their "pretty" stage.

NUTS Collect and shell out the black walnuts now that their husks have dried.

GAME Many firearm hunting seasons open.

DECEMBER

GAME Trapping season comes into full swing as hunting season starts to taper off.

GREENS Wild edibles can still be found despite the colder weather.

CATTAIL Dig in the mud for cattail rootstocks and extract the starch for flour.

TEAS Break up the twigs of black birch, spicebush, and sassafras for spicy hot teas.

170 STOCK YOUR SURVIVAL PANTRY

Any food is better than no food when you're facing an emergency, but not all foods are equal when it comes to a survival stash. First, you'll need enough calories to keep you going. Second, you'll need a healthy blend of macronutrients (protein, fat, and carbohydrates). Vitamins, minerals, and fiber are important, too. And third, the food should be something that is easy to prepare or requires no cooking. If all of that isn't enough, you also have to consider factors like shelf life, food allergens, and, oh yeah, taste. That deal you got on a case of pickled pigs' feet won't seem so great when you have to live off hooves for a week. Get ready to read the labels as you put together a survival pantry.

171 STORE THE TOP TEN STAPLES

Most of our grandparents probably focused their meals around a few important staple items. Look a few generations further back and you might find nothing but those staples. Buy these critical top ten items and store them in insect- and rodent-proof containers in a cool, dry, dark place.

RICE Properly stored, white rice can last for decades—the flavor and texture may suffer a little with age, but there are few better staple items.

BEANS High in protein, beans are a great staple food item. Cook them together with rice, or separately, by boiling them in water. Make bean soup to stretch your food even further.

PASTA Pasta could outlast us all if stored in a cool, dry, dark container. All you need is boiling water and you'll have an energy-packed meal.

SALT Preserve and flavor your food with salt, a once highly prized commodity. Store iodized salt for table use and for making brines. You'll also need natural salt without iodide to ferment vegetables, such as sauerkraut and pickles.

BAKING SODA AND POWDER As anyone who bakes knows, baking soda and baking powder are essentials. Baking soda is also good for cleaning and deodorizing. Both can last for years if stored in airtight containers.

FATS AND OILS Shortening and oil are the calorie powerhouses of your food storage. They'll also be the first thing to go bad, so rotate your stock every six months for best results—or annually at the very least.

SUGAR White sugar can be stored indefinitely in a dry location. Although it's not particularly nutritious, it does provide calories, and it'll sweeten foods and can be used to brew alcohol.

HONEY Even though real honey crystallizes and solidifies over time, nothing diminishes its life span. Magical honey can last indefinitely due to its antimicrobial properties.

DRIED FRUIT Nutrient-dense and flavorful, dried fruit is great for long-term storage. Keep a variety on hand, such as raisins, prunes, cherries, blueberries, apricots, and pineapple.

COFFEE AND/OR TEA If you need your caffeine to get going in the morning, consider some shelf-stable sources. While some might think of them as luxuries, others call them essentials.

172 WEIGH YOUR OPTIONS

Buying a large volume of food is a serious investment in your future survival—and it can wind up being a bad one if you end up stuck eating hundreds of meals that you don't care for just to get rid of those supplies. There are plenty of food-storage options out there, ranging from age-old preservation methods to the latest technological advances. Let's look at the pros and cons of the two most popular food-storage systems, freeze-drying and canning, to find out which side you really want to land on.

	FREEZE-DRIED	CANNED
PROS	These foods are lightweight and have a long shelf life. With the heavy water removed, most freeze-dried meals are a fraction of the weight of the original food, which make it an ideal choice for backpacking.	Availability, cost, and durability are the three main perks of canned foods. Any grocery store will help you stock your larder, and the cans are rodent- and insect-proof.
CONS	Boiling water is required to prepare most freeze-dried foods, and they can carry a hefty price tag. Cost can add up fast if you are purchasing for a large group or a long time span.	Canned foods are heavy, don't last as long as freeze-dried goods, and the heat used to can the food often destroys many of the vitamins. You'll also need a can opener in many cases.

173 PLAN FOR ATTACK

If you're stocking a survival pantry, you face two major security hazards: cold and rats. I recommend a stockpile of both freeze-dried and canned food. The diversity allows you to cover a variety of situations: If rodents get into your freeze-dried pouches, at least the cans are still good, and if the cans unexpectedly freeze or burst, the freeze-dried pouches are unharmed. Go with a single strategy if you know the major risks at your storage site (freezing temps or a likely animal raid), but if you have a rarely visited site in a cold area, double up your security by placing freeze-dried pouches in tightly sealed metal cans or boxes. This takes care of both the critters and the cold.

174 PLAN YOUR MENU

Yes, you could probably live off a pallet of canned peaches, but after the thirty-third can, you may not want to. It's easy to add to your survival stockpile by throwing random things into the cupboard. But a better plan is just that: a plan.

Figure out some complete meals your family would gladly eat, then stock enough food to supply those meals. Some people even store their assorted menu items together.

Everything on this grocery list can be eaten right out of the package—just add a little hot water for the oatmeal—and it can create three days of meals for a family of four.

BREAKFAST The three breakfasts are the first things on the list. Granola and milk will make one breakfast meal, and the oatmeal will make two more. There's one extra packet at each meal for the hungriest survivor.

LUNCH AND DINNER Your lunches and dinners can be a rotation of soups, pastas, and chili, with vegetables on the side (or added to the meal). Add a can of tomatoes or corn to the chili and green beans or other veggies to your soups.

SNACKS The cookies and energy bars are there to fill in for dessert, eat as a snack, and keep everyone happy.

SHOPPING LIST

1 box instant oatmeal (10 packs, your favorite flavor)

1 package shelf-stable milk (3 Tetra pak blocks, 1 cup/236 ml each)

1 package granola

8 cans soup

12 cans prepared pasta (like ravioli)

12 cans vegetables

4 cans chili

1 tin butter cookies (or similar long-lasting treats)

1 box energy bars (12 bars)

175 BRING WILD EDIBLES INTO THE MIX

After eating a number of canned or freeze-dried meals, you won't believe how delicious some fresh food will be. If you properly identify and harvest wild edible plants, you can add something to your meals that will be most welcome. Use these options when it's time to survive.

WILD SALAD Any raw, edible leaves, greens, or flowers can be turned into a vitamin-packed salad. All you need to supply is the dressing. Store some bottles of oil and vinegar, as they have a long shelf life, loads of calories, and do not require refrigeration after opening.

VITAMIN TEA Pine needle, mint, and sassafras teas are a good way to keep everyone hydrated. You can also get vitamin C from the pine and minerals from the sassafras.

WEED STIR-FRY Roots, shoots, flowers, and buds can be sautéed or stir-fried into a delicious and nutrition-filled meal.

176 TAKE A SPIN ON ROTATION

Rotating your stock is all about timing! You want to eat up your aging food and replace it with fresher products while allowing plenty of buffer time—you don't want your oldest items to expire the day after the emergency begins. These tips will get you going in the right direction.

STEP 1 Plan for success while you're still standing in the store. Look at comparable products, or the boxes at the back of the shelf, to find the longest shelf life or most distant expiration date.

STEP 2 Once you get home, use a permanent marker to write the expiration date in bigger script on the bottle, can, or jar you bought. This saves time later when you're inspecting your supplies.

STEP 3 Place the new item in the back of the pantry, ideally behind another of the same item. If you always add to the front, sooner or later, you'll have a dusty old can of beans in the back that expired ten years ago. So always add to the back and use from the front.

STEP 4 Pick a date. Write a note on your calendar to inspect your food storage every season. This helps you to spot any trouble (like pests) and catch aging items. Many products can be safely used past their expiration date, but it's best if you don't have to eat old food.

177 SAMPLE THE VARIETY

A wide range of foods will keep up morale much better than a monotonous menu, as will keeping a secret stash of goodies. Add these snacks and other consumables to your stockpile, and use as directed.

CHOCOLATE Few things perk people up like this sweet treat. Store chocolate chips and bars.

SYRUPS Maple syrup, chocolate syrup, whatever syrup—it'll turn anything into a dessert.

CANDY Bring out some of their favorite candies and watch kids of all ages light up.

WINE Everything tastes better in the wilderness, including a nice glass of your favorite vintage. Try boxed wine if you don't want to lug bottles around.

LIQUOR Whether it's medicinal or not, there are many uses for this nonspoiling liquid.

CANNED MEATS AND FISH Why not? You only live once, and cholesterol really doesn't count in survival.

PEANUT BUTTER As stress levels rise, so do cravings for fatty food. Fortunately, this nutritious snack food contains heart-healthy fat.

178 WHIP UP SOME JERKY

With effective food-preservation techniques, carnivores can turn their success in the wild into a series of future feasts. Dried meat can last for a long time, and it doesn't require any special equipment to create. Here's an age-old technique for making jerky at home or in the wild.

SELECT Get some fresh, raw meat. Cooked meat will go bad in a few days and lead to food poisoning. I recommend using red meat or fish, but with this technique, you can use meat from any mammal, bird, fish, or larger reptile.

PREPARE Slice your pieces very thin and cut across the grain (perpendicular to the long bundles of muscle fibers that appear as lines in the meat). Trim off all visible fat, as it will turn rancid in the dried meat. While the meat is still juicy, sprinkle on a little salt, sugar, or spices such as pepper, ginger, cumin, or chili powder. These are optional, but a good idea, as salt creates a less hospitable environment for bacteria.

DRY Hang your jerky slices on an improvised rack (this can be twigs and branches around camp). You can dry your jerky near a small smoky fire to add smoke flavoring and keep flies away, but don't dry it directly over the fire—it'll cook and then go bad on you. The drying process may take several days, depending on the humidity; turn each piece a few times throughout. Don't leave your jerky out overnight, and don't ever leave it unattended (you need to avoid dampness as well as birds and other jerky-stealing critters). When it becomes slightly brittle, it's done. Red meat jerky will turn a purple-brown color. White meat jerky will be a pinkish-gray.

STORE Store your jerky somewhere dry and safe from pests, and cook it before eating. You can toast it over the fire or pound it up with a rock and throw it in a soup or stew.

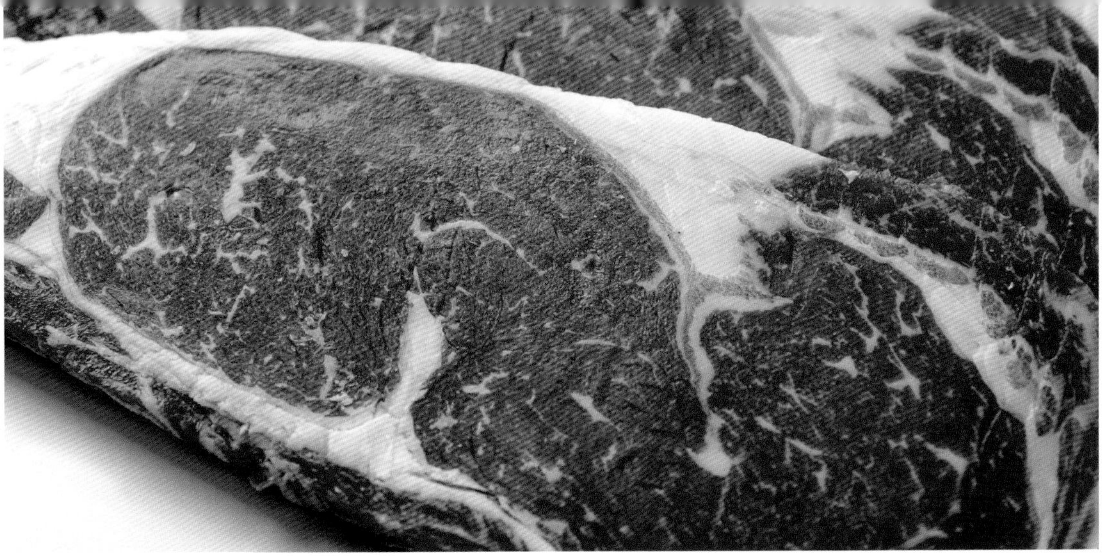

179 RENDER THE FAT

Fat is a little tricky to keep on hand, especially in a raw state, as it goes bad fairly quickly. Cooks of yore used rendering as a way to store fat at room temperature without it spoiling too quickly. Rendering involves cooking the fatty animal tissues for a long time at low temperatures and then filtering the fat for storage.

At home, a slow cooker will suffice, but in the backwoods, rendering over a fire can be a bit trickier. Having said that, it's worth the trouble.

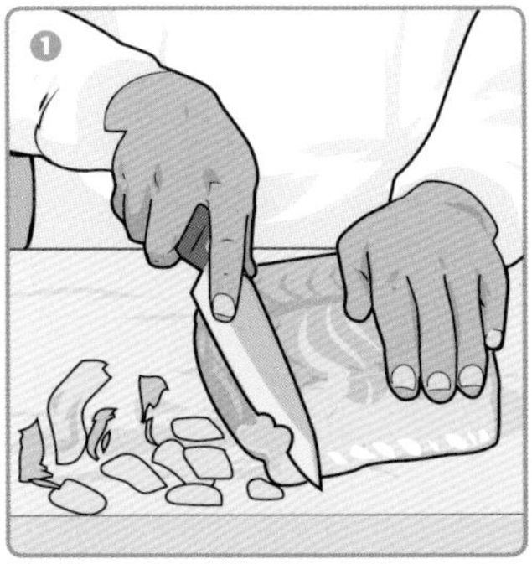

STEP 1 Cut your animal fat into 1-inch (2.5-cm) cubes, removing all visible meat, veins, and nonfatty tissue. Drop the cubes into a pot with water that's about 4 inches (10 cm) deep.

STEP 2 Bring the fat and water mixture to a low simmer, trying to keep the temperature under 150°F (65°C). If the water starts to boil, the fat will probably burn. Keep the pieces simmering for three to five hours.

STEP 3 When it seems like most of the fat has liquefied, let it cool just a little and strain through cheesecloth. In the field, you'll have to get creative to make a suitable filter—I've used T-shirt material. After pouring your grease through the filter cloth into another container, you can simmer a little longer (thirty minutes or so) and filter once more.

STEP 4 Pour your final filtered fat into small jars or cans and keep them in the coolest, darkest place available. Your fat should last several weeks in warmer weather, or several months in colder weather. Just make sure to eat it before it turns rancid. If it starts to smell bad, use it for something other than eating (it can still be a handy nonedible grease).

180 FREEZE IT RIGHT

If you have access to a freezer or you're hanging out at the South Pole, letting the meat freeze can be the easiest preservation method. In cold climates, a shed can be just as cold as a freezer. To freeze, tightly wrap cut meat, and loosely wrap animal quarters or large pieces. Using wax paper or butcher's paper works well, and a vacuum food sealer works even better. Thaw it when ready, and it's like fresh meat again.

181 CAN YOUR MEAT

The ability to preserve and store your own food is a great skill set for the prepper, homesteader, and anyone else who wants to take charge of what they eat. Canning and storing meats at room temperature may be a little scary for beginners, but home canning is very similar to commercial-canning practices and, when properly done, is safe and the results are long lasting. Canning can save you money, and it can also help you build a pantry that will turn your self-sufficient friends green with envy.

GATHER THE GEAR You'll need a pressure canner, jars, rings, lids, a jar-lifting tool, a jar funnel, some salt, and your meat. Small jars are the safest, as they reach higher temperatures in the canning process.

FILL THE JARS Use a jar-filling funnel to add your fresh meat or cooked leftovers to a clean canning jar. Add half a tablespoon (7–8 g) of salt to 2-cup (1/2-l) jars. Add a little less than a tablespoon (15 g) of salt to 1-quart (1-l) jars. Wipe any food from the jar rim after filling, as food particles can break the seal if stuck between the jar mouth and the lid. Pour water in the canner until it is over 2 inches (5 cm) deep, and lower the jars into the canner.

BOIL THE JARS Screw the lid on to the pressure canner and bring it to a boil with the weight off the steam vent. Once it begins boiling, cover the steam vent with the weight and adjust your heat to maintain the pressure at the cooker's recommended poundage for meat processing: 10 pounds (4 kg) is a typical weight for meats. Process 2-cup (1/2-l) jars for up to an hour and a half.

COOL IT DOWN Lift the jars out of the hot water with canning jar tongs and set them on a towel on your countertop to cool down.

CHECK THE SEAL After the jars have been at room temperature for several hours, check the lids to make sure they have "sucked down" and formed a vacuum. You'll typically hear each jar pop as it cools and seals. After sealing, the lids should be solid and unable to flex. If any of the jars don't seal after cooling, use the contents that day and try to determine if the lid or the jar were bad. Check the jar mouth for nicks, cracks, or other damage. If damaged or malformed, the jar should be used for other purposes.

STORE YOUR FOOD Store your canned jars of food in a cool, dry, dark place and use within one year for best results.

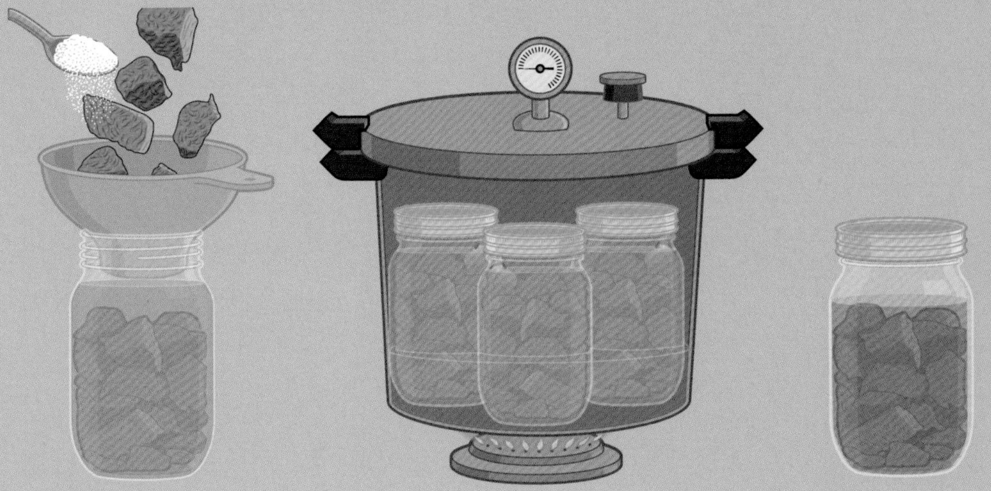

182 SUPERPLANT: YARROW

PICK NATURE'S PANACEA

If I only had access to one medicinal plant, I'd want that plant to be yarrow. Over the centuries, yarrow has been used to prevent infections and break fevers, as a battlefield dressing for bleeding wounds, and to brew beer and make savory foods. Yarrow (*Achillea millefolium*) is a European plant that was brought to North America by settlers. The fernlike leaves can be found year-round in the lower half of the United States, but the biggest leaves are usually found in summer. The plant blooms at the height of summer, with a stalk that is about 2 feet (60 cm) tall with a flat-topped cluster of white flowers—like a triangular cluster version of Queen Anne's lace.

CHURN UP A BETTER BUTTER

Is there anything butter can't improve? If there is, I don't want to know about it. But what if you could make your butter better? My favorite food use of yarrow is to blend finely chopped fresh yarrow leaves into salted butter. The resulting herb spread is amazing on bread, vegetables, and even melted over a hot, juicy steak.

BREW YARROW BEER

According to some beer historians (yes, that's a real job!), the use of yarrow predates the use of hops to brew beer. This isn't surprising, since yarrow inhibits bacterial growth in wounds—and therefore also fights against spoilage. To craft a yarrow brew, you'll need a 1-gallon (4-l) glass jug, a fermentation lock to fit, 1.5 pounds (0.7 kg) of dried amber malt extract, 2 tbsp. (10 g) dried hops, 1 ounce (30 g) fresh yarrow leaf, water, 1 package of ale yeast, table sugar for carbonating, a few screw-top bottles, and cheap vodka to sanitize your equipment.

STEP 1 In a stainless steel or enamel pot, boil 1 gallon (4 l) water with the malt extract and hops for exactly sixty minutes. (Watch that it doesn't boil over.) During the final fifteen minutes of boiling, add the yarrow leaves to the wort (unfermented beer).

STEP 2 Cool and strain the wort into a clean glass jug. Let cool to room temperature.

STEP 3 Add the dried ale yeast to the brew and shake it up.

STEP 4 Add the sanitized lock and set the jug in a sink for a few days, as the malt and hops are usually very foamy. If fermentation (bubbling) doesn't occur within a day, your yeast was dead, or your brew was too hot and killed it. Add more yeast to save the batch.

STEP 5 After a bubbly first week, clean the airlock and put it back on the jug quickly (you need to keep oxygen out). After another three weeks, the sediment should be thick at the bottom of the vessel, the bubbling should have stopped, and the ale should be starting to clear. It will be completely flat when it has finished fermenting.

STEP 6 Carefully pour the flat beer into a clean container, leaving the sediment in the original jug. Add 2.5 tbsp. (30 g) table sugar per 1 gallon (4 l) of beer and mix with a sanitized spoon. The remaining yeast in the beer will eat up the sugar and carbonate your ale. Prepare your funnel and sanitized bottles and caps for bottling. You'll need about 8–10 soda bottles and caps per 1 gallon (4 l) ale. Keep the beer at room temperature for one week to fully carbonate, then chill the bottles and enjoy this delicious heritage beer.

LEARN THE BENEFITS

The genus name *Achillea* is derived from the Greek hero Achilles, who reportedly carried yarrow to treat his army's battle wounds. This medicinal use is reflected in some of yarrow's common names, such as staunchweed and soldier's woundwort. These are just a few of its many uses.

STYPTIC Yarrow can stop bleeding quickly due to its astringent and vasoconstricting properties.

ANTIBACTERIAL The crushed leaves contain compounds that have an antibacterial action. This leaf material can be applied directly to wounds or soaked in water to make a tea that can be employed with a hot compress.

DIAPHORETIC A strong yarrow tea can increase perspiration, helping to break a fever.

ANESTHETIC Crushed fresh leaves can have a numbing action—though not for everybody. For some, it desensitizes the nerves and helps with toothaches, cold sores, and boils.

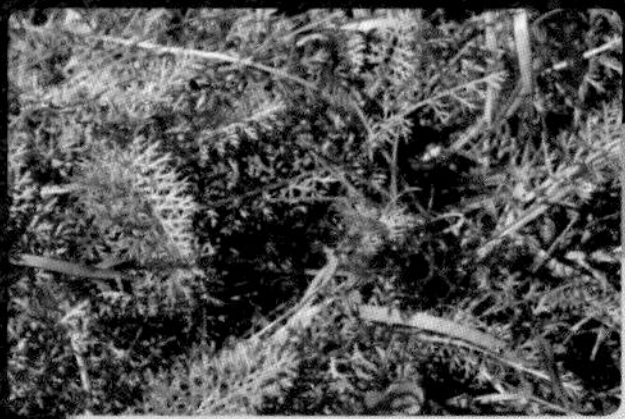

GET THE RIGHT PLANT

When crushed, the leaves and flowers of yarrow will have a pleasant, spicy smell. Most folks agree that it smells like rosemary, oregano, and other cooking herbs. The leaves should be hairy or fuzzy, especially on the stems. If the leaves are smooth-stemmed, don't even touch them. If you've already crushed them to smell the plant's odor and you smell something bad, wash your hands immediately. Fool's parsley (*Aethusa cynapium*) and poison hemlock (*Conium maculatum*) leaves are poisonous or fatal if eaten, and their leaves can resemble yarrow when young—but will have a bad odor reminiscent of chemicals or cleaners.

183 GROW YOUR OWN INVESTMENT

With a measure of patience, a few good seeds, some rich soil, and a sunny location, you really can grow your own food pantry—and the best way to look at home gardening is as an investment. Sometimes the bugs or neighborhood deer will be the ones capitalizing on that investment—but when you're lucky, you'll have so many vegetables you'll have to give them away.

The labors of gardening are richly rewarded—there's something extremely satisfying about setting the table for your family with food that you grew yourself.

When starting out, the most important decision you will make isn't which seeds to buy, but where to plant them.

You'll need to consider the soil composition and the amount of light your garden will receive. Pick the best agricultural soil you have on your property (talk to someone at your county's Agricultural Extension Office to consult their extensive soil maps). Once you know where the good dirt is located, select a section of your best soil that gets at least ten hours of direct, uninterrupted sunlight each day, and start your work.

Choose well and wisely, and soon your family table will be laden with grains, herbs, fruits, and vegetables of all shapes and sizes.

184 LAY IT ALL OUT

Found the perfect garden spot? Now you need to orient your beds or rows on a north–south axis, so that all the plants get an equal amount of sun. Plant the tall guys (like corn, pole beans, and tomatoes) at the north end of the beds or rows, so they don't shade any of the shorter plants. If you're using barrels, containers, or other vessels for your garden, you should still place the tall ones in the back. Avoid placing containers or crops too close to metal siding or similar reflective surfaces during the hottest times of the year, as the plants can literally cook in the hot sunshine.

185 SPREAD YOUR ROOTS

Vegetables need to grow in loose, rich soil, and without competition. You should remove the sod from any new garden spot and deeply dig and chop the soil with a shovel (or till it with a rototiller machine). Deeply, by the way, means at least 1 foot (30 cm)—but 2 feet (60 cm) is better. This is the hardest work in gardening, but the payoff is huge. Here's why.

BENEFITS

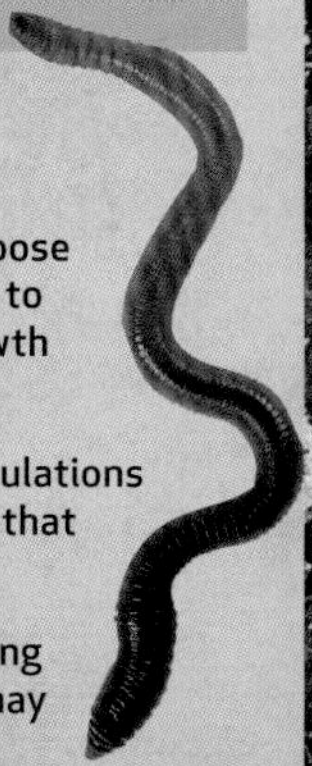

Deep root growth pulls in more nutrients for your vegetables.

Plants grow larger root systems in loose soil, providing a better water supply to each plant and allowing healthy growth even during droughts.

Deeply worked soil grows larger populations of earthworms and other organisms that encourage plant growth.

Work now and kick back later: Working your soil to a 2-foot (60-cm) depth may allow you to skip a year of tilling.

186 BREW COMPOST TEA

Here's a great way to make the most of your leafy leftovers and give your garden a nourishing drink. Obviously, this isn't the kind of tea you drink, but it's a nourishing infusion that can get your garden the minerals and nutrients it needs to flourish. Start by establishing a compost bucket in your kitchen, and throw all of your vegetable and fruit waste into it. As it gets stinky, move it to a compost pile outside.

STEP 1 Shovel some nicely decomposed compost into a burlap sack. The more "mature" your compost is, the better this will work, so turn your pile frequently to let everything rot nicely.

STEP 2 Gather up the sack and tie it off securely, then affix it to a nice sturdy stick or dowel.

STEP 3 Steep your "tea bag" in a bucket of water, stirring frequently, until the water is a rich brownish color. This means the nutrients from the compost have enriched the water.

STEP 4 Remove the bag and decant your tea into a watering can or spray bottle.

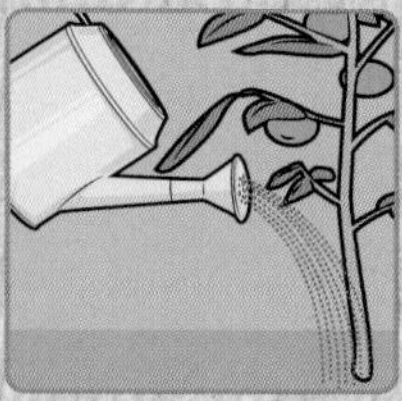

STEP 5 Use this tea when you water and watch your garden flourish!

187 DON'T FORGET TO WATER

Unless you get a solid, heavy rain every other day in your garden, you'll need to water your plants. This can be done with collected rainwater (a great choice) or with a garden hose. Water deeply and thoroughly every other day. Make sure you water in the morning, if possible. Watering in the evening or at night can encourage fungal diseases, and watering in the heat of a sunny afternoon will cause the droplets of water to burn the plant leaves like tiny magnifying glasses.

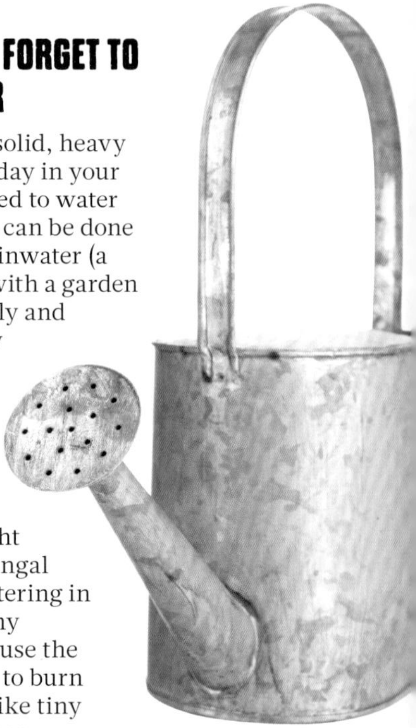

188 HONOR THE AMENDMENTS

Well-decomposed compost is always welcome in the garden. The good stuff will be aged, very dark brown or black in color, and will have gone through a high-heat stage of decomposition to kill diseases and weed seeds. Add all you can to your garden, blending it with the soil or applying on the surface as a "top dressing." You can also add sand to clay-filled soil, add clay to sandy soil, or add aged manure to any soil at all.

189 PLANT ACCORDINGLY

When it's time to plant, you can sow seeds directly into the dirt, or you can plant seedlings that have been growing in small containers. Either way, water the new plants deeply in order to settle the soil around them. Keep in mind that seedlings can suffer from transplant shock if planted in hot, dry soil; plant them in the evening to allow them to adjust to their new home overnight.

190 GROW HARDY HERBS

Some tough herbs can stay alive from season to season, through even the coldest winters. Plants that survive and bloom year after year (or continue to grow throughout) are known as perennials.

You can grow these woody-stemmed plants near your kitchen door in most climates, and when you're tired of eating the same vegetables over and over, pop outside and grab some fresh herbs to transform a tired meal into something new.

Perennial plants also represent a great financial investment, as your plants will live for multiple years and growing seasons. So prepare your soil for a few long-term residents, and plant a few. Some popular perennials are sage, rosemary, oregano, thyme, and tarragon.

191 EAT ON THE CHEAP

It's easy for new gardeners to spend a lot of money on gizmos and tools in their excitement to get started—but neophytes can grow vegetables with little more than a shovel, hoe, and seeds. To feed your family on just a few bills a day, grow staple crops that can become wholesome replacements for more expensive meals. For instance, grow a row of potatoes and plan two dinners a week around a potato-based main course. Plant a variety of beans, and cook them up as a soup entrée. Sow the seeds that will result in the makings of a great stir-fry. These little changes add up to big savings over time.

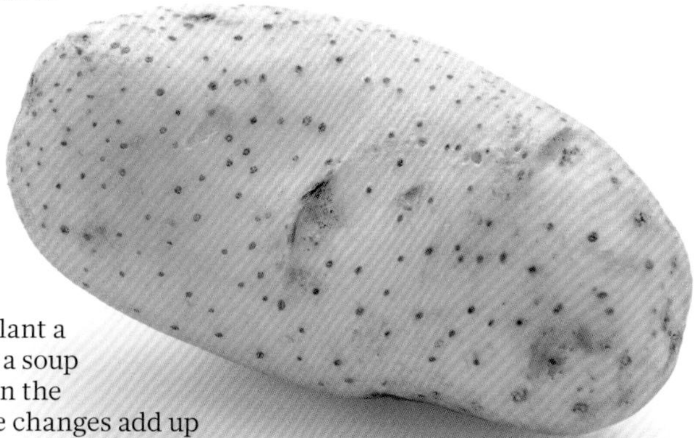

192 FEED THE FAMILY

Let's say you have a family of four to feed and you're on a budget (who isn't these days?)—what kind of impact can your home garden have on the family dinner table? Depending on your menu and your garden's success, your agricultural activities can make a major difference. You might be growing your own food to sell or trade, or just for the unparalleled taste and freshness. Or you might be nurturing a survival garden, in which case the most important consideration should be the caloric value of the food you'll grow. You can't live off salad—there simply aren't enough calories and nutrients in leafy veggies to sustain a human being. In that case, rather than growing a bunch of space-hogging, low-calorie vegetables, try something from one of these healthy, higher-calorie categories instead.

PEAS AND BEANS	SEEDS AND ROOTS
Peas, peanuts, soybeans, navy beans, chickpeas, dry shelling beans, kidney beans, lima beans, fava beans, and black-eyed peas	Sunflowers, parsnips, carrots, turnips, rutabagas, sweet potatoes, and white potatoes

193 DON'T OVERLOOK THE WEEDS

Since we've devoted part of this book to wild edible plants, it would be a shame to overlook them when they unexpectedly spring up in the garden. Think of your weeds as a bonus rather than a nuisance. Make sure you can positively identify the plants, and treat them like valuable vegetables. Frequent edible garden weeds include dandelion, chickweed, plantain, clover, chicory, lamb's quarters, sorrel, and violets.

194 SAVE YOUR SEEDS

The ultimate way to be frugal with your garden is to save the seeds from this year's plants and replant them next year. This is most easily accomplished when you're growing single varieties of each vegetable, to avoid unpredictable results due to cross-pollination. Let veggies mature completely, remove the seeds, dry them, and store for next year.

195 STORE SEEDS RIGHT

Seeds can last for many years if properly stored. Once you've made your garden plans and decided which plants to grow, follow these steps to store your seeds for the long haul of winter—or multiple winters. If you're shopping for seeds, know that spring seeds often go on sale in late summer.

KEEP THEM DRY Store the seeds in a dry place, as they'll go bad if they become damp. Use a watertight container and some desiccant packs (repurpose the silica gel packs that come in so many products) to soak up moisture.

KEEP THEM COOL Store them in a cool place like your fridge. They may sweat a tad when coming out of cold storage, so keep an eye on them.

KEEP THEM IN THE DARK Some seeds are sensitive to light and will refuse to grow if they've been exposed for any length of time, so be sure to keep them somewhere dark. Most storage places that are dry and cool will also be dark—but it's worth making sure.

CHECK THE HUMIDITY Double-check your storage spot with the following 100-point rule: Add the temperature (in Fahrenheit) of your storage space to the humidity percentage and make sure the total is under 100. For example, a 60°F environment at 30 percent humidity makes for a "score" of 90 points. That's below 100, so it passes the test. When possible, lean toward the drier side, and your seeds will sleep happily for years.

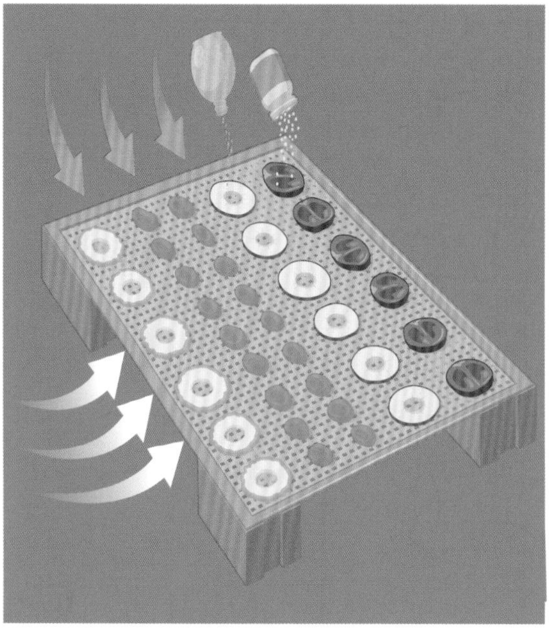

APPLES	Antioxidants, fiber
APRICOTS	Fiber, irons, vitamins A and C
BLACK CURRANTS	Manganese, iron, potassium, vitamin C
BLUEBERRIES	Antioxidants, vitamins A, B, and E
CHERRIES	Antioxidants, beta-carotene, folic acid, fiber
FIGS	Iron, folic acid, potassium
MANGOS	Antioxidants, fatty acids, vitamins A, C, and E
PEARS	Fiber, vitamin C, copper
TOMATOES	Antioxidants, lycopene, vitamin C

196 DRY IT OUT

Drying can allow us to enjoy our foraged edibles and home-grown vegetables long after they've been harvested. Electric-powered home dehydrator units are a great way to preserve many foods while cutting down the food's weight and volume—but they're expensive. Luckily, you can make your own from something you already have around the house: window screens.

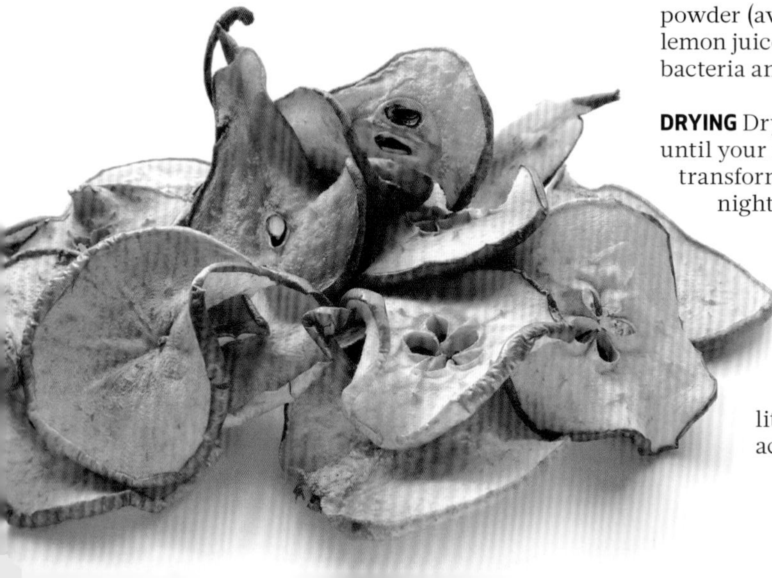

PREPARING Pop the screens off your windows and set them up on a few cinder blocks so air flows underneath. Avoid old metal wire screens, as metals can leach into your food—it'll not only taste bad, but might be toxic (especially in the case of galvanized wire).

PROCESSING Cut fruits and bulky vegetables into thin slices and coat with a little fruit preservative powder (available at most grocery stores) or dip in lemon juice. Acid makes the food less inviting to bacteria and helps preserve nutritional qualities.

DRYING Dry in the sun for a day or more, until your food seems to have completed its transformation. Bring the screens in each night to avoid dampness and animal thieves. This drying method works best with apples, pears, carrots, squash, and zucchini, as well as leafy things like herbs (which can be dried without mincing), and fleshy foods like tomatoes. The fleshier vegetables can be sprinkled with a little salt to help extract the water and act as a preservative.

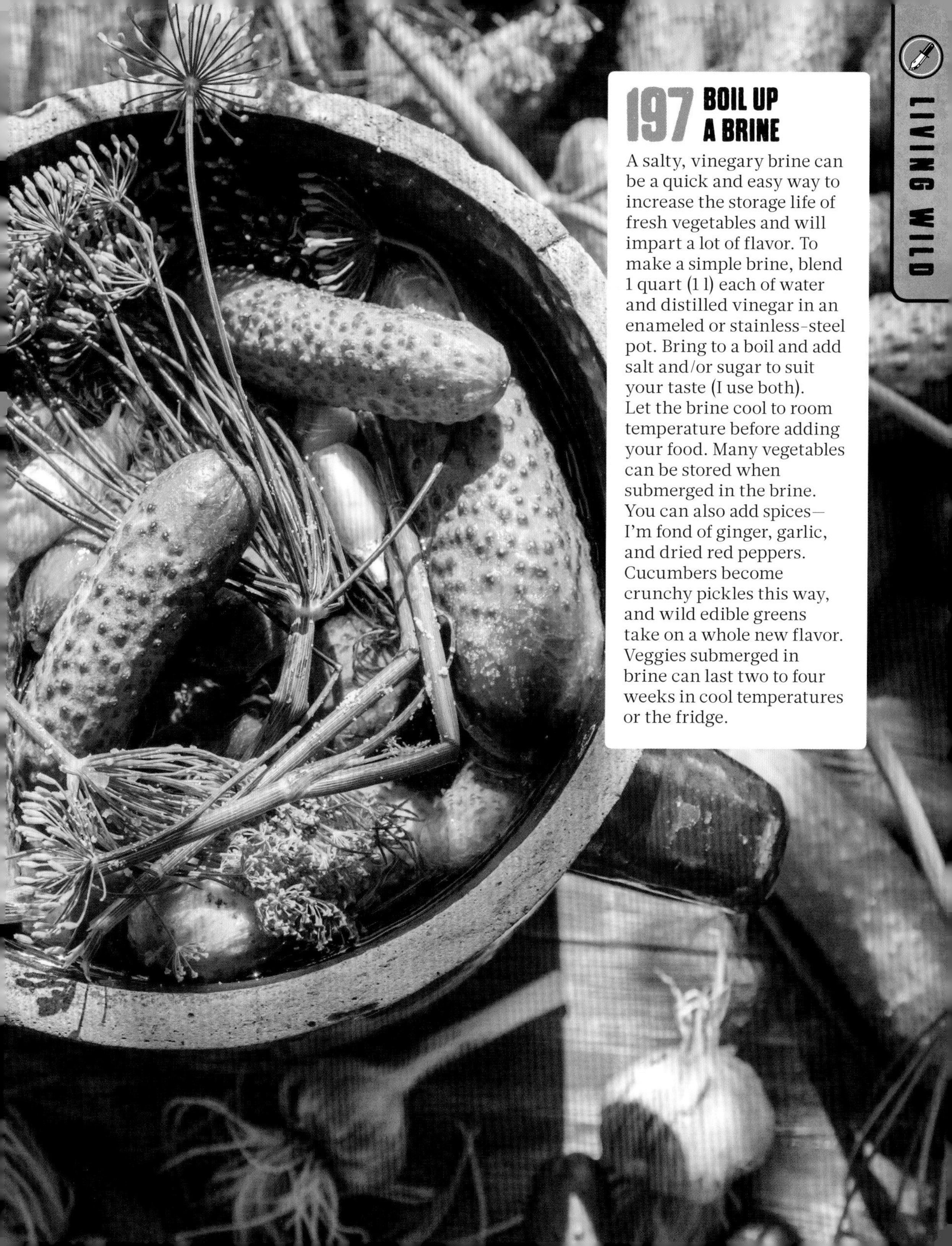

197 BOIL UP A BRINE

A salty, vinegary brine can be a quick and easy way to increase the storage life of fresh vegetables and will impart a lot of flavor. To make a simple brine, blend 1 quart (1 l) each of water and distilled vinegar in an enameled or stainless-steel pot. Bring to a boil and add salt and/or sugar to suit your taste (I use both). Let the brine cool to room temperature before adding your food. Many vegetables can be stored when submerged in the brine. You can also add spices—I'm fond of ginger, garlic, and dried red peppers. Cucumbers become crunchy pickles this way, and wild edible greens take on a whole new flavor. Veggies submerged in brine can last two to four weeks in cool temperatures or the fridge.

198 FERMENT SOME KRAUT

From sauerkraut to kimchi, fermented vegetables are popular around the world. Cabbage, one of the most popular veggies to ferment, contains the organisms necessary for the process, and these steps are all it takes.

STEP 1 Chop or shred your cabbage into small strips. Rinse and then drain for five minutes.

STEP 2 Place enough cabbage in a large glass jar or glazed crock to cover the bottom by about 2 inches (5 cm). Sprinkle with non-iodized salt (table salt won't work), and then mash with a wooden spoon, potato masher, or kraut stomper. You should start to see juices forming as the salt pulls liquid out of the cabbage. Add another thick layer of cabbage and more salt, and repeat until the container is full or you run out of cabbage.

STEP 3 Place a weight on top to keep the cabbage submerged in the liquid. You can use a small jar, boiled rock, or weighted kraut stone. Cover with a clean cloth and allow the kraut to naturally ferment for a week or two, then remove the scum that floats to the top before eating. Refrigerate your excess, can it in jars with a water bath, or store in a cool place like a basement. With open-air storage, make sure to keep the weight in place.

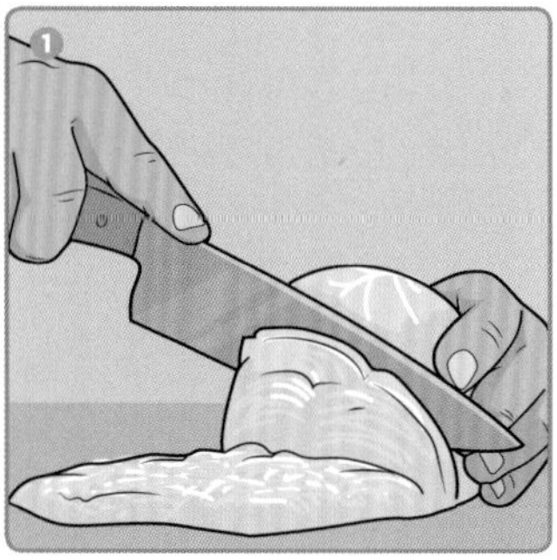

199 STORE VEGGIES UNDERGROUND

You don't always have to harvest your vegetables when they're finished growing. A few root crops can actually be stored in the soil until you need them. If your ground doesn't freeze solid in the winter, consider leaving a patch of carrots or a row of potatoes in the ground where they grew. This frees up storage space in smaller homes, and it can help you to ration food by only digging up what you need. Parsnips can also be treated this way, and some people even prefer the flavor of older parsnips, as the sugar level increases over time. Turnips, however, are not a good candidate for this storage trick, as they can become woody and tough.

200 SUPERPLANT: ECHINACEA

FIGHT INFECTIONS WITH ECHINACEA

Echinacea, also commonly called the purple coneflower, is a native American perennial wildflower best known for its ability to stimulate the immune system. Echinacea preparations are used against colds, flu, minor infections, and a host of other ailments. Several echinacea species native to North America were originally used as medicines by Great Plains tribes, who then showed them to the settlers.

From 1916 to 1950, echinacea was listed in the U.S. National Formulary as a recognized medicinal ingredient. But the discovery of antibiotics and a lack of scientific support for echinacea caused it to fall out of favor. It has been regaining support in recent years, however. The juices and solid materials of several species are now used medicinally—treating the first signs of the common cold and minor fungal infections.

MAKE A TINCTURE

An alcohol-based tincture is usually the easiest way to use echinacea. There are no tablets or juices required, and you don't even need to bother with hot water.

STEP 1 Dry your own echinacea roots or purchase some from a reputable provider, and get the highest-proof vodka (or any clear liquor) that your local liquor store carries.

STEP 2 Place the roots in a glass jar, cover with liquor, and screw on an airtight lid.

STEP 3 Store in a cool, dark place, and shake for a few minutes every few days. Do this for six to eight weeks.

STEP 4 Strain the liquid off the roots and bottle your echinacea tincture for use against future colds. When you feel a cold coming on, place the tincture under your tongue or in water. Use 20 drops every two hours for the first day of symptoms, then decrease to three times daily for up to ten days.

USE WISELY

Echinacea has been employed to treat a vast range of ailments, as noted below, but be aware that it will cause a rash in those allergic to ragweed, marigolds, mums, or daisies, and it can be harmful to those with autoimmune disorders. Be smart about your usage.

Flu	Syphilis	Insect stings
Urinary tract infections	Typhoid	Hemorrhoids
Genital herpes	Malaria	Rheumatism
Blood poisoning (septicemia)	Diphtheria	Migraine headaches and physical pain
Gum disease	Boils and abscesses	ADHD
Tonsillitis	Ulcers	Acid indigestion
Streptococcal infections	Eczema and psoriasis	Dizziness
	Skin wounds, burns, and UV damage	Snake bites

CONCOCT A COLD-KILLER

You can create a tea from several different parts of the echinacea plant and even blend different species together for maximum benefit against the common cold.

FIRST Before flu season hits your area, harvest and dry (or purchase) leaves, flowers, and stems of *Echinacea purpurea* and *Echinacea angustifolia*. Make sure you're 100 percent positive about the identification of these plant parts, then dry them in a shady spot—they'll be brittle in about two weeks.

SECOND Blend together two parts dried root, two parts dried leaf, and one part dried stem. Pulse this in a blender or food processor until finely chopped. Store the blend in a glass jar in a cool, dry, dark location until needed.

THIRD Place about 1 ounce (28 g) of this blended echinacea material into a tea ball or reusable cloth tea bag. Steep the tea material in a small cup (200 ml) of very hot water for fifteen minutes. Drink five to six cups of this tea on the first day of cold symptoms, and then reduce by one cup of tea per day over the next five days.

201 POUR A CUP OF MEDICINE

Because hot water draws out plant compounds more effectively than cold, there's no better way to get plant medicine into your body than by drinking a warm mug of wild-medicine tea. Tea also helps replace the water that some ailments can cause you to lose, especially when you've experienced symptoms such as diarrhea, profuse sweating, or vomiting. A few strong teas can even be used as skin washes, helpful for rashes and other topical ailments. And there's nothing wrong with drinking medicinal tea as a tonic, both for the taste and to maintain good health.

202 HEAL WITH JEWELWEED TEA

The maddening itch of poison ivy is something that most outdoor lovers know well and dread appropriately. Poison ivy, poison oak, and poison sumac are all capable of working their ills upon us year-round, as even dead vines can release the rash-causing compound. But the shiny, oily springtime leaves of poison ivy seem to be the worst ones of the bunch. After exposure, washing immediately with soap and water can help. But if you lack suds, you can try this traditional native plant remedy that I have used successfully on many occasions.

STEP 1 Find and identify the jewelweed plant (*Impatiens capensis*), which grows in moist, shady areas in the eastern United States. Collect several plants, and crush the juicy purplish stalks into a slimy paste. Place this green mush into a pot, and cover with just enough water to submerge.

STEP 2 Heat the mixture for ten minutes. You may bring it to a simmer, but don't let it boil. Strain out the plant material and let cool to room temperature.

STEP 3 Use a cloth to scrub the jewelweed tea briskly over all the skin that poison ivy may have touched. Scrub for two minutes, then rinse with clean water. Using this remedy within the first hour after poison ivy exposure should make the rash minimal or nonexistent.

STEP 4 To store your tea, freeze it. Jewelweed tea has no shelf life as a liquid, and must be used the day it's made if not frozen. An easy way to make the jewelweed useful throughout the year is to pour the tea into an ice cube tray. Just melt one or two when you need a treatment.

In the absence of hot water, you can also use crushed jewelweed directly on your skin. Crush the juicy stems, scrub the snotty-looking mush all over the affected area for two minutes, then rinse with clean water. If you're outside the hour-after-exposure limit, you can still experience some relief from using jewelweed as a wash. If you already have blisters and itch, then you got into the ivy yesterday. Jewelweed will cool the itch, but it won't help as much once the rash has erupted.

Young jewelweed

Adult jewelweed

Jewelweed flower

203 BREW THE PERFECT CUP

There seems to be some confusion about tea making, at least in the foraging and survival realms. Many people complain about their wild tea tasting bad. After a few quick questions, I usually figure out that it was the process, not the materials, that tripped them up. Follow these brewing guidelines and you'll produce some outstanding teas.

TEA TIPS

Teas are made through a process called infusion, where the plant material soaks in a bath of scalding hot water. Never boil your tea! If you do, you're making a decoction, which is generally used as a topical remedy and not for drinking.

Don't ignore water quality and safety. If you're making tea from a stream or other wild source, boil the water for ten minutes, then remove it from the heat before you add the plants. This way, you've disinfected the water without boiling your tea.

Keep it covered! Any kind of lid on the tea vessel will help to keep the oils (which are responsible for a good portion of your tea's taste) in your brew. Open tea pots lose flavor.

204 LOOK AT YOUR HERBAL CHOICES

Plenty of commercial herbal teas boast medicinal properties. But which wild tea is right for your ailments? Study this list—and what's growing around you—to get the right plant for your needs.

PEPPERMINT (*Mentha piperita*) Peppermint tea is excellent for soothing an upset stomach. Add 1 tbsp. dried leaf or 2 tbsp. fresh leaf to 1 cup (250 ml) hot water, cover, and steep for ten to fifteen minutes. Peppermint tea can also help with hangovers. Note: Pregnant or nursing women, anyone with gastroesophageal reflux disease (GERD), or anyone with liver disease should avoid ingesting strong peppermint teas or products.

AMERICAN GINSENG (*Panax quinquifolius*) Teas from different species of ginseng are used in many countries as a tonic and energy booster. Add 1 tbsp. dried root steeped in 1 cup (250 ml) hot water for thirty minutes, which will yield a tea that revitalizes and invigorates. It's even touted as an aphrodisiac—though your results may vary.

PINE NEEDLE (*Pinus* spp.) Stave off scurvy with this survival classic. Pine needle tea is loaded with vitamin C. In fifteen minutes, 2 tbsp. of fresh chopped needles added to your mug of hot water will give you a tea that has five times your USDA daily allowance. Note: Pregnant women, or women who may be pregnant, should not drink pine needle tea.

YARROW (*Achillea millefolium*) Yarrow has over 200 different active compounds, many of which are antibacterial, antiviral, and antifungal, and yarrow tea has potent medicinal properties. Place 1 tbsp. dried yarrow leaf or 2 tbsp. fresh leaf in 1 cup (250 ml) hot water and steep for fifteen minutes to create an immune system–boosting tea. Double the amount of leaf in the batch to induce sweating, which can detox the body and help break a fever. Note: Yarrow should not be used by pregnant or nursing women, and it can cause skin irritation.

205 INFUSE HERBAL OILS

The best way to add medicinal qualities to fat is a liquid oil infusion. And the optimal kind of oil infusion is a slow one done at room temperature.

Place the dried herbs in a jar with a watertight lid. Cover with organic, cold-pressed olive oil. Seal the lid and shake the jar every couple of days for the next six to eight weeks. Strain out the herbs using cheesecloth, and bottle the oil. This oil can be taken internally, as it's nowhere near the strength of commercially manufactured essential oils.

If you don't have two months to wait for an infused oil, a little heat can speed up the process. Place your dried herbs in the bottom of a slow cooker and cover with oil. Turn the heat to its lowest setting, cover, and leave on low heat for 24–48 hours. Cool and strain the oil, and pour it into dark glass bottles for best storage results. Only use dried herbs for oils and tinctures, as fresh herbs release too much water into the medicine.

206 MAKE A QUICK BALM

The outdoors can turn even the toughest hands into a rough, scratched mess. During everyday outdoor activities or an emergency, you can make a balm from several natural oils. This type of topical medicine is thicker than lotion (more like a salve) and typically contains more volatile oils than other skin remedies, working to restore your skin's health by replacing the oils and moisture it lacks. The balm provides the oil directly, and your skin provides the needed moisture underneath the oily coating. Here are two ways to make a balm that just might save your hide.

PLANT OIL BALM The best field-made balm I've ever gotten was made from oily tree nuts. Shell out the nutmeat from hickory, pecan, beech, or walnut, crush it into a paste, and rub it into your dry skin. In a survival scenario, you may be better off eating those nuts for their high-calorie content, but for everyday outdoor activities, you can probably afford this nonfood use. Should you ever need a more refined skin product, simmer the crushed nutmeats in a little water for thirty to forty-five minutes. This will bring the oil to the surface as a liquid, which can be skimmed off and used as a lotion.

ANIMAL FAT BALM The lard, tallow, marrow, and fat of game animals can be the most abundant source of oil in hunting and survival situations. It can be wiped on your skin as a solid or liquid, raw or cooked—although cooked is the safest approach, as it destroys any pathogens. Bear fat is my favorite choice because it penetrates your skin so deeply. It's also great for conditioning other skins (like leather).

207 MELT SOME LARD SALVE

Although it smells a little strange, lard can make a fine one-step medicinal salve for a variety of uses. The process is easy and the results are healing. Yarrow is an outstanding herb to blend with lard, but many medicinal plants can make friends with this greasy substance. And you thought lard was bad for you!

YOU'LL NEED

1 cup (250 g) lard: organic and preservative-free would be best; vegan-friendly shortening can also be substituted

6 tsp. (30 g) dried herbs: plantain leaf for cuts and burns, chickweed for itching, yarrow for bleeding control and antiseptic, or another herb based on your needs

Cheesecloth

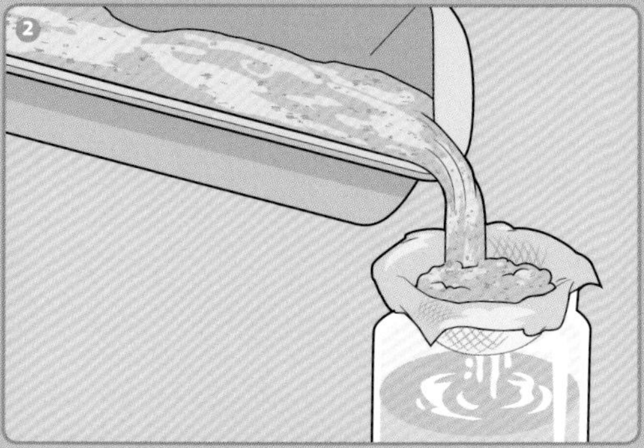

STEP 1 Place your lard into an oven-safe dish (not aluminum) and heat slowly until liquefied. Stir the dried herbs into the oil. Bake in the oven at the lowest possible temperature—no more than 200°F (93°C)—for three hours. You can also use a pan on your stove top on the lowest heat setting for a few hours, or use a slow cooker on low heat for 24 hours.

STEP 2 Allow the mixture to cool just slightly. You'll want to strain it through the cheesecloth while it's still a warm liquid. Make sure to squeeze all of the oil from the cloth.

STEP 3 Before the lard stops acting like a liquid, pour it into a clean, wide-mouth jar or several small jars. As it cools, the lard will become semi-solid and reach its normal, room-temperature consistency.

That's it! You've created an easy medicinal salve. Store it somewhere cool (if you're at home, put it in the fridge), and use it or toss it within a few months of production, as lard tends to go rancid pretty quickly (especially in warmer conditions).

208 SOAK UP SOME ALCOHOL

A simple and effective way to preserve the medicinal quality of a plant is to make a tincture from it, using a food-grade alcohol. Tinctures are more powerful and last longer than dried herbs, and you can even mix up your own combination formulas. Just avoid rubbing alcohol or anything with methanol as an ingredient, as these are not safe. All tinctures should be made with food- or beverage-grade alcohols.

STEP 1 Gather the appropriate dried herbs and select a glass jar (preferably wide-mouthed) with a tight-fitting lid. Purchase the highest-proof vodka you can find to act as the solvent and preservative of this tincture. (Moonshine is also acceptable.)

STEP 2 Cut, crush, chop, or otherwise break up the dried plant material and pack it tightly into the jar. Pour enough vodka over the plant material to just cover it, then lid the jar.

STEP 3 Let the jar sit for six weeks in a cool, dark place, like a cabinet. Take it out once a day to shake it, but avoid exposing your jar to sunlight, as UV rays can have a negative effect on tincture-making.

STEP 4 After six weeks, use a cloth to strain out the plant material and bottle your tincture in a dark glass. Use as directed for your specific ailment (see item 211). You can also use any tincture as a disinfectant, due to its alcohol content.

209 PICK A POULTICE

Plantain (*Plantago* spp.) is known for being a handy field remedy—and also may be the first thing you grab at home if you get stung or bitten by a venomous insect or arthropod. Take several leaves of any plantain species (the older and more bitter, the better), and grind or chew them into a paste. Put this paste directly on the bite or sting, and the pain will start to ease. Keep the poultice moist, and secure it in place with a bandage or dressing. Change it every few hours or at least once a day—though you probably won't need to keep it on that long, as beestings and similar wounds should be much better within a day. Based on your needs, you can add fresh red clover flowers, stinging nettle root (an antihistamine), or yarrow to the plantain poultice.

210 BE AN INFORMED INFUSER

As with prescription medicines, often a tincture that's beneficial for many people can be bad news for a few. Know yourself and your health status, and don't treat herbs lightly.

IF YOU	STAY AWAY FROM
May be pregnant	Black cohosh, catnip, comfrey, goldenseal, yarrow, barberry, feverfew, juniper, cedar, mugwort, pennyroyal, mint (especially peppermint), pine, pokeweed, thuja, wormwood, angelica, and mayapple
Are nursing	Aloe vera, basil, borage, bugleweed, coltsfoot, comfrey, elecampane, ephedra, parsley and sage (galactofuge in both reduces milk flow), and wormwood
Have a heart condition, high blood pressure, or high cholesterol	Bilberry (can increase the risk of bleeding with anticoagulants); echinacea (can increase the risk of liver damage with medications prescribed to lower cholesterol); garlic (a natural blood thinner); ginger, ginseng, and St. John's wort (affect how the body absorbs prescription medications)
Have diabetes	Balsam poplar, birch, clover, horse chestnut, meadowsweet, willow, and wintergreen
Have liver problems	Black cohosh, colt's foot, comfrey, pennyroyal, sassafras, and wormwood

211 LEARN TINCTURE TREATMENTS

Make these tinctures to relieve numerous common ailments.

BURDOCK ROOT (*Arctium lappa*) Burdock aids liver function and treats arthritis and rheumatism, as well as skin problems like psoriasis, eczema, acne, and dandruff.

DANDELION ROOT (*Taraxacum officinale*) This tincture can stimulate the liver and treat gallbladder problems, digestive upset, hypoglycemia, high blood pressure, and recent-onset diabetes.

ECHINACEA ROOT See item 200.

HAWTHORNE BERRIES (*Crataegus oxyacantha*) These berries treat both high and low blood pressure, and relieve insomnia, heart palpitations, and arteriosclerosis.

NETTLES LEAVES AND ROOTS (*Urtica urens*) A treatment for allergies and asthma, nettles can also be used as a tonic for the stomach, urinary system, and lungs.

212 BREW A HOT OAK COMPRESS

Crush up a few handfuls of oak acorns and boil them in 1 quart (1 l) of water for thirty minutes or until the water is dark brown. Soak a clean cloth in this water and, while it's still hot (105–110°F/40–43°C), apply it to the injury. This can ease the pain of puncture wounds, ingrown toenails, boils, infected hairs, and a host of other ailments. Reheat the liquid and reapply the compress as needed. Do not use on sprains unless you alternately ice the injury.

213 TAP A TREE

The ubiquitous, familiar maples (genus *Acer*) produce a watery sap that you can use as drinking water—and, of course, to make delicious syrup.

The sap flows in the late winter when nighttime temperatures are below freezing and the days are warmer. The sap is slightly sweet right out of the tree, as it is 3–5 percent sugar by volume. You can tap most maple trees, but avoid Norway maples, *Acer platanoides*, and any others with milky sap.

Bore a hole by drilling through the bark, about 2 inches (5 cm) into the sapwood, angling the hole upward. Any reasonable-size drill bit can work, but $^{7}/_{16}$-inch (11-mm) holes match the commercially available tree taps known as spiles. Once you've drilled your hole, you can hammer in a spile and hang a bucket or jug on it to collect the sap.

If you can't find a supplier of spiles, use whatever you have. Half-inch vinyl tubing works well, as will bamboo, PVC pipe, and metal pipe pieces. All you really need is something to channel the sap so it drips into your container. Plastic drinking water jugs are fine for sap collecting, as are the classic metal buckets. In recent years, I've started using plastic vinegar jugs, which have thicker walls and are stronger than water jugs, and they are less likely to burst during a cold snap due to freeze expansion.

214 FOLLOW THESE TAPPING TIPS

Collecting the tree sap is pretty easy, but there are a few tricks to this trade. Keep these pointers in mind, particularly when dealing with maples.

TOP TAP TIPS

The sap flows best on the south side of the tree, which gets the most sun exposure.

You can put in one tap for each foot (30 cm) of diameter on the tree trunk.

Younger trees can be more productive than older trees.

If you're using it for drinking water, sap doesn't keep long before souring—so treat sap like milk: Keep it cold, keep it clean, and do something with it sooner rather than later.

If the sap has turned cloudy and smells sour (usually after sitting for more than a week), it has become a breeding ground for bacteria and should be discarded.

Collect your sap each day to avoid overflowing containers and wasted sap.

The sap doesn't run the same every day, even on the same tree.

Make as many taps as you can to make this venture worthwhile.

215 BOIL SOME TREE SUGAR

To turn sap into syrup, grab the largest pot you own and a reliable heat source, and head outside. Boiling indoors is never a good idea, as every surface will be covered with condensed water. Use a wood fire or propane burner to bring the sap to a boil, and keep it boiling until it visibly thickens. It should look like new motor oil (in color and viscosity) when it's close to done.

Dip a spoon in and allow it to cool for a moment, then see how it pours. If the syrup forms a curtain-like sheet off the spoon edge, you're done. If it's still runny, boil off more water. Be aware that there is a fine line between too watery and too dry. If you overcook the sap, it will crystallize into a solid upon cooling. This is fine if you're trying to make maple candy, but not ideal if you've got plans for pancakes.

You'll need 10 gallons (38 l) of sap to make 1 quart (1 l) of syrup. That may sound like a lot, but each tap into a productive tree can yield 1 gallon (4 l) of sap per day at the height of the sap run. Keep your finished syrup in the fridge to prevent mold, or process the syrup in jars in a water bath canner for long-term storage. Fittingly, sugar maple has the highest sugar percentage in its sap, whereas other trees (including other maples) have about half as much sugar. Regardless of the species used, once the sap is reduced to syrup, it has about 100 calories per ounce (per 30 ml).

216 EXPLORE YOUR CHOICES

Maple isn't the only tree that can produce sap water and syrup. Sycamores (*Platanus occidentalis*), birches (genus *Betula*), and hickories (genus *Carya*) are also contenders for both, and black birch is particularly delicious. Walnuts (genus *Juglans*) can also be tapped for drinking water, but they're not particularly tasty for syrup. You can even mix and match to create your own syrup blends.

217 BREW SOME MAPLE WINE

One of my all-time favorite home-brewed beverages is something I call maple wine. Knowing that the American founding fathers used maple syrup in beer recipes, and being a big fan of mead (a honey wine), I put these two concepts together. Here's a quick rundown for the best homemade wine I've ever had.

STEP 1 Boil down your sap to 1 gallon (4 l) of fluid. Check the sugar content with a triple hydrometer (if you have one, the specific gravity should read 1.100 or near it; if you don't, just hope for the best). Let it cool to room temperature, and sanitize a 1-gallon (4-l) glass jug, a stopper, and a wine lock (available at home-brew supply stores).

STEP 2 Pour the syrup water into the jug and add a small packet of red wine yeast. Plug the jug with the stopper and a water-filled wine lock. Keep the jug in a dark place with a 60–70°F (16–21°C) temperature for two months. It should bubble for weeks, and finally start to settle after a month and a half.

STEP 3 Pour the wine off the sediment into a new container. If it hasn't cleared, add a hot wine finings mix (again from the supply shop) and wait a week. Pour off the sediment again, then bottle or drink, and enjoy this smooth and silky wine that tastes of caramel.

218 MEET THE BEES

Humans have craved and collected honey for thousands of years—an ancient Spanish cave painting (dating back around 8,000 years) depicts people collecting wild honey. All this time, and our love of this sweet food hasn't changed at all. At 304 calories per 100 grams (about 5 tablespoons), it's also a very valuable wild-food source. Whether you are a beekeeper or a wild honey collector, it pays to know the bees that are working hard for you.

THE QUEEN One solitary queen bee is the ruler and mother of her hive. She may lay 2,000 eggs each day when at the peak of her fertility. The queen is the largest bee in the hive, about 1 inch (2.5 cm) long, and she can live for several years. Her welfare affects that of the entire hive—so take good care of your queen.

THE WORKERS The worker caste of bees makes up the main population of any hive—and, as their name implies, they do all the work. These busy bees are almost half an inch (12 mm) in length and are responsible for gathering pollen and defending the hive. They carry the pollen from flowers on their hind legs, make the honey, build the combs to store the honey, and take care of the eggs and newly hatched larvae. The worker's sting is painful to humans and other hive raiders, but it is fatal to the bee that delivered it. (Wonder why? Well, some of the bee's innards are torn out as the barb lodges in its foe. Aren't you glad you asked?)

THE DRONES Drone bees are few in number in any hive. They are about the same size as the workers, but are generally stockier and have larger eyes. The stingless drones spend all their time near the queen, as their only job is to mate with her. Might sound fun, but it's typically fatal for the drone.

219 GET THE RIGHT GEAR

You may not need any specialized equipment to purchase a "super" (short for superhive) full of honey bees and set it up on your land. But when it comes time to collect the honey, you'll need a few unique items.

BEE SUIT A bee suit is a set of coveralls, generally white or light-colored. The suit should have a wide-brimmed hat with a veil to protect your head and neck from stings. I recommend gloves.

HIVE TOOLS You'll need a smoker to calm the bees as you start to dismantle their home, and a small pry bar to pry apart the lid and frames. Grab an uncapping knife to cut the beeswax combs open so you can extract the honey.

EXTRACTOR Getting honey out (without comb damage) is tricky unless you have access to a centrifuge. This can be a motor-operated device or a hand-crank model. The extractor spins the combs, releasing the honey via centrifugal force.

220 SET UP A COLONY

Beehives have come a long way from the coiled-straw skeps and hollow logs that our ancestors used. Since the 1850s, most beekeepers use specialized boxes called supers. Supers hold a number of frames with wax foundation sheets stamped in them, upon which the bees build combs for raising their young and storing their honey.

These bee boxes and frames have about 1/5 inch (5 mm) of open space between them—just enough room for a single bee to get through. This "bee gap" keeps the bees from gluing all the frame parts together with propolis, a gummy substance they create from plant resins.

Some beekeepers will sell the super with a colony of bees already inside, allowing a beekeeping beginner to get off to a quick start.

Whether you're a beginner or already maintaining your flock (or swarm), follow these tips in order to maintain your super and keep your bees healthy.

PRO TIPS

Set up your hive in a dry location, and in an area with good drainage. Use blocks, bricks, or posts to create a stand to support the super. This keeps the colony drier, discouraging disease and mold.

Keep it sheltered—the hive needs to stay out of the wind in cold weather. Deep cold can kill the bees, and even an unseasonable chill can reduce the worker bees' efficiency.

The super should be in a sunny location in order to take advantage of solar heat. The hive's interior temperature is usually around 93°F (34°C), which is regulated by the bee's body heat and activity.

221 FEED YOUR BEES WELL

Many different trees and plants can provide the food sources that bees require. Worker bees will travel up to 1.8 miles (3 km) from the hive to forage for their favorite nectar and pollen, but a closer supply of food generally makes for a more efficient use of their time and energy.

Set up your super near an area that has abundant flowers, orchards, and crops that the bees enjoy. Fields of clover and alfalfa are a great food resource in agricultural areas. Orchards of apples, oranges, and other fruits can provide another bee hot spot. Your bees will also enjoy wildflowers such as asters, goldenrod, dandelion, and sage.

Avoid areas with large concentrations of toxic flowers. Don't keep your super near large stands of mountain laurel or rhododendron, as the honey your bees produce may take on toxins from the poisonous flowering shrubs.

Once you get the hang of it, just one super of bees can yield a huge amount of honey, with the average established hive creating 30–60 pounds (14–27 kg) of honey in a calendar year. The late Ormond Aebi, an American beekeeper, still holds his 1974 world record for honey obtained from a single hive: 404 pounds (183 kg) in one year.

Learn to live wild and give something back.

Throughout this book, you have seen strategy after strategy for collecting wild foods. Plants, mushrooms, fish, birds, mammals, reptiles, shellfish, and insects are at once survival foods and culinary frontiers. Sure, some of these foods may not be palatable to you—everyone's tastes are different—but these foods all share one common trait: calories.

In essence, you are trying to preserve the calories you currently hold in your body and provide additional calories to cover the workload of your daily tasks. Since we live in an unprecedented age of plenty due to agricultural advancements, global shipping, and indefinite food storage, it's easy to eat too many calories in our modern lives—giving calories a bad rap. But if you're in an emergency scenario without much of a food supply, calories will soon be the most important thing you can get your hands on.

I want this book to put you on the path of our forebears—to learn the value of the calorie-rich wilderness and to exercise mastery of your wild-food resources. And in that mastery, I hope you'll exercise restraint. Once you begin to see food all around you, the open-eyed will observe how vulnerable many plants and animals have become. Be conservative in your approach to wild-food collection. Leave some plants and animals for your next trip and for those who will follow you.

I want you to become a hunter, trapper, angler, and forager, but I want your great-grandchildren to have the same opportunity. Be careful out there.

And enjoy your wild food!

—Tim MacWelch

INDEX

G

H

I

J

K

L

M

N

O

P

T

U

V

W

Y

FROM THE AUTHOR

This one is for my students! Your years of support and encouragement have been both humbling and empowering. It's always a good time when we go out into the woods, hunt down wild edible plants, make medicines and wild brew, track animals, and chow down on a primitively cooked feast—but it's more than just fun for me. You have let me live my dream, and for that, I gratefully offer this book as my way of saying thanks.

I'd also like to thank my team at *Outdoor Life*: John Taranto, Andrew McKean, Alex Robinson, Gerry Bethge, and Martin Leung. It's a privilege to work with you guys every week. And thank you to my friends at Weldon Owen Publishing. Bridget Fitzgerald, you have been a phenomenal editor, helping me to find the words that you knew I meant to say. And to the artists of the group, Barbara Genetin, William Mack, and Conor Buckley, your talent with photos and illustrations has made this book even better than I could have imagined.

Thanks also to my family, for continuing to put up with me when I'm in "writer mode" (grouchy). And to you, the reader, I thank you most of all. I hope this book will give you that push out the door to practice these skills, and bring you a greater sense of meaning and appreciation for the wild things around you.

ABOUT TIM MACWELCH

Tim MacWelch is the author of the *Prepare for Anything Survival Manual* and has been an active practitioner of survival and outdoor skills for over 26 years. His love of the outdoors started at a young age, growing up on a farm in the rolling hills of Virginia. Eating wild berries, fishing, and learning about the animals of the forest were all part of country life. Tim became interested in survival skills and woodcraft as an offshoot of backpacking as a teen—while out in remote areas, it seemed like a smart plan to learn some skills. The majority of his training over the years has involved testing survival skills and devising new ones, but the biggest leaps forward came from his experience as a teacher.

Tim's teaching experiences over the years have been rich and diverse, from spending hundreds of hours volunteering to founding his own year-round survival school 18 years ago. He has worked with Boy Scouts, youth groups, summer camps, and adults in all walks of life, as well as providing outdoor skills training for numerous personnel in law enforcement, search and rescue organizations, all branches of the United States Armed Forces, the State Department, and the Department of Justice and some of its agencies. Tim and his wilderness school have been featured on *Good Morning America* and several *National Geographic* programs, and featured in many publications including *Conde Nast Traveler*, the *Washington Post*, and *American Survival Guide*.

Since late 2010, Tim has written hundreds of pieces for *Outdoor Life* and many other publications. Tim's current and past articles and galleries can be found at survival.outdoorlife.com and you can learn more about his survival school at www.advancedsurvivaltraining.com.

ABOUT OUTDOOR LIFE

Since it was founded in 1898, *Outdoor Life* magazine has provided survival tips, wilderness skills, gear reports, and other essential information for hands-on outdoor enthusiasts. Each issue delivers the best advice in sportsmanship as well as thrilling true-life tales, detailed gear reviews, insider hunting, shooting, and fishing hints, and much more to nearly 1 million readers. Its survival-themed Web site also covers disaster preparedness and the skills you need to thrive anywhere from the backcountry to the urban jungles.

A NOTE TO READERS

PHOTOGRAPHY CREDITS

Photography courtesy of Shutterstock, with the following exceptions: *Peter Barrot / Digital Studio:* cover, 7, 167 *Bear Archery:* 41 (recurve) *Denver Bryan:* 95 *© Macduff Everton/Corbis:* 158 *Mark A. Garland / USDA, Natural Resources Conservation Service:* 126 (Indian cucumber root, Indian cucumber) *Judy Hertz, Garden in a City blog:* 121 (spicebush) *Mitch Kezar/Windigo:* Hunting introduction *Taylor F. Lockwood:* 115 (showy flamecap, scaly chanterelle, death angel), 118 (hen of the woods) *William Mack:* 6 (carved fish stick) *Tim MacWelch:* 118 (oyster), 119 (black walnut, hickory), 120 (bittercress, wild lettuce, plantain, clover, chickweed, wood sorrel), 122 (redbud, birch), 123 (curly dock), 124 (wild grape, autumn olive, cherry), 125 (burdock), 129 (wild grape, autumn olive, cherry), 132 (pokeweed berries, horse nettle fruit), 143 (dandelion), 202 (young jewelweed, adult jewelweed) *Paolo Marchesi:* 39 *Marlin Firearms:* 35 *Matt Nager / Redux:* photo of Andrew McKean *PSE Archery:* 41 (longbow) *Remington:* 35 (semiautomatic) *© Jessica Rinaldi/ Reuters/Corbis:* 11 *Dan Saelinger:* 4 (center crickhopper, righthand plug, lefthand and righthand spinners, lefthand and righthand jigs, righthand fly), 35 (single shot, lever action, pump action, modern sporting), *© Josef Scaylea/Corbis:* 36 (mountain man with muzzleloader) *Benjamin C Tankersley/For The Washington Post:* Author Photo *Thompson Center Arms:* 35 (muzzleloader) Nathaniel Welch: 37 (hunter)

ILLUSTRATION CREDITS

Conor Buckley: Icons, 09, 29–30, 169, 179, 186, 198, 207; *Tina Cash Walsh:* 138, 213; *Hayden Foell:* 65, 94, 110–112, 165, 181; *Vik Kulihin:* 63, 67, 69, 78, 80, 82–84; *Liberum Donum:* 85, 135, 161; *Christine Meighan:* 07, 10, 14, 21, 23, 26, 52–52, 69, 72, 75, 96, 99, 154, 162, 196; *Lauren Towner:* 45–46, 148, 168; *Gabhor Utomo:* 117

weldon**owen**

PUBLISHER Roger Shaw
ASSOCIATE PUBLISHER Mariah Bear
EDITOR Bridget Fitzgerald
CREATIVE DIRECTOR Chrissy Kwansick
ART DIRECTOR William Mack, Allister Fein
DESIGNER Barbara Genetin
ILLUSTRATION COORDINATOR Conor Buckley
MANAGING EDITOR Lauren LaPera
PRODUCTION MANAGER Binh Au

P.O. Box 3088
San Rafael, CA 94912
www.weldonowen.com

Weldon Owen would like to thank Jan Hughes, Katharine Moore, John Taranto, and Andrew McKean for editorial assistance, and Larry Sweazy for indexing services.

Originally published in 2014.

ISBN 13: 978-1-68188-539-1

10 9 8 7 6 5 4 3
2022 2023 2024

Printed in China

OUTDOOR LIFE

2 Park Avenue
New York, NY 10016
www.outdoorlife.com